The Space In-Between

POST-CONTEMPORARY INTERVENTIONS

Series Editors: Stanley Fish and Fredric Jameson

A Book in the Series

LATIN AMERICA IN TRANSLATION | EN TRADUCCIÓN | EM TRADUÇÃO

Sponsored by the Duke–University of North Carolina

Program in Latin American Studies

THE SPACE IN-BETWEEN

Essays on Latin American Culture

■

Silviano Santiago

Edited by Ana Lúcia Gazzola, with an introduction by

Ana Lúcia Gazzola and Wander Melo Miranda

Translated by Tom Burns, Ana Lúcia Gazzola,

and Gareth Williams

Duke University Press   Durham and London

2001

©2001 Duke University Press
All rights reserved
Printed in the United States of America on acid-free paper ∞
Typeset in Monotype Garamond by Keystone Typesetting, Inc.
Library of Congress Cataloging-in-Publication Data appear
on the last printed page of this book.

Contents

∎

Introduction: Silviano Santiago, a Voice In-Between   1

1. Why and For What Purpose Does the European Travel?   9

2. Latin American Discourse: The Space In-Between   25

3. Eça, Author of *Madame Bovary*   39

4. Universality in Spite of Dependency   53

5. The Rhetoric of Verisimilitude   64

6. Worth Its Weight: Brazilian Modernist Fiction   79

7. The Permanence of the Discourse of Tradition in Modernism   93

8. Repression and Censorship in the Field of the Arts during the 1970s   111

9. Literature and Mass Culture   119

10. The Postmodern Narrator   133

11. Worldly Appeal: Local and Global Politics in the Shaping of Brazilian Culture   147

Notes   175

Index   185

The Space In-Between

Introduction

Silviano Santiago, a Voice In-Between

■

Among present-day Brazilian critics, Silviano Santiago occupies a unique place owing to his pioneering development of concepts that have nowadays become current coin in Brazilian and international criticism. Developed in several of his writings since the end of the 1960s and the beginning of the 1970s, concepts such as the space in-between and hybridism are central for an innovating thought that managed to articulate from a Brazilian and Latin American perspective the strategic relation between notions of dependency and universality.

The differentiating feature of the role played by Santiago in the Brazilian cultural scene is his circulation within challenging theoretical spaces and distinct *loci* of enunciation. The movement among theory, fiction, criticism, and poetry also confers on his work the discursive mobility that characterizes the traveling intellectual in postmodernity. The possibility of this circulation is doubtlessly related to his professional experience, from his work as an active film critic at the Center of Cinematographic Studies in Belo Horizonte, where he did his undergraduate work at the Federal University of Minas Gerais, to his years of graduate study at the University of Paris, Sorbonne, where he wrote his dissertation on the genesis of André Gide's *Les Faux-Monnayeurs,* based on an unpublished manuscript of the author he had discovered in Rio de Janeiro. While he was writing the dissertation, Santiago went to the United States to teach Brazilian and French literatures. He taught at various institutions, including the universities of New Mexico, New Jersey, New York, Texas, California, and Indiana, the University of Toronto, and the University of Paris. In 1970, he was awarded tenure at State

University of New York at Buffalo, but he decided to return to Brazil as a professor at the Catholic University of Rio de Janeiro. His experience during this period was decisive, for he was responsible for the introduction of poststructuralist thought into Brazil, particularly the work of Jacques Derrida, which he was one of the first to study systematically, as can be seen by the publication of *Glossário de Derrida* [Glossary for Derrida], which he edited in 1976. The publication of *Uma literatura nos trópicos: ensaios sobre dependência cultural* [A literature in the tropics: Essays on cultural dependency] (1978) opened the way for a deconstructionist reflection on Brazilian culture, which was consolidated in the 1980s with the essays collected in *Vale quanto pesa: ensaios sobre questões político-culturais* [Worth its weight: Essays on political-cultural questions] (1982) and *Nas malhas da letra* [In the meshes of the letter] (1989). He has recently edited the important collection *Intérpretes do Brasil* [Interpreters of Brazil] (2000), with eleven classical works of Brazilian culture. Also worthy of mention is Santiago's academic leadership: he has been the advisor for more than forty dissertations, a consultant to government agencies for the definition of a policy for supporting research in his field, and a professor responsible for creating various courses that proposed a reordering of the Brazilian literary canon in the light of the theories that informed his intellectual production. In this way, he has contributed decisively to the formation of generations of scholars, to the academic consolidation of literary and cultural studies in the country, and, especially, to the updating of Brazilian critical thought.

To his broad critical activity and theoretical reflection must be added Santiago's artistic production, which functions as a supplement to what was left open in these areas. Among works that include novels, short stories, and poetry are *Em liberdade* [In liberty] (1981); *Stella Manhattan* (1985, English translation by George Yudice, published under the same title by Duke University Press in 1995); *Viagem ao México* [Journey to Mexico] (1995); *Keith Jarrett no Blue Note* (1966); and *De cócoras* [On squatting] (1999).

The essays in this volume were chosen with the aim of offering an articulate vision of Santiago's critical work, from his reflections of a more inclusive character on the status of Latin American literature to those that focus on specific questions of Brazilian culture. Such questions constitute a theoretical field that defines the problematics of cultural difference from a point of view that evades the traditional studies of source and influence in comparative literature. This cultural perspective gives the essays in this volume a broader reach than that of a study of a specific, national literature.

In these terms, Santiago shows himself to be immune to evolutionist concepts and firmly opposed to ethnocentric ones. This can be seen particularly in the essay "Why and For What Purpose Does the European

Travel" and in the essay with the provocative title of "Eça, Author of *Madame Bovary*," whose arguments are supplemented by "Latin American Discourse: The Space In-Between" and "Universality in Spite of Dependency." In the first essay, Santiago focuses on the pedagogical and modernizing function of the European traveler in the New World. His interest in the question of travel is related to a long tradition of travelers in Brazil, who, since the colonial period, in cultural and artistic missions or in response to the expansionist interests of their countries of origin, contributed to the gradual constitution of an image of nationhood for internal and external consumption. Most of the texts by these travelers try to "impose a meaning on the Other in the very place of the Other," as Santiago points out. In opposition to Umberto Eco's *Travels in Hyperreality*, Santiago prefers the concept of *supplement*, a counterpart offered by the so-called New World for the constitution of a new regime of alterity. In this way, America is perceived as excess whose supplementary status defines the force-field within which both the American and European identities are configured; the latter is then displaced from its hegemonic centrality by the notion of a "happy and affirmative copy."

Santiago had worked on these notions in his earlier essays "Latin American Discourse: The Space In-Between" and "Universality in Spite of Dependency." In these essays, the ideological fallacy in which notions like source and influence are often clothed is dismantled, and the value of the (peripheral) copy with respect to the (hegemonic) model is recovered. Their relation comes to be seen no longer as the dead-end of dependency and the impossibility of Latin American cultural identity, but as a process of differentiated repetition in which the insertion of the native culture into the universal totality is sought. By the overturning of values such as "backwardness" and "originality," what is affirmed is the value of the text of the colonized culture as space in-between, which retroactively affects the text of the dominant culture, thus creating the possibility for a concrete evaluation of the universality of the texts of the metropolis. .

The approach to peripheral or reflexive literatures, therefore, passes through a discussion of dependency made from a comparativist perspective—as Santiago warns, by way of Antonio Candido—in characterizing the object of study of comparative literature: "The object must be double, since it is made up of literary works produced in different national contexts, which are, nevertheless, analyzed and contrasted for the purpose of both broadening the limited horizon of artistic knowledge and the critical vision of national literatures."

It is not, of course, a question of a mechanical reduction of the text to the social process from which it originates or of ignoring this relation. It is a question of making the two interact, holding in view the movement of the producer-subject through the corridors of a library whose books, inevitably out of place, will seem to him strange and familiar—whether because they are depositories of a "foreign sign," or because they are the constant object of appropriation and digestion, defined by "a kind of global translation, pastiche, parody, digression," and situated in a cultural context marked by something similar to the Freudian *Unheimliche.*

The notions of the original and the copy are seen as fundamental in this process: presuppositions such as identification, plagiarism, and transgression inherent in these notions are discussed by a return to the innovative works of Jorge Luis Borges, especially "Pierre Menard, Author of the *Quijote.*" From this short story, Santiago takes the metaphors of the *visible* and *invisible* texts he uses as the operational concepts that allow for the reading of the relationship between dominant and dominated literatures. Its "originality" lies in the invisible dimension of the copy. Thus, there is an acceptance of the dominant culture as imprisoner and, at the same time, an active revolt against this imprisonment. If the concept of prison form (taken by Santiago from the poetry of Robert Desnos) is seen as the initial obstacle to the sphere of effective action of the dependent production, its working-out will allow the reader to establish a dialogue with the model borrowed from the dominant culture, which in turn will reveal the difference established by the copy. From this point of view, the decolonized text of the dominant culture begins to have unforeseen richness and energy, "because it contains within itself a representation of the dominant text and a response to that representation within its very fabrication. And this is a cultural response which creates a means of gauging universality which would be as efficient as those already known and catalogued."

The initial step in the deconstruction of the notions of original and copy is taken by Santiago in "Universality in Spite of Dependency" through the "archaeological" withdrawal of the critic to the beginnings of the formation of discursive practices among us, that is, at the moment when the impasses of the European holy wars are displaced from their context of origin to the New World. The result of this displacement is seen as an imposition of an ethnocentric cultural standard, evident, in the Brazilian case, in the catechistic work of Anchieta, which introduced the Indian into a field of struggle that was not his, requiring his introjection of a strange sociopolitical and socioeconomic context—that of the unity of the Church and of the constitution of the strong European state.

The conversion of the Indian at the end of the sixteenth century displaced him from his culture and he, divested of this true alterity and reduced to a simulacrum of the European, began to memorize and live a

European fiction. The foundation of schools in the same century would reinforce the didactic character of the colonizing process and the role of memory as its fundamental prerequisite. This is so because an alien history was narcissistically imposed as material for memorization, making uniform the different existing civilizations, westernizing the newly discovered, and strategically imposing European history as universal history. Later, the institutionalization of the dominant class as proprietor of a cultural discourse will take place, by the hierarchical suppression of native or Negro values, through the preservation of European culture as exclusive proprietor of knowledge and truth and as the culture of reference that establishes the hierarchies. In "The Rhetoric of Verisimilitude," Santiago offers an enlightening example of this dilemma, based on an analysis of Machado de Assis's *Dom Casmurro.* This essay is seminal for the development of the critical fortunes of the oeuvre of the greatest Brazilian novelist. Santiago analyzes the discourse of the narrator as spokesman for class values derived from the Brazilian rhetorical tradition and religious instruction inherited from the colonial period.

Developing further his reflection on the periods of the fashioning and consolidation of "Brazilian intelligence," Santiago focuses on the dilemma that will permeate its subsequent impasses. His decentralizing, historico-anthropological approach is not a question of abstract reason but is based on the political and cultural causes of the problem. When he uses anthropological discourse and contrasts it with historical discourse to fill certain methodological gaps of which the latter does not seem aware, he detects a possible identity for the Brazilian cultural product. This occurs precisely because he does not place at a lower level the determining factor of this equation—the position occupied by the intellectual in the peripheral cultures—which only the interaction of both discourses can situate more clearly, effectively, and adequately. The intellectual is explained and at the same time destroyed by historical discourse, in the sense that we have been living "a fiction since they made European history our history." The intellectual is recovered and constituted, though not explained, by anthropology, "since what is considered by History to be superstition constitutes the concrete reality of our past," and he ends up by being constituted as a cultural being in an ambivalent space in-between, drawn within the limits of the two disciplines.

It is from this place that Santiago speaks, and it is by taking up this position that he manages to expose the demotion of the dominated culture's product, from the initial simulacrum of the model of the metropolis, through the moment at which it begins to be questioned, to the phase of its being effectively surpassed. Exemplary, in the two latter cases, are the author's studies of the literary production of the modernists. Santiago approaches modernism as the surpassing of the model by the copy, the parodic appropriation of the discourse of the Same by the Other who subverts it. The paradigmatic example of *Macunaíma* by Mário de Andrade uncovers the new circulating space of the text-of-difference and of the clash of unequal voices that compose it: "It is in this not very pacific space in-between that the Brazilian intellectual finds today the volcanic soil where he may unrepress all the values destroyed by the culture of the conquerors . . . , that the novelist sees in the mirror not his own reflected image, but that of an anthropologist who does not need to leave his own country."

The question of the copy is not exhausted, however, in the virulent gesture of desecration, decentering, and the dismantling occasioned by parody, in the context of a country that attempts through modernization to break with the old, dominant oligarchies. After its renovation by the tropicalist movement that arose in the sixties, the parodic discourse became more commonplace, but in recent years it has lost its oppositional force and its reason for being, and has been substituted by pastiche.

More than a mere artistic technique of appropriating the discourse of the Other or a new fashion from the hegemonic centers, pastiche is taken by Santiago as an operational category which, on sharply differentiating itself from parody's firm opposition to the past, allows the understanding of the dialogue between the past and the present—without undervaluing the first term of the relation—in a space in which different and opposed elements live together, in a soil where figures that contradict each other coexist.

On the horizon opened up by this operational category, it is possible to recover, in a more adequate way and without any kind of prejudice, the reason for the permanence of the discourse of tradition in the world of certain modernist achievements. In the countercurrent of the readings centered on the idea of "the tradition of rupture" (Octavio Paz), Santiago shows how "the discourse of tradition was activated by the first (Brazilian) modernists, and right at the beginning of the movement," on the basis of the recovery of the Baroque of Minas Gerais as a mark of national identity, and in later developments such as the participation of intellectuals like Mário de Andrade and Carlos Drummond de Andrade in state projects related to the preservation of the historical patrimony of the country. In the literary aspect, Santiago emphasizes the importance of Christian discourse in the works of an important poet like Murilo Mendes as a sign of the permanence of tradition in modern Brazilian poetry.

The critical recovery of the historicity of Brazilian modernity situates the readings of Silviano Santiago within the scope of postmodern thought and creates a conceptual field that makes a more rigorous evaluation of contemporary cultural production possible. The systematic reflection of Santiago on Brazilian literature after the military coup has filled a gap in the general picture of Brazilian criticism. He allows for a firmer grasp of the process of flux and reflux of contemporary literary production in relation to an already established tradition. In his studies on Brazilian prose of recent decades, Santiago foregrounds the "formal anarchy" that characterizes it, although he calls attention to two dominant trends that at first are defined by the camouflaged or displaced approach to the situations vetoed by the censorship and repression of the military regime. In "Repression and Censorship in the Field of the Arts during the 1970s," Santiago discusses the type of narrative characterized by fantastic, oneiric discourse that in a disguised way radically criticizes the macrostructures of power and the authoritarian microstructures of daily control. He also focuses on the reportage-novel, which imitates journalistic language and thus dislocates to literary space the question of police violence and arbitrariness during the military dictatorship. He calls attention to the discrepancy between the reduction of the already small Brazilian literary public, provoked by the impact of repression and censorship, and the large number of politically committed works produced in the period, which have great value for postmodern Brazilian culture.

In the same way, the discussion of the relation between literature and mass culture offers the critic the opportunity to evaluate in what form the consumption of imported models (in this case the American cinema of the 1940s) reintroduces in other terms the question of the "contradiction between backwardness and modernity." As he returns to his reflection on recent literature, but now by way of a "detour of mass culture," Santiago foregrounds the gap between the value of the literary object and its recognition by its contemporaries. This is the starting point for his argument that literature has the ability to mobilize tradition and generate "posterior spaces" where alternative forms of understanding history are realized.

Generating these alternative forms is the role of contemporary fiction, as discussed by Santiago in "The Postmodern Narrator." Taking up Walter Benjamin's classic formulation on the narrator, Santiago departs from it when he proposes a new type of narrator in postmodernity. Distancing himself from experience and at the same time confusing himself with it, this narrator decenters the place of the subject of writing and history and identifies himself with the reader in the gaze they cast together on the Other. Uttered by a narrator more and more molded by the mass media, the contemporary narrative for Santiago is a testimony of the experience of the gaze in postindustrial society.

The main questions addressed in the essays of this volume converge in the final text, "Worldly Appeal," which discusses the politics of identity and globalization in modern Brazilian culture. Santiago concentrates on an examination of decisive moments of the constitution of the political thought of nationhood and cosmopolitanism in Brazil. Both perspectives, the national and the cosmopolitan, are emblematic of the space in-between of Brazilian culture, pulled toward the worldly appeal (Joaquim Nabuco) as well as the "localist unrepression" (Mário de Andrade). The notion of the consciousness of underdevelopment is added to this dilemma by the Marxist analysis of the historical process of the country, carried out by the writers of the 1930s and Caio Prado Jr. This notion will be paramount for the critical debate in Brazil in the following decades. As he demonstrates the unfolding of these questions up to the present time, Santiago calls attention to "the return to a new cosmopolitan realignment of the instinct of nationhood, now dealing with a globalization produced by the hegemonic force of U.S. pop culture." In this scenario, he overcomes the pervasive dilemma of Brazilian culture by rejecting the Manichaeist opposition between the theories of national identity and those of globalization.

This deconstructive affirmation of the voice in-between is the stand that best represents Santiago's contribution to the fashioning of a critical thought on Brazil and Latin America.

Ana Lúcia Gazzola and Wander Melo Miranda

1. Why and For What Purpose Does

the European Travel?

■

FOR RENATO

I consider invalid the opinion of those who search, having already found.
—*Paul Valéry*

The last book by Umberto Eco published among us, *Travels in Hyperreality: Essays,* is useful for asking once again a question that always occurs in the discussion of the relationship between the Old and the New World, ever since the latter was revealed to Western European consciousness: Why and for what purpose does the European travel?

Years ago, it was fashionable for American historiography to try to explain the reason why the New World did not manage to discover the Old one. Among many hypotheses, one was most seductive because it pointed to the scientific superiority of the Occident. It was said that discovery had not taken place because our pre-Columbians did not know the compass. Gradually, with the recent studies of political anthropology carried out or inspired by Pierre Clastres, we will discover that there must be other reasons, or at least different reasons from those dictated by victorious European ethnocentrism. But let us consider, for the time being, the classical question formulated above.

FIRST RESPONSES

Camões told us that, when the European traveled, it was to propagate Faith and the Empire, and he was right. But, rather than making the Portuguese responsible for the colonization of other peoples, he gave the responsibility for the job to the pagan gods. This was a decoy pointed out by Voltaire in the *Essay on Epic Poetry* (1733): "The main goal of the Portuguese, after the establishment of their commerce, was the propagation of their faith, and Venus sees to the success of the enterprise. Seriously, such an absurd marvel disfigures the entire work in the eyes of sensible readers." António José Saraiva adds one more contradiction to this one: in the epic poem, the humans behave like gods and the gods like humans. The Portuguese argonauts, such as, for example, Vasco da Gama, are decent, perfect, Olympian, while the gods engage in merely mortal intrigue, victims of their own feelings (love, hatred, etc.). This is why Saraiva could come to the conclusion that mythology, in Camões, is the transposition of historical reality.

At any rate, Camões's answer has at least one major advantage: it does not emphasize the gratuitous aspect of the journey, that of pure and simple curiosity for what is different, for the Other (for the aboriginal, different from and symmetrical to the European). The emphasis on curiosity would reduce the whole question of the discovery and colonization, of the conquest, to a mere intellectual exercise on the dissatisfaction of the white man, "naturally" inclined to universalism, with his own civilization. It would result in a mere variation on the manner in which the European searches for knowledge: he travels because he is curious about what he does not know. The unknown is what instigates his knowledge. Camões insists, to the contrary, on the expansionist and colonizing goal of the journey. So much the better.

The navigators and the colonizers were not truly curious about the Other and dissatisfied with the European reality of the time; this was true in relation to those who remained in Europe, with the burden of religious intolerance and the Inquisition, such as Montaigne. As far as I know, Montaigne never traveled outside Europe, but he had the brilliant idea of taking from the Other (or, more specifically, from the anthropophagous who visits Europe) his potential to contest the organization of the modern European state, conferring on it the status—here, surely—of an object of knowledge, of intellectual curiosity (read the chapter "Des cannibales" in his essays).

The point is not that the Portuguese had not felt in their own skin the outrages of the Inquisition. They were not insensitive, as Camões was not, to the "rough, dark, and vile sadness" the nation was going through. But they were unable to understand and criticize the wave of religious intolerance that ravaged the continent with the religious and social standards opened up by the maritime discoveries. Diego Bernardes, for example, tells us, in "An Answer to Dr. António Ferreira," of the atmosphere prevailing in Portugal, but he does not establish Montaigne's enlightened counterpoint. So he says:

A medo vivo, a medo escrevo e falo,
hei medo do que falo só comigo,
mas inda a medo cuido, a medo calo.
[I live in fear, I write and speak in fear,
I even fear what I only tell myself,
but still in fear I take care, in fear I keep silent.]

On the other hand, Sá de Miranda, at least in the turns of comparison, abandons the European frontiers and enters Egypt, where he finds in the behavior of thirsty dogs on the banks of the Nile the way to survive those negative times: (inguisi tion)

Farei como os cães do Nilo
que correm e vão bebendo.
[I will do as the dogs of the Nile
that run as they drink.]

This is stated in a "Letter to the King D. João III." Isn't he the clever fellow?

Even the Puritans, who moved to America once and for all, and who could at first be considered dissatisfied with European intolerance, did exactly the same, as they took to the other place the intolerance that had victimized them, reaffirming it even more vigorously because the historical and social obstacles existing in Europe were lacking. Thus, the contact with the New World does not change the Puritans' world view; on the contrary, it provides them with a guarantee—legitimized by the theory of predestination—that they are making the right journey. It is no coincidence that the "bible" of the American Puritans, *Pilgrim's Progress,* presents salvation through faith by means of an allegorical journey. The difficulties for the soul to reach the safe port that God represents are the same undergone by the traveler confronted with an insurmountable natural obstacle. In other words: one can only attain one's deepest religious being through the hardship of a journey:

This hill, though high, I covet to ascend;
The difficulty will not me offend;
For I perceive the way to life lies here:
Come, pluck up, Heart, let's neither faint nor fear:
Better, though difficult, the right way to go
Than wrong, though easy, where the end is woe.

As paradoxical as it may seem, the best answer and the most radical of all is provided by inertia. What Camões's masterful creation tells us is that the truly dissatisfied person with the Portuguese reality of the time is the inert Old Man from Restelo, the figure who remained in the port criticizing the navigators, and even the first navigator: "*Oh! maldito o primeiro que no mundo / Nas ondas vela pôs um seco lenho.*" ["Be damned the first man who in the world / In the waves placed a sail a piece of dry wood."] The Old Man asks the navigators the reason for the journey since there is so much to be done in the country itself and surrounding areas. Wouldn't it be better to spend so much energy and money transforming the country into a model of equilibrium and civilization? Addressing the "glory of command" that constitutes the motivation for travel, he asks:

A que novos desastres determinas
De levar estes Reinos e esta gente?
Que perigos, que mortes lhes destinas,
Debaixo dalgum monte preminente?
Que promessas de reinos e de minas
De ouro, que lhe farás tão facilmente?
Que fama lhe prometerás? Que histórias?
Que triunfos? Que palmas? Que vitórias?
[To what new disasters are you determined
To lead this Kingdom and these people?
What dangers, what deaths do you have for them,
Underneath some overhanging mountain?
What promises of kingdoms and mines
Of gold will you make them so easily?
What fame will you promise? What stories?
What triumphs? What laurels? What victories?]

Fernando Pessoa must have been thinking of the Old Man from Restelo when he imagined the verses that celebrated the Fifth Empire:

Triste de quem vive em casa,
Contente com o seu lar,
Sem que um sonho, no erguer de asa,
Faça até mais rubra a brasa
Da lareira a abandonar!
[Sad is the one who stays at home,
Contented with his homestead,
Without a dream, that in the lifting of wing,
Would turn redder the embers
In the fireplace left behind!]

I also remember that, during the first space explorations by NASA back in the 1960s, there was an obscure reader who wrote letters to *Time* and *Newsweek* repeating the lessons of the Old Man from Restelo: he asked the

American government if it wouldn't be better to spend all those federal resources on programs to improve the quality of life of poor Americans. From this point of view, the answer to the initial question would be quite interesting: the European travels because he is insensitive to the problems of his own people, because he does not have a high sense of justice. (In the contemporary world, the same conclusion would be valid in reference to Americans and Soviets.)

Colonization through the spread of Faith and the Empire is the negation of the values of the Other (Camões unfortunately was not lucid enough to realize that the coin has two sides). To be more precise, it is a triple negation of the Other: first, from a social standpoint, because the Indian loses his freedom as he becomes the subject of a European crown. Second, the Indian is forced to abandon his religious system (and everything implied by it in economic, social, and political terms) and is transformed—by the power of catechism—into a mere copy of the European. Third, he loses his linguistic identity, gradually expressing himself through a language that does not belong to him. As António Ferreira says in his exaltation:

> Floresça, fale, cante, ouça-se viva
> A Portuguesa língua, e já onde for
> Senhora vá de si soberba, e altiva.
> [Flourish, speak, sing, listen to itself and live
> The Portuguese language, and wherever it goes,
> It shall lordly go, haughty and proud.]

Therefore, colonization through the expansion of Faith and of the Empire is above all the lack of respect (and not mere intellectual curiosity) in relation to the Other; it is intolerance with the values of the Other. It is the main effect of the narcissistic European gesture that aimed at seeing its own image repeated throughout the universe. In full glory, the so-called universal history begins with European expansionism. The New World is only the occasion for another mirror, and the native is the clay to mold a double, similar figure—and add more violence and destruction.

From such a situation does Saint Francis Xavier escape in his pilgrimage through Japan. He believed in a "universal" that transcended linguistic differences and that, in its turn, was transcended by Western reason. Pierre Chaunu says this about him: "Trusting in universal revelation, or rather, the universality of Western reason, [Saint Francis Xavier] believed he could find terms in the Japanese language that translated Christian concepts, since he thought of crystallizing around Japanese words the forgotten notions of a latent monotheism, and he resurrected beyond paganism the data of universal revelation."

Before his death, the Apostle would find out that it was a mistake to think that there could be preestablished harmonies between Japanese and European thought.

A PARENTHESIS

Let us not discuss the aspects of colonization that have a clearly economic character, since in this case we would have to leave aside the question referred to in the title and would have to try to answer a narrower but more urgent question: Why and for what purpose does the black African travel? It is obvious that the *why* in the question is merely rhetorical, since the Africans traveled without their own motivation and the journey had a narrow and specific goal. The Europeans not only liked to travel, but they also really wanted the Africans to go with them, without bothering to ask them if that pleased them. But we have come to realize that Camões's answer also ignored a very important aspect of the question: the expansion of Faith and Empire was built on basis of one of the most unjust socioeconomic systems man was capable of inventing—that of black slavery in the New World.

THE ETHICS OF ADVENTURE

One thing would become clear as time went by: it appears that the European travels because he does not like to work, but on the other hand we must admit that, in the end, he does work, for no ship can reach its destination by itself. It is more correct to say that there is a hierarchy in work: the noble type as opposed to the undignified. Noble work is that which is justified by the ethics of adventure, which, in its turn, in a rather unethical manner, justified and legitimized everything, so that the action of the adventure would be entirely fulfilled, including black slavery.

There is no doubt that one of the major interests of the novel written from the nineteenth century on is to institute as truthful and just an ethics of adventure for modern man. We can mention Daniel Defoe, Chateaubriand, even and especially Joseph Conrad, and more recently Michel Butor. It is obvious that the arguments raised by the novelists are convincing, so convincing that we are finally seduced by them, and we forget what remains hidden. Isn't seduction the enticement through a transitory intensity, as illustrated by the myth of Don Juan?

To make the ethics of adventure fascinating and seductive, those novelists and others made a single individual responsible for the burden of agency. In this way, questions of a collective and ideological nature (such as colonization and exploitation) become abstract, and the reader's spirit is subdued by the formidable evidence of such heroes of our time in lands other than the European lands.

It is fantastic, in this phase, how religious oratory tried to justify action (in this case, religious proselytism) in the most varied ways, with the single aim of devaluing the priests that would not go planting, as Padre Antônio Vieira said. It was he who made the famous pun between "Paço" and "passos" mentioned in the *Sermão da sexagésima:* "Ah Dia do Juízo! Ah pregadores! Os de cá, achar-vos-ei com mais Paço; os de lá, com mais passos." [Oh Judgment Day! Oh preachers! In the ones from here, I will find more Court; in the ones from over there, more steps.] Manuel Bernardes, up against the wall of his personal defects, is led to justify himself: he wants "to compensate by flights of the pen the steps that, due to his ailments, he could not take in the mission." Frei Antônio das Chagas also considers less valuable the joyful delights of mysticism: "Sanctity does not consist in praying a lot, but in working a lot. There is more value in a single day in which you perform deeds of charity, or humility, or obedience, or patience, than in a month of contemplation, ecstasy, and rapture."

THE CORSAIR AND THE DUTCHMAN

The one who is capable of unmasking the modern adventurer protected by the ethics of adventure would be the corsair. This would be the adventurer devoid of the objective rationalization that would make greedy sailors into heroes. The corsair is then much closer—as a deconstructive metaphor—to the navigator and the colonizer that spread Faith and the Empire.

What is fascinating about the ethics of adventure—now seen from this new angle—is that nothing, absolutely nothing, has an owner. The navigators discovered what had already been discovered. That is why they call themselves inventors. The "invention of America" is an ethnocentric historiographical attitude. "At once he teaches, subjugates, domesticates the barbarian," says António Ferreira's verse in praise of the Portuguese conqueror. They tread, touch, take, possess: land, vegetation, animals, and women (I have forgotten to mention that the ethics of adventure is exclusively masculine—as mentioned in the medieval *cantigas de amigo* [a friend's songs], later on by Pero Vaz de Caminha, and recently in a rough voice by Guimarães Rosa when he created Diadorim). In everything that surrounds the adventurer, there is a state of complete availability, if I may take the expression used by another traveler, André Gide.

Or wouldn't it be fairer to say, in the company of a Gide traveling in North Africa, in his turn aided by Bougainville's wonder as he saw the Polynesian islands, all of them aided even further by Diderot's enlightened comments on Bougainville's text—wouldn't it be fairer to say that the things of the world have no owner and that the concept of *property* is the manner by means of which the European manifests himself as he deals either with his own kind or with the Other, or as he deals with things?

The European conqueror usurps, and as he disguises this gesture with the notion of property, he institutes as indispensable for the future social contract the notion of *theft* and the resulting and indispensable punishment: jail, in short. The notion of property can only be considered as legitimate and current after the first major theft is accomplished. The redemption of the adventurer would be in the radical imposition of a code of conduct (or of justice) that would be valid for everyone but himself. Could one invent a fairer definition for the role of European civilization in the New World? Diderot says emblematically in the *Supplement to Bougainville's Journey,* a text that would be better analyzed by our anthropologists: "Cet Otaïtien qui courut à ta rencontre, qui t'accueillit, qui te reçut, en criant taïo, ami, ami, vous l'avez tué. Et pourquoi l'avez-vous tué? Parce qu'il avait été séduit par l'éclat de tes petits oeufs de serpent. Il te donnait ses fruits; il t'offrait sa femme et sa fille; il te cédait sa cabane, et tu l'as tué pour une poignée de ces grains, qu'il avait pris sans te les demander." [This Tahitian that came to meet you, welcomed you, greeted you shouting *taïo,* friend, friend, you killed him. Why did you kill him? Because he had been seduced by the shine of your serpent's eggs. He gave you fruit; he offered you his wife and his daughter, he gave you his hut, and you killed him for a handful of these grains he had taken without your consent.]

When this code of conduct turns against him (and there are such cases), the adventurer will be forced to become an eternal traveler—a nationless person very close to a corsair. He is tied to his ship and to the constant mutability of the journey. Wouldn't the myth of the ghost ship be a kind of Montezuma's revenge (as they say in Mexico) against those who take possession but whose possession cannot be considered evil? With no resting place or rest, lonely and landless, the captain of the ghost ship is forced to live the ethics of adventure in a state of purity—like a curse.

The myth of the ghost ship (or of the wandering Dutchman), in this sense, would occupy a large space within the answer I am trying to organize, because it establishes the difference between the adventurer and the colonizer. When the ship finally anchors in a port, when the adventurer can become sedentary, meeting the wife who promises eternal loyalty and forms with him the patriarchal family, at that moment the colonizer appears—and it is he who, still sustained by the ethics of adventure, distorts it, using it as a justification for this thirst for control and power.

Transformed into a colonizer, the navigator can no longer work. If work on the land had been considered noble, he would not have needed to leave his homeland. He would entirely agree with the Old Man from Restelo and would not travel. If he traveled, it is because he considers sedentary work undignified, and this type of work is the fate of those who are defeated by him. Black slavery—in the adventurer's code and exclusively under this perspective—is justified by the supremacy of courage and adventure, by the "victory" of the European against his Other. On land, the adventurer can never be a farmer; he prolongs his previous life as a sailor by becoming a hunter or a *bandeirante* [explorer]. Due to this, he considers the rules of domination and submission as natural, since he sees himself in a world where everything but himself is game and prey animal. The debasing of the human condition in slavery is a consequence of "defeat," and the mere sedentary work in the farmland is the lord's "payment."

The theories of the supremacy of the white race, established by the conscious or unconscious racism of the nineteenth century, do not discard the metaphorization of human relations by the relationships between men and animals. They do not discard the white man's position as a "*hunter*" (of animals, of women, and of nonwhite men). If Darwin's evolutionist discovery puts us on another level in order to question man's origin scientifically, there is no doubt that the struggle for life works perfectly as a justification for the victory of the European from the great discoveries onward as a form of supremacy, including racial supremacy. Man is the wolf of man—this would be the proverbial form of the ethics of adventure when it is transformed into a standard of conduct on land.

THE TEACHING OF THE MODERN

Camões's answer to the question that has motivated these comments is no doubt valid for as long as the New World is a colony of the Old. Since the struggles for freedom and independence and since independence itself, the goal of the journey takes new directions. It becomes the urgent requirement for the young nation to continue the process of westernization that it started on without requesting it. The journey of the European has a predominantly pedagogical and modernizing function. The European travels, then, as a member of a cultural mission and often at the request of the interested country. He brings his diploma, preferably a university degree, in his luggage.

In the specific case of Brazil, it would be tiresome to list all the cultural missions that came after the French mission of 1816, whose aim was to establish and direct schools of sciences, arts, and trades. It is never excessive to recall that the University of São Paulo (USP) was founded by a mission, formed by young, inexperienced professors that later become great names in their areas of expertise.[1] USP has established a model that is still used whenever there is a desire for a quick updating of science and culture. The model has become more complicated lately, as our institutions of knowledge have been demanding more autonomy. The Brazilian counterpart was demanded in the journey trade. Since then what was only "cooperation" (the famous *coopération technique* of the French) has become a *covenant*. In other words: things must be carried out in the form of an exchange, as the New World also has something to offer.

We can hardly compare the role of a cultural mission to the recent phenomenon of the Brazilianists from the United States. These have not had a teaching role in our educational and research institutions (if I am allowed a pun, I would say that they had, rather than a teaching [*docente*] role, a role in relation to a sick [*doente*] country). The Brazilianists have made a reputation through their taste for research on primary sources. They were interested in recovering material which, in their opinion, was not apprehended in an adequate, rigorous, and scientific manner by the natives. This material would be, to stay close to the discourse of the Cold War and the Cuban Revolution, the "new riches" the country had to offer to the new conquerors: its political, social, economic, and cultural history. The United States, as the leading nation of the first world, could not ignore what was going on south of the border.

I have referred to the "new riches" above because it was the Europeans who came to know our "old riches." I am referring, of course, to the constant voyages of naturalists (mineralogists, botanists, biologists, etc.) who came to the New World to make it known in the eyes of contemporary science. I remember quite clearly a short story by J. J. Veiga, "A usina atrás do morro" [The sugar-mill behind the hill], where, maliciously, the installation of a big foreign factory cannot be disconnected from the previous stay of an European naturalist in the small village.

In a contemporary and entirely computerized world, this naturalist "prospecting" does not have to be done *in loco*. Quite the contrary. The modern argonauts (including the Brazilianists, let us not forget and let us warn our best students of the topic) have renounced the turbulent waters of the ocean; from the sky, with powerful, efficient airships and delicate, sensitive films, they can make a superior and more sophisticated mapping than the one made by the old explorer on land. Jacques Derrida would no doubt be delighted to see that one could better know the *real* through its representation than through empirical exploration.

We can see that, in order to provide an answer to the question on a cultural level and in the contemporary period, we must first come to the conclusion that the knowledge of the New World is not limited to speculative activity or a mere listing of data, and even less so to the task of inter-pretation. On the contrary, if such a thing as knowledge that turns into action exists, it was the knowledge produced, in the past, about "American" nature and the knowledge produced, nowadays, about the "history" of the underdeveloped countries. One should not think, however, that I am think-ing in Manichaean terms (heroes and villains of the New World, liberators and spies); I only wish to emphasize that knowledge produced in an aca-demic and disinterested manner—which happens quite often—ends up fall-ing into the trap of colonialism or neocolonialism. The practical orientation given to knowledge is rarely operated by its real discoverer.

If in the past there was an instructive difference between navigator and colonizer, we must now distinguish between the researcher and the indus-trialist. There is an ethics of knowledge inspiring the best researchers, and this ethics forbids that the material produced be used for social and eco-nomic domination. But, fortunately or unfortunately, knowledge—after it is formulated and publicized—exists indiscriminately for everyone. Nothing therefore prevents less scrupulous minds from taking possession of it with the aim of exploiting or destroying others. This seems to have been the dilemma that took the scientist Nobel from inventor to sponsor. The latter erases the wastage of the former, although he gives incentive to him. Of all the prizes, the only one to be saved is the Nobel Peace Prize but even it has lost some luster lately . . .

THE ANTHROPOLOGIST

Within the scope of the present discussion, one of the best and most in-structive books that provides an answer to the initial question is Claude Lévi-Strauss's *Tristes tropiques*. The anthropologist would be the *unhappy con-sciousness* of the European traveler and colonizer. He would be doubly un-happy, first of all, because the anthropologist discovers for the West and accounts for the destruction of the Other in the name of the ethnocentric conquest to which he gives continuity. Second, because he is the one capable of giving voice to an "already dead" knowledge (that of the destroyed peoples), and this knowledge—in a clear-cut opposition to his own—is of a limited utility for the country where it was generated and which now wants to be modern. In the cultural mission we were talking about, the anthropol-ogist is the antipode of the teacher, let us say, of nuclear physics.

The anthropologist, still according to Lévi-Strauss, embodies the very contradiction between the Old and the New: very often he is, in his home-land, a person dominated by new ideas and by revolutionary praxis; when he steps onto the land of the Other, he becomes conservative, since he tries to preserve, with his limited resources, a civilization that no longer exists; he tries to turn the eyes of a country modernized by neocolonialism toward what remains of an identity gradually lost through westernization.

A spirit contemporaneous to the anthropologist's but moving in the opposite direction is that which pervades someone like Antonin Artaud. Weary of the increasing sclerosis invading the European bourgeois stage, Artaud leaves in search of "theatrical" expressions in which the foundations of scenic experience had not yet been stifled by the process of commercialization and professionalization of modern times. It is in this sense that, like a new Montaigne, he turns against the moribund European theater (in what he considers a rejuvenating force)—that breath of the sacred and of violence, of myth and ritual, that gradually vanished from the Western stage through good scenic behavior, the one mandatory requirement of naturalist bourgeois theater.

THE TOURIST

After tracing a wide genealogical panorama, we realize that Umberto Eco's *Travels in Hyperreality* is both instructive and desolating. The European is now disguised as a tourist in the New World and, in a brotherhood with his peers from all over the world, grasps with eyes and words the obvious on which the internal and external tourists in the United States feed. His only difference: his gaze assumes it is superior and critical. Superior it certainly is all the time, since the text itself explores the original place of the legitimate discourse on the New World–Europe. Critical it might be, but original it is not, as we shall see.

What I call obvious is whatever is "cultural" and feeds the tourist industry in the United States: from Disneyland to wax museums, from museum-castles to zoos, from replicas of Superman to holograms. The industry of tourism is the bureaucratized substitute and negation of the old spirit of adventure, since it places in the aisles of ships and planes armies of civilians marching in search of cultural leisure.

Umberto Eco cannot escape—like any other tourist—the contingencies of travel agencies and organized trips. As if he had read all the instructive brochures of the thousand charms of the country to be visited, he departs with an exclusive and preestablished itinerary, repressing any other element of the country that would in some way distort his conscientious cultural mission. He says: "The theme of our trip . . . is the Absolute False; thus we are only interested in absolutely false cities." In other words: he will find in the States what he already knows and what the tourist brochures have presented in detail. Maybe he will take the trip only to be able to describe in a more realistic manner (isn't it a general belief that the report about what one has witnessed is more real?) the absolutely false.

The trip and the traveler are, then, totally dispensable. Thank you very much and *ciao,* if we had the European insolence. They are not that dispensable, when one thinks in terms of this long genealogy I have described. The condition of the traveler (of the wiseacre traveler, the one who thinks he knows more than the natives) is indispensable to the European who wants to impose a meaning on the Other in the very place of the Other. The American intellectuals do not see what only I can see. What I see, says Eco, is "snubbed by the European visitor and even by the American intellectual himself." Montaigne, as we have seen, did not have to travel in order to learn from the Other the distortions of his own culture. He and Alexis de Tocqueville, in the nineteenth century, are the major exceptions that confirm the rule of self-sufficient travelers.

Umberto Eco considers himself original in relation to his contemporaries and his peers. This is why he takes (so he believes) a perspective that differs from the one usually taken by Europeans and Europeanized Americans. These people think of the United States as only the "country of skyscrapers of glass and steel, of abstract expressionism" (of which Jackson Pollock is an example). Eco also goes that far: he assumes that he is more American than Americans, something like the real American, since he has discovered (would that be the verb?) the preference for a copy more real than the real and that founds the hyperrealist style of production of Europeanized Americans (and *also,* obviously, of the Europeans who gradually become more Americanized—but that Eco doesn't want to see).

AN ECHO OF THE FALSE

Eco says: "The point is to find out from which basis of popular sensibility and manual ability the contemporary hyperrealists take their inspiration and why they feel the need to play to exasperation with this tendency." Eco's search would thus be a kind of archaeology (in the sense that Nietzsche and Foucault give to the term) of American highbrow production, a search for a popular "foundation" that it ignores, if it ignores it. Rather, it knows it so well that the most challenging part of its production is founded on what Eco intends to "discover" for his contemporaries and peers.

The impression one has is that specifically artistic knowledge (the kind that is the work of art and founds it) does not exist for Eco. That is: the work of art does not know. The work of art does not have an autonomous value for Eco. In this sense, it is always insufficient in the spectators' eyes. It necessarily requires a method capable of viewing its own knowledge, a knowledge that, for these reasons, becomes absolutely secondary (in truth, without being so).

A person only knows when he interprets and is in possession of a scientific method (in this case Foucauldian archaeology and Peircean semiotics); in other words, only intellectuals with blinder vision like Umberto Eco can truly "know."

Well, the American work of art is what it is, it has its value because it *interprets* this "foundation of popular sensibility and manual ability." If it were not so, the United States would not be the source of the various movements of pop painting. The preceding statement is so obvious for anyone minimally interested in the relations between art and society in the United States that one is astounded by Eco's archaeological and semiotic levity. It would be more interesting if Eco asked why the contemporary European artist—who, as far as one knows, is deprived of the archaeology of the popular "foundation" to which Eco refers—also creates hyperrealistic art. Would European art be the echo of the absolutely false?

But for this Eco would have to have the intellectual curiosity of Montaigne, Tocqueville, Artaud, and, instead of making only a tourist trip for the American obvious, he would have to wander as well round Europe itself with another world view, perhaps less self-sufficient, certainly less naive and possibly less authoritarian, necessarily original, and thus, completely indispensable.

The New World intellectuals (*noblesse oblige!*) have always had the courage to see what is European in themselves. H. L. Mencken said that American culture was a cold breeze that came from Europe. Oswald de Andrade had no other intention when he expressed his anthropophagous theory. Henry James and T. S. Eliot (and even our Murilo Mendes) decided to accept in its totality the European part that touched them and left for Europe for good. There is no spirit more universalist and less "provincial" than theirs. In this sense, it is quite instructive to read Lionel Trilling's brilliant essay "Manners, Morals, and the Novel."

Am I not just answering another question? Why and for what purpose does the inhabitant of the New World travel?

FORCE AND SIGNIFICATION

Eco's major mistake was to have believed that he could at the same time light one candle for hermeneutics (or archaeology) and another for semiotics. Michel Foucault, in a fine study that has since 1967 derived the implications from the works of Freud, Nietzsche, and Marx for the constitution of a contemporary hermeneutics, arrived at the following conclusion: "It seems to me mandatory to understand something that most of our contemporaries forget, *that hermeneutics and semiology are two ferocious enemies*" (his emphasis).

Foucault's argument is based on the fact that one and the other have an irreconcilable understanding of the status of the sign. Semiology believes that the sign exists primarily, originally, that it exists as a coherent, pertinent, and systematic mark. It is in this sense that semiology allows Eco to establish a "foundation" (original, primary, real) that makes it possible to "explain" hyperrealism as an expression of today's American culture. He is, at the most, semiologically correct.

For hermeneutics (or archaeology) this "foundation" does not exist as something original or primary, it does not even exist as a "foundation," if one thinks of a foundation as the origin and end of something. For the Foucauldian hermeneutics there is nothing primary or original, since the sign itself (considered as original by semiotics) is already an interpretation. Does one need to return to the metaphor of peeling an onion to explain didactically and concretely the hermeneutic movement?

What Umberto Eco calls "foundation" is nothing more than a force (in the Nietzschean sense) among so many other energies that make up the complex American cultural texture. As such, this "foundation" is an interpretation among many others of what has been named "America," and, doubtless, as I will attempt to show, the most European of all interpretations. The meaning imposed by the European on America derives from the force of the violence of the conquest. As a result, the (American) copy as more real than the (European) real becomes the supreme desire of the New World inhabitants in their wish for autonomy. The (American) copy can only be "real" at the moment in which it surpasses the (European) model. That is: the copy is more real than the real when it becomes capable of "influencing" the model.

Hyperrealism is thus a desire. Hyperrealism is the desire of an America that dislocates itself from the condition of being a European copy. And, in art, it is the rerouting of an art that is not going to manifest itself as the mere repetition of the model. The copy gradually imposes itself as real: the real thing, according to the Coca-Cola advertisement analyzed by Eco. America is this *excess* that marks its own presence. As excess, it is supplementary. The supplement is already more meaningful than the whole (Europe) it supplements—a hypothesis.

The archaeology of America leads us back to the violence of the conquest (and not only to the sign that represents it as a copy), to the violence that imposed on the Other his inexorable condition as a copy. A bottomless foundation without the foundation of an "identity" that is established insofar as we enter the vertigo of the well of the past and free the sign (of the European signification conferred on America) from its condition of original and retain only the understanding of a force that is violence and that necessarily requires other forces as an affirmation of its own becoming. It is in this differential clash of forces (and not only in the *symptom* of these forces concretized in the form of a sign) that one can reveal the "identity" of an America: yesterday, a bitter and unhappy copy; today, a happy and affirmative copy; always, inexorably, a copy.

As Jacques do Prado Brandão has warned me via Thomas Mann: "The well of the past is very deep." Should we not say rather that this well is bottomless?

Translated by Tom Burns and Ana Lúcia Gazzola

2. Latin American Discourse:

The Space In-Between

■

*The land turtle who owned no more than a soft white shell allowed himself to
be bitten by a jaguar who was attacking him. The wound was so deep that
the jaguar became stuck to the land turtle and finally died. The land turtle
made its shell from the head of the jaguar.*—*Antonio Callado,* Quarup

*Before all else, negative work. One must free oneself from a whole array of
notions connected to the idea of continuity. . . . For example, the notion
of influence provides a magical rather than a substantive foundation to acts
of transmission and communication.*—*Michel Foucault,* Archeology of
Knowledge

Montaigne opens chapter 31 of his *Essays,* in which he addresses the question of the cannibals of the New World, with a precise reference to Greek history. This very same reference will also allow us to inscribe ourselves within the debate about the position that Latin American literary discourse occupies in its conflictive relationship with Europe. Montaigne states the following: "When King Pyrrhus entered Italy, after examining the formation of the army sent by the Romans to meet him, he said: 'I do not know what barbarians they are (for the Greeks called all foreign nations barbarian), but the disposition of the army I see before me is by no means barbaric.' "

Montaigne's quotation—clearly metaphorical to the degree that it announces the internal organization of his chapter on South American, or more precisely Brazilian, cannibals—essentially reveals the trace of the eternal conflict between civilization and barbarism, colonizer and colonized, Greece and Rome, Rome and the provinces, Europe and the New World, and so on. But, on the other hand, King Pyrrhus's words, dictated by a certain kind of pragmatic wisdom, fail to hide the surprise and wonder of what remains an extraordinary discovery: that the barbarians do not behave as such.

It is at the moment of combat—that decisive and revealing instance in which two enemy forces must face each other, brutally displaced from their condition of economic inequality and embodied exclusively within the immediacy of war—that King Pyrrhus realizes that the Greeks have underestimated the military prowess of the foreigners, the barbarians, the Romans. The superiority established by the Greek soldiers prior to the armed conflict, which was a great source of pride and conceit among Greek officers, was above all produced by the economic fissure that governed relations between the two nations. But as soon as one sets aside the restricted realm of economic colonialism, one can understand that very often it is necessary to invert the values of opposing groups and perhaps question the very concept of superiority.

As can be seen in this extract from the *Essays,* rather than revealing an *ordonnance de l'armée* portraying Greek prejudices about the Romans, what was witnessed was a well-organized army that had little to envy in those of civilized peoples. However, notions derived from quantification and colonialism are suddenly inadequate, as King Pyrrhus's words reveal an irrepressible compromise with the qualitative judgment implied by his admiration. In spite of their social and economic differences, the two armies are equal on the battlefield. And even if they were not in equilibrium, it is still worth recalling the unusual circumstances of the Greek monarch's death, since the contemporaneity of this unexpected incident holds a clear warning for the powerful military nations of today: Pyrrhus, king of Ephesus, "was murdered in the seizure of Argos by an old woman who hit his head with a tile thrown from atop a roof," as we are delightfully informed by the *Petit larousse.*

Let us then discuss the contemporary space in which King Pyrrhus's wonder is articulated, together with the possible inversion of values implied.

I

First we must establish a number of distinctions in order to further delineate and define the topic at hand. For didactic purposes, let us analyze relations between two civilizations that are completely foreign to one another and whose first encounters can only be characterized by mutual *ignorance*. Since the last century, ethnologists, in their desire to demystify the sanctioned discourse of historians, have been united in acknowledging that the victory of the white man in the New World is due less to reasons of cultural distinction than it is to the brutal imposition of an ideology that produced a recurrence of words such as "slave" and "beast" in the writings of both Portuguese and Spaniards alike.[1] Such expressions are much more revealing of a relation of domination than they are a translation of a desire to know. Thus it is along these same lines that Claude Lévi-Strauss writes of a psycho-sociological inquiry that was undertaken by the monks of the order of St. Jerome. When asked if the Indians were capable of "living for themselves, like the peasants of Castile," the response was negative: "Strictly speaking, their babies might; besides, the Indians have such profound vices that one can even doubt it; proof of this are the following: they avoid the Spaniards, they refuse to work without pay, yet they are so perverse that they give their goods away, they refuse to shun those whose ears have been cut off by the Spaniards. . . . It is better for the Indians to become enslaved men than to continue living as free animals."[2]

In stark contrast, however, and according to the information provided by Lévi-Strauss in *Tristes tropiques,* the Indians of Puerto Rico devoted themselves to capturing whites in order to drown them. Afterward, they stood guard over the ocean, watching out for corpses for weeks on end in order to determine whether they were subject to the laws of putrefaction. Not without irony, Lévi-Strauss concludes: "The whites would invoke the social sciences while the Indians placed more trust in the natural sciences; whereas the whites proclaimed that the Indians were beasts, the latter were happy to take the former as gods. While both were equally ignorant, the latter belief was at least worthier of men" (p. 83).

Violence is always practiced by the Indians for religious purposes. Faced with the whites, who considered themselves to be the bearers of God's word, each and every one a prophet, the reaction of the Indian is to test to what extent the words of the Europeans translate into transparent truth. One must wonder, however, whether the experiences of the Puerto Rican Indians could not be justified by the religious zeal of the missionaries. Their successive sermons preached the immortality of the True God and the resurrection of Christ: as a result, the Indians were more than eager to witness the biblical miracle and experience religious mystery in all its enigmatic splendor. Thus, for the Indians the proof of God's power should reveal itself not so much through the passive *assimilation* of the Christian word but rather through the *vision* of a truly miraculous act.

In this regard, extraordinary information can be gleaned from a letter written by Pero Vaz de Caminha to the king of Portugal. According to this scribe, the Brazilian Indians were *naturally* given to religious conversion since, from a distance, they would *imitate* the gestures of the Christians during the holy ritual of Catholic mass.[3] Imitation—an exclusively epidermic act, a mere reflex of the object on a mirror surface, a ritual devoid of words—is the most convincing argument that the navigator is able to send to his king in order to prove the innocence of the Indians. Faced with the image of these red-skinned figures aping the whites, one wonders whether they were really trying to attain spiritual ecstasy by means of gestural duplication. Did they not believe that they could come face to face with the Christians' God through such "spiritual exercises," just as the Puerto Rican Indians would have bowed before the drowned Spaniard who had escaped putrefaction?

Among the indigenous peoples of Latin America, the European word—uttered and immediately erased—became lost in the immateriality of its voice. Never solidifying itself in a written sign, it was never capable of positing, indivisibly, in *writing [écriture]* the name of the divinity. The Indians accepted only the oral transmission of events as legitimate communicative currency, whereas the conquerors and the missionaries insisted on the benefits of a miraculous conversion, achieved by passive assimilation to an orally transmitted doctrine. To establish the name of God is equivalent to the imposition of a linguistic code in which His name circulates with obvious transparency.

To unite not only religious representation but also European language: such was the task to which Jesuits and conquerors dedicated themselves from the second half of the sixteenth century in Brazil. Theatrical representations performed in Indian villages included an episode from *Flos sanctorum* with dialogue written in Portuguese and *tupi-guarani,* or, to be more precise, with the text in Portuguese and its translation in tupi-guarani. Moreover, there are many testimonies of witnesses who insist on pointing out the *realism* of these representations. A Jesuit priest, Cardim, tells us that the spectators could not hide their emotion and tears before the live portrait of the martyrdom of Saint Sebastian, patron saint of Rio de Janeiro. Religious doctrine and European language contaminate the savage mind as they stage the piercing of the human body with arrows, a body that is similar to other bodies which, for religious reasons, could encounter a similar fate to that of the saint's. Gradually, theatrical representations propose a substitution that is definitive and unavoidable: from now on, in this newly discovered land, the linguistic code and the religious code become inextricably linked thanks to the intransigence, cunning, and power of the white man. By the same token, the Indians, losing their language and their concept of the sacred, receive the European substitute in exchange.

Preventing bilingualism means both preventing religious pluralism and imposing colonial power. Within the conqueror's formulations, singularity is the only thing that counts. One single God, one King, one language: the true God, the true King, the true language. As Jacques Derrida wrote recently: "The sign and the name of the divinity have the same time and the same place of birth."[4] One slight correction is required in the last part of the sentence; namely the addition of a prefix that might update the statement to become ". . . the same time and the same place of rebirth."

The expansion of this colonialist renaissance—itself a repressed product of that other Renaissance that was taking place simultaneously in Europe—appropriates the sociocultural space of the New World and inscribes it, by conversion, into the context of Western civilization, conferring on it, moreover, the familiar social status of the firstborn. America is transformed into a copy, a simulacrum that desires to be increasingly like the original, even though its originality cannot be found in the copy of the original model, but rather in an origin that was completely erased by the conquerors. Through the constant destruction of original traces, together with the forgetting of the origin, the phenomenon of duplication establishes itself as the only valid rule of civilization. Thus it is that we see all around us the birth of those European-named cities, whose only originality is to be found in the fact that they always carry the adjective "new" before the name of origin: New England, Nueva España, Nova Friburgo, Nouvelle France, and so on. With the passage of time, however, this adjective can, and often does, come to have a meaning other than its dictionary definition since, strangely enough, the word *new* comes to mean *outmoded,* as in this beautiful sentence of Lévi-Strauss: "The tropics are not so much exotic as they are outmoded" (p. 96).

Neocolonialism, this new mask terrorizing the countries of the third world at the height of the twentieth century, is the gradual imposition in another country of values rejected by the metropolis. It is the exportation of objects that are out of date or obsolete in neocolonialist society, which is nowadays invariably transformed into a society of consumption. Today, when commands are given by technocrats, inequality becomes scientific and prefabricated; inferiority is controlled by the hands that manipulate generosity and power, power and prejudice. Let us turn once again to Montaigne: "They are savages, just like we call savages the fruit that nature, exclusively by itself and its natural progress, has produced; as a matter of fact, we should preferably call savages those that we have changed by means of our artifice and deviated from the natural order. In the former, the true, most useful and natural virtues and properties are live and vigorous, while we have degenerated them in the latter, merely adjusting them to the whims of our corrupted taste."

In its turn, colonialist rebirth engenders the new society of the mestizo, whose main characteristic is that, in him, the notion of *unity* is turned upside down and contaminated in a subtle and complex mixture of European and autochthonous elements—a kind of gradual infiltration achieved by "savage thought," that is to say, by the opening up of the only possible path that could lead to decolonization. This path leads in a direction opposite to that traveled by the colonizer. In their wish to exterminate the indigenous race, the colonizers would collect the infected clothes of smallpox victims in the hospitals in order to hang them, together with other gifts, along the routes most usually frequented by the tribes. In the new, indefatigable movement of opposition, of racial contamination, of sabotaging the cultural and social values imposed by the conquerors, a wider transformation operates on the surface, but nevertheless corrects the two principal systems that contributed to the spreading of Western culture among us: namely, the linguistic code and the religious code. These rubrics lose their status of purity and are gradually enriched by new acquisitions, minute metamorphoses, and uncanny corruptions that transform the integrity of the Holy Book, the European Dictionary, and its Grammar. Hybridism reigns.

The major contribution of Latin America to Western culture is to be found in its systematic destruction of the concepts of *unity* and *purity*:[5] these two concepts lose the precise contours of their meaning, they lose their crushing weight, their sign of cultural superiority, and do so to such an extent that the contaminating labor of Latin Americans affirms itself as it becomes more and more effective. Latin America establishes its place on the map of Western civilization by actively and destructively diverting the European norm and resignifying preestablished and immutable elements that were exported to the New World by the Europeans. Since Latin America can no longer close its doors to foreign invasion nor recuperate its condition as a "paradise" of isolation and innocence, one realizes with cynicism that, without such resignifications, its product would be a mere copy—silence, a copy that is frequently outmoded due to that imperceptible retrocession of time that Lévi-Strauss talks about. Its geography must be one of assimilation and aggressiveness, of learning and reaction, of false obedience. Passivity would reduce its effective role to disappearance by analogy. While maintaining its place in the second row, it must nevertheless mark its difference and its presence, very often presenting itself as avant-garde. Silence would be the response desired by cultural imperialism, or the re-sounding echo that achieves little more than tightening the conquering powers' noose.

To speak, to write, means to speak against, to write against.

II

If ethnologists are the ones who are truly responsible for the demystification of the discourse of History, if they contribute decisively to the cultural recuperation of the colonized peoples by removing the veil from cultural imperialism, then what would the role of the contemporary intellectuals be, when faced with analyzing relations between two nations who are partaking of the same culture—Western culture—but in a context in which one maintains economic power over the other? If, through their writings, ethnologists have succeeded in resurrecting dismantled cultures as artistic objects of richness and beauty, how, then, should the contemporary critic present the complex system of works that have been explained up until now through a traditional and reactionary critical methodology, whose only originality is to be found in the study of sources and influences? What would be the attitude of an artist from a country positioned in obvious economic inferiority to Western metropolitan culture and finally to the culture of his own country? Can the work of art's originality be grasped if it is considered exclusively in terms of the artist's indebtedness to a model that was necessarily imported from the metropolis? Or, rather, would it not be more interesting to high-light the elements of the work that establish its difference?

Answering these questions cannot be an easy or a pleasant task for it is necessary to declare for once and for all the collapse of a method that is deeply rooted in the academic system: namely, the study of sources and influences. Since certain university professors speak in the name of objec-tivity, encyclopedic knowledge, and scientific truth, such critical discourse occupies an essential position in contemporary critical practices. But we must now locate it in its true place. Such criticism merely reveals the indi-gence of an art that is, a priori, poor, due to the economic conditions in which it must survive. It merely sheds light on the lack of imagination of artists forced, due to the lack of an autochthonous tradition, to appropriate models disseminated from within the metropolis. Such a critical discourse parodies the quixotic search of Latin American artists as they underline their secondary position in relation to the beauty, power, and glory of works created within the colonialist and neocolonialist center. It reduces Latin American artists' creative production to the parasitic condition of a work feeding off another without ever providing anything in return; a work whose life is limited and precarious since it is enclosed in the radiance and prestige of the original, of the trendsetter.

The origin is the pure and unattainable star that contaminates without ever sullying itself, and which shines for the artists of Latin American countries whenever they depend on its light for their creative expression. It illuminates the movement of the hands yet simultaneously subjects them to its superior magnetism. Since any critical discourse that speaks of influences establishes this star as the only value that matters, to establish the bridge— and thus reduce the debt and distance between the artist, a mortal, and that immortal star—is surely the essential role and function of the Latin American artist in Western society. In addition, he must fully understand the implications of the movement toward the star that the critic mentions and do so in order to inscribe his project on the horizon of Western culture. The place of the parasitic project still and always remains subject to the magnetic field opened up by the main star, the expansion of which dismantles the originality of the parasite and confers on it, a priori, a parallel and inferior meaning. Thus the magnetic field organizes the space of literature through this unique force of attraction that the critic chooses and imposes on Latin American artists, this group of anonymous corpuscles that feed on the generosity of the trendsetter and the encyclopedic memory of the critic.

Let us just say parenthetically that the critical discourse that we have just described in its most general teams does not differ greatly from neo-colonialist discourse: after all, both speak of deficient economies. Indeed, it might be necessary some day to write a psychoanalytic study of the pleasure that appears on the face of some college professors when they discover an influence, as if the *truth* of a text could only be ascertained through debt and imitation. It is a curious truth that preaches the love of genealogy and a curious profession which, with its gaze turned toward the past and to the expense of the present, establishes value as dependent on the discovery of a contracted debt, a stolen idea, or a borrowed image or word. The prophetic, cannibalistic voice of Paul Valéry calls us: "nothing more original, more intrinsic to itself than feeding on others. But it is necessary to digest them. The lion is comprised of ingested sheep."

Declaring the collapse of a method such as this implies the need to replace it with another, in which the elements that have been forgotten, neglected, or abandoned by detectivesque criticism can be isolated and emphasized for the benefit of a new critical practice which, in turn, will forget and neglect the hunt for sources and influences and establish difference as the sole critical value. The Latin American writer throws at literature that same malevolent, audacious gaze that we find in Roland Barthes's recent reading/writing of Balzac's short story "Sarrasine," which had, in previous generations, succumbed to the flames of immolation. In *S/Z* Barthes proposes, as a point of departure, the division of literature into readerly and writerly texts, taking into consideration the fact that the evaluation that one makes of a text today is intimately connected to a "practice, and this practice is that of writing" [écriture]. The readerly text is that which can be read but not written, not rewritten. It is the classic text par excellence that invites the reader to dwell within the interior of its enclosure. Writerly texts, on the other hand, present a productive (nonrepresentational) model that motivates the reader to abandon his comfortable position as consumer and take the risk of becoming a producer of texts: "to reconstitute every text, not in its individuality, but in its playfulness," states Barthes. In this way, reading, rather than pacifying the reader or guaranteeing his place as a paying customer in bourgeois society, awakens him, transforms and radicalizes him, finally accelerating the process of expressing his own experience. In other words, it invites him to praxis. Let us quote Barthes again: "Which texts would I accept to write (rewrite), desire, and affirm as a power in this world which is mine?"

This question, which reflects a restless, dissenting, and anthropophagous assimilation, is similar to what writers from cultures dominated by others have been doing for years: reading with the aim of searching for a writerly text that can motivate them to work and that can serve as model in the organization of their own writing. Such writers systematically implement digression, this form, as Barthes points out, so poorly integrated into the discourse of knowledge. Borrowing an expression recently coined by Michel Foucault in his analysis of *Bouvard et Pécouchet,* perhaps it could be said that the second work is thus constructed from a ferocious commitment to the *déjà-dit,* although perhaps it would be more precise to say to the *déjà-écrit.*

The second text organizes itself on the basis of its silent, treacherous meditation on the first, while the reader, now transformed into its author, labors to unearth the limitations, weaknesses, and gaps to be found in the original model. Thus, s/he dismantles and rearticulates it according to her/his own devices and ideological leanings, her/his own vision of the material as first presented in the original. The writer labors *on* another text and almost never exaggerates the role played in her/his work by the reality that surrounds her/him. In this sense, negative remarks dealing for example with the alienation of the Latin American writer are useless and even ridiculous. If the writer speaks exclusively of her/his own life experience, then her/his text remains unnoticed by her/his contemporaries. Thus it is best for her/him to learn first the language of the metropolis in order to then combat it more effectively. Our critical task will characterize itself primarily by analyzing the use that an author makes of a text or of a literary technique that belongs to public domain. It will study what s/he gets out of it and will end with a portrayal of the technique that the same writer constructs in her/his aggressive resignification of the original model: thus s/he will dismantle the principles that posited it as an unreproducible and wholly unique object. In the neocolonial space, the imaginary can no longer be construed on ignorance and ingenuity, nourished by a simplistic manipulation of notions pertaining to the author's immediate experience. Rather, it should affirm itself as a writing *upon* another writing. Since the second work generally embodies a critique of the previous work, it asserts itself with all the demystifying violence of an anatomic plate revealing the internal architecture of a human body. Propaganda is effective precisely because it speaks the language of our time.

The Latin American writer plays with the signs of another writer and of another work. The words of the other present themselves as objects that fascinate his eyes, his fingers, and the writing of the second text becomes partially the story of a sensual experience with foreign signs. Sartre has perfectly described this sensation, the adventure of reading, when he tells us of his childhood experiences in the family library: "The dense memories and the sweet nonsense of peasant children, I hopelessly searched for them in myself. I have never played in the dirt, I have never searched for birds' nests, nor collected plants, nor thrown rocks at birds. However, books have been my birds and my nests, my pets, my stable, and my field."

Since the sign is often presented in a foreign language, the work of the writer becomes a kind of global translation, a pastiche, a parody or a digression rather than a literal translation. The foreign sign reflects itself in the mirror of the dictionary and in the creative imagination of the Latin American writer, and disseminates itself throughout the blank page with the grace and nonchalance of a hand sketching lines and curves. During the process of translation, the imaginary of the writer is always on stage, as in this beautiful example borrowed from Julio Cortázar.

The main character of *62,* an Argentine, sees the following magical sentence drawn on the mirror of the Parisian restaurant where he is going to have dinner: "Je voudrais un château saignant." But instead of reproducing the sentence in the original, he immediately translates it: "I would like a bloody castle." Written on the mirror and appropriated into the visual field of the Latin American character, *château* is removed from its gastronomic context and inscribed into a feudal, colonialist context, the lord's dwelling, *el castillo.* And the adjective that merely indicated the customer's preference for rare steak becomes, in the pen of the Argentine writer—*sangriento*—the obvious sign of an uprising, a desire to destroy the château, the castillo, to put it to fire and sword. The *translation* of the signifier posits a new meaning as well as suggesting the name of the person who best understood the New World in the nineteenth century: René de Chateaubriand. It is by no means coincidental that, before entering the restaurant, Cortázar's character buys a book written by another tireless traveler, Michel Butor, in which he talks about the author of *René* and *Atala*. So the customer's statement uttered in all its gastronomic innocence, "je voudrais un château saignant," is viewed on the surface of the mirror, of the dictionary, by an imagination that is already laboring under the influence of Butor and the situation of any South American in Paris, "I would like a bloody castle."

It is difficult to define whether it is the sentence that attracts the South American's attention or if he sees it because he has just raised his eyes from Butor's book. In any case, one thing is clear: the readings of the South American writer are never innocent and they never could be.

From the book to the mirror, the mirror to the gluttonous customer, the château to its translation, Chateaubriand to the Latin American writer, the original to the aggression—it is in these completed transformations[6] and in the final stillness of coagulated desire, in writing, that we can elucidate the contemporary critical space in which we must begin reading the romantic texts of the New World. This is the space in which, although the signifier may remain the same, the signified disseminates another inverted meaning. Let us take, for example, the word *Indian*. In Chateaubriand, as in many other European Romantics, this signifier becomes the origin of a whole literary theme telling us of escape, travel, and the desire to evade the narrow contours of the European homeland. Rimbaud, for example, opens his "Bateau Ivre" with an allusion to the "Peaux rouges criards," which, in its childish innocence, foreshadows the cry of rebellion that we hear at the end of the poem: "I miss Europe and its ancient parapets." However, when that same signifier—Indian/redskin—appears in the American Romantic text, it becomes a political symbol of postindependence nationalism finally raising its free voice (or apparently free voice, as is unfortunately too often the case). And if among Europeans that signifier expresses a desire for expansion, among Americans its translation reveals a desire to establish the limits of the new nation, a form of contraction.

Let me pause for a moment and closely analyze a short story by Jorge Luis Borges whose title in itself reveals our very purpose: "Pierre Menard, Author of the *Quijote*." Pierre Menard, novelist and symbolist poet but also a tireless reader, a devourer of books, is the ideal metaphor for disclosing the role of the Latin American writer, since he lives between the assimilation of the original model, that is, between the love and respect for that which is already written, and the need to produce a new text that confronts and sometimes negates that original. Pierre Menard's literary works were first zealously classified by Mme. Bachelier: they consist of the works published during his lifetime and read with pleasure by his admirers. But, the narrator tells us, Mme. Bachelier omits the most absurd and most ambitious of his projects from Menard's bibliography: that is, his desire to rewrite the *Quijote:* "He did not want to compose another *Quijote,* which would have been easy, but the *Quijote* itself." Mme. Bachelier's omission, the story's narrator states, stems from the fact that she was unable to *see* Pierre Menard's *invisible,* "subterraneous, endlessly heroic, unrivalled" work. The few chapters written by Menard are invisible because the model and the copy are identical; there is no difference in vocabulary, syntax, or structure between the two versions, one by Cervantes, the other Menard's copy. The invisible work is the paradox of the second text that completely disappears and thereby opens the space of its most evident signification: the cultural, social, and political situation in which the second author is located.

Nevertheless the second text can be *visible:* thus it is that the story's narrator can include Paul Valéry's poem "Le cimetière marin" in Menard's bibliography after all, since, in the poem's transcription, Valéry's decasyllables have become alexandrines. Indeed, the aggression against and the consequent transgression of Valéry's model-poem are revealed precisely within these two syllables added to the decasyllable, a small sonorous and differential supplement that reorganizes the visual and silent space of Valéry's stanza and poem and also modifies the internal rhythm of each verse. Hence the originality of Pierre Menard's *visible* work resides in that small but violent supplement that inscribes its presence on the blank page and provokes a rupture between model and copy, finally locating the poet in his challenge to literature and the work that serves as his inspiration. "The lion is comprised of ingested sheep."

According to Pierre Menard, if Cervantes had not "rejected the cooperation of chance in the construction of his text," he did assure, however, "the mysterious duty of literally reconstituting his spontaneous work." In Menard, as in many Latin American writers, there is a rejection of the "spontaneous" and an acceptance of writing as a lucid and conscious duty. Perhaps it is time to suggest, as a revealing image for the underground and endlessly heroic endeavor of the Latin American writer, the very title of the first section of Borges's collection of short stories: "The Garden of Forking Paths." Literature, the garden; the writer's task, the conscious choice before each fork rather than the calm acceptance of chance invention. Knowledge is conceived as a form of production. The consumption of the book through reading already implies the organization of a writing praxis.

The project of Pierre Menard therefore rejects total freedom in creation, which is, after all, a power traditionally conferred on the artist as an element that establishes identity and difference in Western neocolonialist culture. Freedom, in Menard, is controlled by the original model, in the very same way that the citizens' freedom in colonized countries is put under close surveillance by metropolitan power. Menard's presence—difference, writing, originality—inscribes itself within the transgression of the model, within a subtle and imperceptible movement of conversion, perversion, and inversion.

The originality of Pierre Menard's project, its visible and written aspect, derives from the fact that he refuses to accept the traditional notion of artistic invention since he himself denies the total freedom of the artist. Like Robert Desnos, he proclaims *formes prisons* his site of elaboration. The Latin American artist accepts prison as a form of behavior, and transgression as a form of expression. This, no doubt, points to the absurd, the torment, beauty, and vigor of his visible project. The invisible becomes *silence* in his text—the presence of the model—while the visible becomes a message that constitutes absence in the model. Let us quote Pierre Menard once again: "My solitary game is ruled by two diametrically opposed laws. The first one allows me to practice formal or psychological variations; the second one obliges me to sacrifice them to the 'original' text."

As so often mentioned in Borges's short stories, the Latin American writer is a devourer of books. He reads constantly and publishes occasionally. Knowledge never corrodes the delicate and secret mechanisms of creation; quite the contrary, it stimulates his creative processes, since it is the organizing principle of textual production. In this sense, Latin American writers' strategies of reading and producing are similar to Marx's strategy as recently discussed by Louis Althusser. Our reading is as *guilty* as Althusser's since we read Latin American writers "by observing the rules of a reading whose impressive lesson is given to us in their own reading" of European writers. Let us quote from Althusser once again: "When we read Marx, we are faced with a *reader* reading out loud Quesnay, Smith, Ricardo, etc. before us in order to support his argument with whatever they said that he considers to be true, and to critique whatever he considers to be false."

Contemporary Latin American literature gives us a text and at the same time opens up a theoretical field whose elaboration can be inspiring. This theoretical field undermines the principles of academic practices interested exclusively in the *invisible* areas of the text, in the debts contracted by the writer. At the same time it rejects the discourse of pseudomarxist critique that preaches a direct praxis of the text. Rather, the new theoretical field suggests that the efficacy of such readings is the result of facile interpretation. Such theoreticians forget that the effectiveness of a critique cannot be measured by the sloth it inspires in its reader; on the contrary, it should decondition the reader and make his life impossible within bourgeois consumer society. Facile reading confirms the ideas of neocolonialist forces who insist that the country is in the state it is because of the laziness of its inhabitants. The Latin American writer demonstrates that we should free ourselves from the image of a smiling carnival and fiesta-filled holiday haven for cultural tourism.

Somewhere between sacrifice and playfulness, prison and transgression, submission to the code and aggression, obedience and rebellion, assimilation and expression—there, in this apparently empty space, its temple and its clandestinity, is where the anthropophagous ritual of Latin American discourse is constructed.

Translated by Ana Lúcia Gazzola and Gareth Williams

3. Eça, Author of *Madame Bovary*

■

FOR HEITOR AND TEREZINHA

. . . which texts would I agree to write (to rewrite), to desire, to put forth as a power within this world which is mine?—Roland Barthes, S / Z

The allusion in the title is obvious: Jorge Luis Borges and his story "Pierre Menard, Author of the *Quijote,*" published in *Fictions*. Less obvious, however, are my intentions: to trace the ways in which the proximity of Flaubert and Eça de Queirós in the European literary space, or even the intrinsic connection between *Madame Bovary* and *O primo Basílio* [Cousin Basilio], are different from or even the opposite of the relations proposed in Borges's story. The contemporaneity of the French and Portuguese writers, together with the precedence of the French text over the dependent Portuguese text, will lead us inevitably to what has been the banquet of traditional criticism: the search for and the study of sources.

I

In the specific case of "Pierre Menard," three centuries separate the model from its copy. Moreover, no lexical, syntactical, or structural violation is found in the second version that might produce a clear difference from the first. These are three centuries in which events and discoveries have produced definitive and unpredictable disjunctions—including what the book *Don Quixote* itself meant in the seventeenth century—that changed the meaning of Cervantes's work when analyzed both within the historical context, "the century of the Battle of Lepanto and of Lope de Vega," and within the historical context of the critic and the reader. Between the book's publication and its prestige as a literary classic one encounters its inclusion in the delicate and flexible system of History, together with its status as a transformational agent within the system to which it now belongs, by rights that have also been acquired by literary critics and historians. The accommodation of the work to History and the threat of it being cast into the oblivion of the library catalogue can only be annulled by a critic who renders it contemporary—transforming it into a prisoner of his own historical context. If the work is the same (no matter the century in which it is read), it is the name of its *second* author (that is, of the critic) that stamps the work with its new, original meaning.

As the Argentine writer proposes, the copy can also not be identical to the original, in which case it forms a part of the modernizing game, "Christ on a boulevard, Hamlet on Cannebière, Quixote on Wall Street." This is a modernizing game that appropriates the theater and cinema of a certain period and clarifies it for its contemporaries by bringing it up to date, centuries later, with the aid of modern techniques or accessories. The main function of these elements is to disclose those aspects of the original that would otherwise be comprehensible only as a result of beginner's luck. This kind of critical transformation can be found in 1925, in the poet Manuel Bandeira, a contemporary of Pierre Menard, who took two poems (one from Bocage and the other from Castro Alves) and "translated" them (the term is his) into the language and typography of the Brazilian avant-garde of the time, adding that "my purpose was to translate with the greatest fidelity and without allowing any personal feeling to slip into the translation: I hope I have achieved this." He ended by stating that the translation of Castro Alves's poem, "O Adeus de Tereza," "is so far from the original that to the uninitiated it appears to be a creation."

On the other hand, and still in reference to Borges's text, we could speak of the possibility of restructuring the complementary characters, Don Quixote and Sancho. For example, this would be the case of the novelist Daudet, who, by creating Tartarin, attempted to unite "in *one* figure the Ingenioso Hidalgo and his squire." Tartarin would be the typical by-product of Christian theory, which, from the beginning of the nineteenth century, insisted on mixing the grotesque with the sublime—the theory of Victor Hugo's *homo duplex* as expressed in his "Preface to Cromwell," and reworked later by Baudelaire as the angel and the beast, the two postulates. Finally, the copy could even signify the *total identification* of one author with another. This would be typical of a certain kind of criticism, exemplified by Georges Poulet, who, on the opening page of *Les chemins actuels de la critique* [Current trends of criticism], states that "there is no true criticism without the coincidence of two consciousnesses."

And yet, as stated above, in Pierre Menard's project the model and the copy are *identical,* rendering his version of *Don Quijote* different from all his previous production in which he invariably added similarities. The narrator of Borges's story—and this would be the raison d'être for his writing—proposes a new cataloguing of the complete works of Pierre Menard under two headings: their *visible* and their *invisible* features would be taken into consideration, the latter determining his *endlessly heroic* work, his "peerless" work.

Thus, in the catalogue of the *visible* works established by the story's narrator, we could include the poem "Le cimitière marin" [Sea cemetery], by Paul Valéry, since in Menard's transcription Valéry's decasyllabic lines are transformed into alexandrines. The *transgression of the model,* therefore, occurs in the two syllables added to each verse, thereby reorganizing the visual space of the stanza and the poem and modifying the internal rhythm of the verse. In this sense, but now in the merely visual field, one might recall Robert Desmos's disobedient translation of the poem "Our Father" published in *L'Aumonyme* (1923). I say the visual field because in the auditory, sonorous field the poem represents no transgression—for the sound of the combined words constitute, phoneme by phoneme, the whole of the Catholic prayer. Following is Desnos's double rendering of sound and spacing:

> Nounou laissez-nous succomber à la tentation
> et d'aile ivrez-nous du mal.

But in the case of Menard's *Don Quijote* the texts are identical, and if, in order to construct his novel, Cervantes "did not refuse the collaboration of chance" or of invention, Pierre Menard, on the other hand, has "adopted the mysterious duty of literally reconstructing a spontaneous work." Pierre Menard's *Quijote* can thus find its raison d'être and metaphorization in the title of the first section of Borges's *Fictions:* "The Garden of Forking Paths," in which the narrator's conscious choice of paths produces his destiny rather than positioning him as an invented product of chance.

Pierre Menard's project therefore rejects the *freedom* of creation (on both visible and invisible levels), which in our culture has traditionally produced identity and difference, plagiarism and originality. This is a problem that the French structuralists attempted to resolve in a gesture similar to that of the Spanish Hidalgo as they attempted to codify each and every *récit.* This is precisely the growing freedom that Roman Jakobson talks about in his article "Two Aspects of Language and Two Types of Aphasia":

> There is, then, in the combination of linguistic units, an ascending scale of freedom. In the combination of distinctive features in phonemes, the individual freedom of the speaker is nonexistent; the code has already determined all the possibilities that can be used in the language in question. The freedom to combine phonemes into words is circumscribed: it is limited to the marginal situation of the creation of words. In forming sentences with words, the speaker is subject to less coercion. And finally, in the combination of sentences in utterances, the action of coercive rules ceases, and the freedom of any individual to create new contexts increases substantially, although one should not underestimate the number of stereotyped utterances.

Prisoner of the dictionary and of syntax, the writer only encounters freedom by hurling himself into the combination of sentences. This problem has hindered enormously the possibility of a literary criticism based on the "second degree linguistics" that Roland Barthes calls for when, in his essay on "The Structural Analysis of the *Récit*" published in *Communication* No. 8, he attempts to establish a homological relation between the sentence and the *discours,* applying to the latter—to the récit—the properties already found and codified by linguistics in sentence analysis.

The originality of Pierre Menard's project, his invisible work, emerges therefore from the fact that by refusing our traditional conception of what invention is he succeeds in denying the freedom of the creator, thus constituting our imprisonment within the workings of the models as the only means of upholding the absurdity of his project. In a letter to the story's narrator, Pierre Menard says: "My solitary game is governed by two polar laws. The first allows me to test variants of a formal and psychological type; the second obliges me to sacrifice them to the 'original' text and to affirm this annihilation irrefutably."

This formulation of literary creation would not be far from the definition proposed by the creator of the formes prisons, Robert Desnos, who, in *L'Aumonyme,* defines the poet as:

	syllabes
Prisonnier des	et non des sens.
	mots
	syllables
[Prisoner of	and not of meanings.]
	words

Let us leave aside the lure of my title and engage the complex problems that emerge from within a number of novels that, with a very short period of time between their publications, all share the same theme. In particular we will examine the problem of the translation from one existing structure in a given culture (in this case the French) to another, or others (in particular the Portuguese and the Brazilian). Thus we will deal with problems of disarticulation and rearticulation, of negation and affirmation, of a violent contradiction transformed into panic in the face of the already militant criticism of Eça de Queirós during the last century. Plagiarism and the accusation of plagiarism haunt the end of the nineteenth century and especially this novelist who, since *O crime do Padre Amaro* [The crime of Father Amaro], found himself charged both in Brazil and Portugal of plagiarizing Zola and *La faute de l'Abbé Mouret* [The fault of Abbey Mouret].

In order to advance our discussion, let us take up once again the visible/invisible, apparent/clandestine dichotomy found in Borges, and try to examine the way in which it is articulated in the relationship between *Madame Bovary* and *O primo Basílio,* and how it could, in a way, reveal the Portuguese novelist's mystery of creation while clarifying not his debt to Flaubert but his enrichment of Emma's story, or, if not its enrichment, at least how poor *Madame Bovary* appears alongside the rich complexity of *O primo Basílio.*

Eça de Queirós's invisible work can be found at the beginning of the novel in the buzzing of the Flaubertian flies that have been attracted by the sugar at the bottom of a cider glass, a choice of beverage that conjures the Norman space immediately opened up by the French novel. This is a buzzing that will later echo in Lisbon, as flies crawl along a table and finally settle on the sugar remaining at the bottom of a teacup that had been served to and drunk by the protagonists. Indeed, the imported nature of the tea immediately denotes the need that the Portuguese have for vicariously living the foreign. In the same vein these flies are transformed into *moustiques* in Robbe-Grillet's more recent *La jalousie* [Jealousy]. But in this novel, rather than being attracted by the sugar, they fly around the kerosene lamp. Their buzzing superimposes itself on the lamp's hissing and is interrupted sporadically by the noise of nocturnal insects or the cries of animals, and especially by the long-awaited sound of the car bringing back the wife that the narrator suspects of being an adulteress. And this in a novelist who has been considered the pope of the *École du regard.*

Continuing along this line but without wishing to exhaust the coincidences found in *Madame Bovary* and *O primo Basílio,* we should speak of our heroines' preferred readings, especially since the romantic novels that they digest, as René Girard has shown in his analysis of the romances of chivalry consumed by Don Quixote, play a fundamental role in the genesis of the analysis of desire. According to Girard, desire is a "simple straight line that unites subject and object," but above this line is the mediating textual object that joins both subject and object. The presence of the mediating object has led Girard to present the problem through the spatial metaphor of the "triangle of desire." Girard notes: "In Flaubert's novels one encounters desire according to the *Other* and the 'seminal' character of literature. Emma Bovary desires through the romantic heroines who have filled her imagination."

In Flaubert's novel one reads: "Later, with Walter Scott, she falls in love with historical facts, dreams of trunks, guard-rooms and troubadours. She wishes she had lived in some old manor, like those high-busted ladies who, under the clover of the ogives, would spend their days, elbow resting on a rock and chin in their hand, watching a knight with a white plume arriving at a gallop from the country on a black horse."

And in Eça de Queirós's novel:

> While single, 18 years old, she had become enthusiastic over Walter Scott and Scotland: she had wished to live then in one of those Scottish castles with the clan's coats-of-arms over the ogives, furnished with gothic trunks and trophies of arms, covered with wide tapestries embroidered with heroic legends that the wind of the lake stirs and brings to life; and she had loved Evandalo, Morton, and Ivanhoe, tender and grave, wearing on their helmet the eagle's plume, fixed on the side by the thistle of Scotland of emeralds and diamonds.

What is even more curious, reminding us not so much of "Pierre Menard" as another Borges story (the first in the *Fictions* collection, "Tlon, Ubquar, Orbis Tertium," which seems to confirm that this is without doubt the *invisible* body of Eça de Queirós's work) is that one does not find this paragraph in the American translation of *Cousin Basilio.* Either Roy Campbell, the translator, or Noonday Press, the publisher, anticipated our reading and simply suppressed any allusion to Walter Scott from these pages. Thus, in the English version, the Portuguese Luisa has never read the author of *Ivanhoe.*

But where the invisibility of *O primo Basílio* is most notable is in the absence of any concept of the city of Lisbon, a cultural center that remains so different from any other European capital city. And herein lies Eça de Queirós's need to portray Lisbon as if it were any small provincial French town, such as Tostes or Yonville. In Tostes, Emma muses: "What would that Paris be like? What a colossal name! She repeated it to herself in a low voice, for the pleasure of it; it sounded to her ears like a great bell in a cathedral! It shone in her eyes even on the label of her pots of pomade."

Both novelists establish Paris as the point of ideal, cosmopolitan reference for their heroines, the geometric place on which the hopes of both the provincial Emma and the provincial Lisbonite Luisa converge.

Paris, center of France for the provinces. Paris, center of Europe for Portugal. In their sharing of the same center, the peripheral Yonville and Lisbon become equal. For Louisa: "And to go to Paris! Especially Paris! But how! She would never really go; they were poor; Jorge was a stay-at-home, so Lisbonite!" Indeed, we could even generalize the allure of Paris for the Portuguese with a few lines from Cesário Verde's "O sentimento de um ocidental" [The feeling of a westerner] or with a letter that he wrote on July 16, 1879, to his friend Mariano Pina: "Your stay in Paris makes me, me particularly, feel quite bad; it generates in me the fixation, the monomania, of going there. I make immense efforts to witness what goes on in that superior world and deplorably neglect what goes on around me. Like an abstract astronomer I point a telescope abroad and, my eyes tired and kidneys pained, look attentively, constantly. Somebody could stab me, which is highly likely, and I would not see who had done it."

This attitude, which is overtly translated into Verde's poetry, led Ramalho Ortigão, in his criticism of Verde's work, to attack him violently for his false dandyism:

> In Portugal there are honest public servants, worthy businessmen, peaceful heads of family, discreet embibers of tea with milk and of pale Colares diluted with Arsenal water, who have decided to follow the Baudelaire style. Since, however, Baudelaire was corrupt and they are not, since Baudelaire was a dandy and they are not, since Baudelaire lived on the boulevard of the Italians and they live on Cabalhoeiros Street, since Baudelaire knew of fashion, elegance, sport, and the *demimonde*, while they only know of cheap fabrics, empty spools, and pincushions by Mr. Marçal Maria Fernandes, tailor of Santa Justa lane, the result is that they have put a false poetry in circulation that belongs neither to the environment in which it was born, nor to that to which it is addressed. (*Farpas*, vol. 10, p. 221)

This criticism is precisely the reaction that was needed to counter the kind of cosmopolitanism that was preached in the Lectures of the Cassino Lisbonense of 1871 or, even before that in 1865, in the famous letter from Antero de Quental to Antonio Feliciano de Castilho: "Nevertheless, whenever one thinks and knows anything in Europe, it is not Portugal, not Lisbon; it is Paris, London, Berlin."

If Borges's analysis of Pierre Menard's invisible work led him to the discovery of his originality, of the truly extraordinary quality of Menard's unfinished project, *Don Quijote,* my examination of the equivalent function in Eça de Queirós leads us only to the worst of what *O primo Basílio* and a great deal of Portuguese production at the turn of the century can offer us. The equation here is inverted: what is imposed in the Portuguese novel, what the reader looks for today in Eça's novel is the *visible,* those details that disclose the difference that the novelist wished to establish with its Flaubertian model, together with the spectacular commentaries that appear throughout the course of *O primo Basílio.*

III

Perhaps I could broaden the debate at this point and reveal the conclusion that I hope to reach. The wealth and interest of both Portuguese and Brazilian literatures in the nineteenth century do not derive so much from the *originality of the model,* from the abstract or dramatic framework of the novel or poem, as from the *transgression* constructed by creating a new use for any model borrowed from the dominant culture. In this way, the work of art is organized by an artist's silent and treacherous meditation, which is designed to surprise the original in its very limitations. The artist thus disarticulates and rearticulates it in accordance with his secondary meditated reading of themes originally presented in the metropolis. The Brazilian romantics, for example, immediately realized this when they began to deal with the theme of the Indian. Idealized and exoticized by Europeans, object of an entire literature of evasion and of flight from the strictures of the European fatherland, a bearer of new values that the New World was attempting to impose on Western culture, the Indian, when produced by the pen of Brazilian writers, was always a political symbol of nationalism, of the search for the roots of Brazilian culture, an unfurled banner that bespoke the recent independence of the country and the need for writers to deal with elements indigenous to their own civilization, which until then had been merely a product of metropolitan colonialism.

Erected on its commitment to the already spoken, to use Michel Foucault's phrase in his analysis of *Bouvard et Pécuchet,* the second work maintains little contact with the immediate reality of its author. For this reason, criticism addressing the alienation of the author is useless and even ridiculous. Rather, one should review the propriety with which the writer utilizes a text that already exists in the public domain, and in particular the tactics he invents in order to assault that original and shake the foundations that grounded it as a unique object impervious to reproduction. The imaginary of the writer is nourished not so much by the experiential manipulation of immediate reality as by the novel's metalanguage. Since the second work generally presupposes the critique of the first, it imposes itself with the demystifying violence of the anatomical plates laying bare the internal architecture of the human body. In this process of demystification, the second discourse presupposes the existence of a prior and similar other, which is both its point of departure and its arrival, a closed circuit in which the decisions to be made by the narrator or by his characters before each "forking" are already more or less foreseen and prescribed by the original.

The freedom to be exercised, then, exists much more on the plane of the general architecture of the novel than in the minute transformations that could be made in the character's behavior. Thus, there is little difference between the suicide of Emma Bovary and the natural death that slowly befalls Luisa. Let us not fall into the trap set by Machado de Assis in his famous criticism of *O primo Basílio:* "Luisa is a negative character and, throughout the action portrayed by the author, more of a puppet than a moral person" for she lacks "passion, remorse and, still less, conscience." Although Machado de Assis doesn't mention *Madame Bovary* by name, he kept the novel intact in his mind while already engaged in a project that would later become *Dom Casmurro,* a third work, therefore. Concerned rather more with the ethical-moral drama of the jealous character than with the secrets of adultery, Machado de Assis could not understand that the game imagined by Eça de Queirós was situated on another level quite different from Flaubert's: that of the repetition that results in profundity. In other words, any commentary on Luisa's attitudes or even on those of her husband cannot be located on the conventional plane of the narrow moral and violent reaction to a cause which is obvious to the reader, but will have to organize itself in accordance with reactions to a previously written text, to a reproduction of the general theme within the interior of *O primo Basílio* itself.

IV

I am obviously referring to the play that Ernestinho writes and rewrites while the action of the novel unfolds and that premieres shortly before Luisa's death. The play is called *Honra e paixão* [Honor and passion], a title that leads us directly to the situation of both Emma and Luisa. The play's argument, sketched out by its author during a small family gathering that takes place in chapter 2, an occasion that the author uses as a means of presenting the main characters in the novel, is as follows:

She was a married woman. In Sintra she had met a fateful man, the count of Monte Redondo. Her ruined husband had a gambling debt of a hundred *contos*. He was dishonored, and was going to be jailed. The woman, mad, runs to some castled ruins where the count lives and lets her veil fall, telling him of the catastrophe. The count throws his cloak over his shoulders and departs, arriving at precisely the moment when the police are taking the man away. "It is a very moving scene," he said, "at night, in the moonlight!" The count reveals himself, throws a pouch of gold at the feet of the police officers, shouting, "Glut yourselves, you vultures!" "Fine ending!" the Counsellor murmured. "Finally," added Ernestinho, summing up, "here is the complicated ending: the count of Monte Redondo and the woman love each other, the husband finds out, flings all his gold at the feet of the count, and kills his wife."

The play's ending, however, brings considerable difficulties to Ernestinho's already troubled life, primarily because his literary agent demands two substantial changes. The final scene will not take place at the edge of a cliff but in a drawing-room, and worse! he wants the husband to forgive his wife. The subject is then put up for discussion among various guests. We should call attention to the opinion of Jorge, Luisa's husband, not only for the sharpness and moral intransigence of his words but also because they reveal the novel's first intervention by the future cuckold. In a way, Jorge's resistance will remain in the reader's mind during the slow unraveling of Luisa's drama, constantly reminding us of the novel's true-to-life outcome. Jorge says: "I speak seriously and I mean it! If the husband is betrayed I'm in favor of death. Over the cliff, in the drawing-room, on the street, but let him kill her. How can I consent that in a case like this, a cousin of mine, someone from my family, of my own blood, be ready to forgive like some infatuated fellow! No, kill her! It's a family principle. Kill her all the sooner!"

Jorge's words, of course, scarcely find an echo among his friends who are all in favor of mercy. But dissatisfied, Jorge insists on the husband's authority over the wife and even transfers the problem onto Ernestinho's personal life, rendering the narrative "real" and at the same time abolishing Eliotian aesthetic distance. His own opinion would be no different: "And here, if instead of talking about the end of an act it were a case of real life, if Ernesto came to tell me: you know, I found my wife . . . I give my word of honor that I would give him the same answer: kill her!"

Everyone violently protests, and henceforth the future injured husband is nicknamed "tiger, Othello, Bluebeard."

It is not a mere coincidence that a series of allusions to Ernestinho, to his play, and to Jorge's reactions become inserted in the development of the plot at exactly those points in which their significance finds parallel meaning in the actions of a particular character. In this way they become a kind of mirror defining the moral limits of the character's attitudes, as if the latter, deprived of the internal landscape that Gide talks about and therefore inscribed in total superficiality, could only see the consequences of his acts on the surface of the mirror which is Ernestinho's text. Therefore, for the further analysis of Eça de Queirós, it is important to rethink the moral categories—lucidity, remorse, expiation, consciousness of evil—established by the Flaubert/Baudelaire axis that was sustained, as we have seen, by Machado de Assis in his unfavorable critique of *O primo Basílio*. Eça de Queirós's art finds its modernity precisely in this taste for the external, for the surface, insofar as it is freed of any involvement in introspection, living skin-deep, to use Jean Cocteau's expression, or even "unfolding-deep," as we shall see presently.

For example, in chapter 7, when Luisa is on her way to the "Paradise" to meet Basilio, she runs into Ernestinho by chance on the street. After complaining once again about his agent, he confesses to Luisa that he has finally decided to pardon his heroine and give her husband a post in a foreign embassy, a decision which contributes to a certain sense of uneasiness in Luisa when she proceeds to meet her lover: "Luisa entered the 'Paradise' quite vexed. She told Basilio of the meeting [with Ernestinho]. Ernestinho was so foolish! He could talk about that later, relay the encounter, someone could ask her who was the friend from Porto . . . —No, really, it's not prudent to come like this so often. It'd be better not to come so much. Someone might find out."

In this same line of reasoning we see that much later, in chapter 9, when Luisa thinks of the reactions that her husband may have when he discovers her adultery, the picture she forms in her imagination is inspired by the intransigent and spiteful Jorge that she learned of in chapter 2: "What would he do if he knew? Would he kill her? She remembered his serious words that night when Ernestinho told them the ending of his drama."

The circle traced around the characters of *O primo Basílio* and *Honra e paixão* draws in tighter, almost completely organizing Luisa's imaginary life. Indeed, from within this form of reflective development, we pass to a form of symbiosis in which the characters of the novel lose their identity in the masks of Ernestinho's characters (actors all of them), as well as in the entanglements of the intrigue established by the Portuguese Dumas *fils*. Luisa's third dream is wholly dominated by the idea of theater, of the play, and by the figure of Ernestinho: Luisa is an actress playing the part of the heroine of *Honra e paixão* when, beneath the features of the count she recognizes, as we also discern, Basilio. In the end the husband, Jorge, appears and despite the dramatist's modifications, plays his role according to the first version, reaping revenge on his unfaithful wife. If the author Ernestinho had already forgiven the wife, in the actress's dream the author continues to exact revenge. Following are a couple of sentences taken from the long passage of the dream: "She was on stage; she was an actress; she was making her debut in Ernestinho's drama; and very nervous she saw before her in the vast whispering audience, rows of black, burning eyes, angrily fixed on her. . . . Basilio repeated on stage, without embarrassment, the libertine delights of the Paraíso! How did she consent? . . . and she saw Jorge, Jorge who advanced, dressed in mourning, with black gloves and a dagger in his hand, the blade shining less than his eyes."

As the novel comes to a close, that is to say, within its nineteenth-century novelistic techniques, as the moment of the hero's or the heroine's death approaches, Ernestinho's play becomes more concrete. In the novel's penultimate chapter, the play premieres with great success. Luisa is already suffering from a strange and undefined disease and could not be present at her friend's success, but Ernestinho visits the couple to relay the good news. At a certain point, the conversation centers on Jorge, and for the first time, the playwright informs him that he had changed his mind about the fifth act of the play (in a conversation that repeats the aforementioned dialogue between Ernestinho and Luisa). As previously in the case of Luisa, shortly before her visit to the "Paradise," the author of *Honra e paixão* activates Jorge's growing awareness of the problem that he is facing in silence, installing in him a certain insecurity that will take over from the peace that he had found in the unconsciousness of passion. As in a Greek tragedy, it is at this moment, when confronted by factors external to him, in the face of outside stimulus, that Jorge understands that he has changed his way of thinking. Eça de Queirós's dialogue is revealing:

"It was Jorge who wanted to kill her," Ernestinho said, giving himself up to laughter.

"Don't you remember that night . . . ?"

"Yes, yes," said Jorge, laughing too, but nervously.

"Our Jorge," said the Counsellor solemnly, "could not maintain such extreme ideas. Surely reflection, experience of life . . ."

"I have changed, Counsellor, I have changed," Jorge interrupted.

The narrative process that we have been analyzing, that is to say, the presence in the novel's interior of a work of fiction that reproduces the novel, or the fact that the novelist dramatizes his ideal within the novel at the level of his characters, immediately positions Eça de Queirós and *O primo Basílio* alongside a number of other works. André Gide is perhaps the first to have called attention to the phenomenon which, according to him, can be found both in painting (the Flemish painters, Velásquez) and in the theater (*Hamlet*). In search of a point of reference Gide compares it to the fabrication of coats-of-arms, in which a central point reproduces the whole in miniature. The author of *The Counterfeiters* concludes: "I so much like to find in a work of art the very subject of the work transposed to the scale of the characters. Nothing illustrates better nor establishes more surely the proportions of the whole."

This might be the fate and originality of the best works written in cultures that remain dependent on another culture: the meditation on the prior work leads the lucid artist to a transgression of the model. The transgression of *Madame Bovary* is concretized in *O primo Basílio* not so much in the change of the title, which at first sight might give us the impression that Eça de Queirós wanted to shift the narrative point-of-view by moving from the adulterous wife to the lover, but in the creation of Ernestinho, whose authorial project is similar in the dialectic of its title, its honor/passion, to that of Eça's and to the drama of Luisa and Jorge. Eça de Queirós makes his characters conscious of their fate before they give themselves up to the adventures that await them; he makes them conscious of their actions through a process of mirroring and unfolding; finally, he has Luisa feel the pain of remorse and expiation oneirically, through a process of symbiosis in which one body gives itself over to the mask of another, which is nothing more than a faithful copy of her own face. And he makes her find in her dream the catharsis necessary to continue surviving. In this phase of oneiric symbiosis, the drama of adultery is no longer articulated on the plane of lucidity but is transported to the imaginary and the unconscious.

On the axis between the imaginary and the unconscious we also encounter the supplement that develops the issue of day-dreaming and the "Bovaryesque" quality of Flaubert's novel. In both *Madame Bovary* and *O primo Basílio* (as René Girard has argued so well with the aid of Gaultier), day-dreaming produces one of the acute forms of triangular desire. Madame Bovary's imagination, which is completely overpowered by her reading of novels, establishes the mediating factor between herself and the love object that she covets. This process is also encountered in Eça de Queirós and I have emphasized that this would be the invisible part of his work. It is enough to quote the following sentence: "She herself would at last have the amorous adventure that she had read about so often in romantic novels!" But just as the Portuguese novelist surpassed his model in creating Ernestinho, who writes *Honra e paixão,* he also enriched the Flaubertian model by introducing the oneiric.

The oneiric becomes the poison cultivated in silence in the scorpion's tail, as a means both of defense and of attack, which in light of the circle of fire, the premonition of death, the absence caused by Basilio's departure, and the husband's cowardly aggressiveness, slowly turns against its own body, injecting into it drop by drop the liquid that it silently manufactured, that poison of remorse, nocturnal purification remaining always on the dark side of daytime, light, and consciousness. If day-dreaming roused desire and the consummation of pleasure in the unforgettable moments of "Paradise," the oneiric on the other hand is nothing more than remorse's powerful return. Little by little remorse establishes its reign in the body freed by pleasure and disobedience to society's code, a reign that is the torture and torment of man's law. Madame Bovary finds her punishment in arsenic, while Luisa, like a scorpion, struggles against the venom cultivated by the nocturnal life of the unconscious.

It would be ridiculous to try to lend Baudelaire's lucidity to Luisa, that is to say, "the consciousness in evil" expressed in the famous couplet:

Tête-à-tête sombre et limpide
Qu'un coeur devenu son miroir.
[Head to head somber and limpid
That a heart become its own mirror.]

On the contrary, Luisa, in her bourgeois Lisbonite mediocrity, lives the only drama that she can live in all its fullness: the unconsciousness in evil.

Finally Flaubert's and Eça de Queirós's visible works meet, intertwine, complement one another, and organize themselves harmonically in the European literary space of the second half of the nineteenth century. The invisible of one constitutes the visible of the other, and vice versa. Eça de Queirós's clandestine work is flung audaciously beyond the borders of little Portugal to be inscribed in the European firmament with the suicide of a scorpion.

Translated by Tom Burns and Ana Lúcia Gazzola

4. Universality in Spite of Dependency

■

FOR HELOÍSA

We are neither Europeans nor North Americans yet nothing to us is foreign for, deprived of an original culture, everything is foreign. The painful construction of our selfhood unravels itself through the tenuous dialectic between non-being and being other.—Paulo Emílio Salles Gomes (1973)

Because the truth (and I don't know whether it is bitter or sweet) is the following: if my generation is obliged (and I don't know whether this is its vocation) to formulate an eminently universalist *reinterpretation of the Brazilian predicament, it could only be achieved through a nationalizing and regionalizing interpretation of Modernism.—José Guilherme Merquior (1980)*

I

It is not every day that humanity's geographical "take" on the world is modified. But rather than producing a positive or fertile shift in the foundations of humanity or the society in whose name one discovers, the expansion of the cognitive horizon usually allows a pioneer to reproduce the sociopolitical and economic conflicts and impasses of his own society—yet to do so always elsewhere under the rubric of occupation. Here is a concrete example: the New World served as a stage to which the unresolvable European religious wars could be displaced. The victorious conqueror ended up introjecting the major dilemmas of the European kings and subjects—their entanglement in the disunity of the Church and the constant wars between different religious factions (Catholics, Lutherans, Calvinists)—into the "unknown" space of America. Thus it is that the "unknown" becomes "known" and the cultural pattern of colonization is established.

The catechism of a José de Anchieta, for example, both prepared the Indian for the "conversion" and "salvation" of his soul and served to locate him unwittingly between the Portuguese and the French, as well as between the Reformation and the Counter-Reformation. It prepared and incited him to fight for issues such as the unity of the Church and the constitution of the European state that simply did not pertain to him or to his people. He was obliged, in other words, to internalize an economic and sociopolitical situation that was not his. Symptomatic of this state of affairs was the devotion for Saint Mauritius, the patron saint of the state of Espírito Santo in Brazil, which Anchieta's text strived to inspire in his converts. Mauritius, a soldier loyal to a pagan emperor, was called to lead his Theban legion into battle against the Christians. In the midst of battle he changed sides and, deciding not to kill the Christians, undermined the supreme power of the emperor, and was duly sacrificed. Mauritius the soldier was a rebel before his pagan brothers whereas Mauritius the convert remained a martyr within the process of Catholic catechism. Thus it is that Saint Mauritius became the patron saint of Espírito Santo in this new dissemination of the faith. As a rebel, martyr, and patron saint he was, above all, a model to be imitated.

The life and martyrdom of the saint serve as symbolic counterpoint to resistance against the French and English corsairs (who were considered to be "heretical") that the Portuguese Christians were attempting to introduce into the Indian mind. The indigenous mind memorized Anchieta's didactic verses, which were placed before him as if they were his own:

> O pecado nos dá guerra
> em todo tempo e lugar.
> E, pois quisestes (S. Maurício) morar
> nesta nossa pobre terra,
> ajudai-a sem cessar,
>
> porque cessando o pecar
> cessarão muitos reveses
> com que os hereges franceses
> nos poderão apertar
> e luteranos ingleses.

[Sin combats us
in all time and places.
And since you desired (Saint Mauritius) to dwell
in our poor land,
help us incessantly,

for when sin ceases,
misfortunes
with which the French heretics
and English Lutherans
could afflict us, will perish.]

The struggle for power and the partition of "our poor land" implies religious division and conflict. But whereas in the Americas land was a stage and the struggle a simulation, in Europe the problem was the concrete reality of *cuius regio, eius religio* [each country has its own religion].

By this time the Indian was no longer considered a tabula rasa by the Portuguese but rather was seen by the Catholic conquerors as overrun by the French or English heretics. Conversion at the end of the sixteenth century created two forms of eviction for the Indian: It displaced him from his culture and, forcing him to resist the "heretics," dislodged him from any practice that was not Catholic. In both cases it obliged him to enter the major conflicts of the Western world without taking part in them as actor but rather as mere reciter. Doubly deprived: European history became indigenous history and the only thing left to him was to memorize and live a European "fiction" (Portuguese, in particular) that was unfolding on the enormous stage which was his own land. And in the twentieth century not even the land belongs to him anymore. Thus the third, last, and definitive act of eviction has been successfully completed by the colonizers.

It is important to mention how, in the modern world, colonization can only be a pedagogical activity, in which memory is the most sought after of talents. This is so to such an extent that our contemporary historians believe that the origins of "Brazilian intelligence" are located in the creation of the schools in the sixteenth century, that is to say, when alien history was imposed as a subject for memorization and learning, and imposed as the only truth. With this in mind, it is hardly necessary to emphasize the violent commitment of "intelligence" to the most fervent manifestations of ethnocentrism. This ethnocentrism translates a precabralian world view that was present in the first colonizers and that construed the indigenous inhabitants as a tabula rasa. What a pitiful "Brazilian intelligence," indeed, raising itself to the level of historical reflection yet always remaining entrenched in sixteenth-century prejudices!

Within this ethnocentric perspective the experience of colonization reveals a basically narcissistic operation in which the Other is assimilated to the conqueror's reflected image, fused to it and losing the very condition of its alterity. In other words, the indigenous loses his true alterity (the condition of being Other, different) and achieves a fictitious alterity (that of being the European's reflected image). The native becomes the European's Other: at one and the same time his specular image and his own suppressed indigenous alterity. The more distinct the Indian the less civilized he is; the less civilized, the more he negates European narcissism; the more he negates European narcissism the stronger and more demanding the force that strives to render him a like image; the more akin to the European the weaker the force of his own alterity. This is how colonization unfolds. This is how "intelligence" was formed in Brazil.

If discovery is driven by the unknown, and a spirit of adventure, courage, and audacity are required, then the experience of colonization requires a *profiteur* spirit, a sword, and false cordiality. False cordiality states that we will be friends provided you obey me; the sword adds: if you do not obey me there will be fire and brimstone. Finally the profiteering spirit concludes that the enterprise remains valid for as long as it is profitable.

The Old Man of Restelo in Camões's *Lusíadas,* together with those readers who send letters to *Time* and *Newsweek* criticizing the NASA program, derive their strength from the moral ambiguity of discovery and colonization. At the quayside pier the old man refuses to embark. He does not act but, rather, speaks, reflecting on the immorality of what he considers to be a useless search for the unknown, precisely because the unknown is in society itself and remains unseen. To civilize the Other is a superfluous task as long as there are "others" (marginalized groups) oppressed by the dominant class, and so on. Why depart when problems at home have not yet been resolved and remain so abundant?

II

We see, therefore, that the maritime discoveries of the modern era, together with the subsequent occupation of the lands discovered by Europeans, brought about the expansion of the cognitive and economic frontiers of Europe. But it also transformed European history into universal History, into a History which initially, for those who were colonized, was nothing more than a story, a fiction. Economic, social, political, and cultural differences were first annulled by violence, thereby transforming the multifaceted medieval world (the specifically European "known" world and its other "unknown" ones) into a whole, narcissistically forged according to the values of the colonizers. Then those very differences were erased by the victorious and exclusive discourses of universal History.

The standard westernization of the different civilizations existing in the newly discovered lands came to dominate the goals of the economic and sociopolitical institutions of the New World, as they positioned the dominant class as the protector and custodian of a Europeanizing cultural discourse that included constant and successive "cordial" assimilations of indigenous or black difference. Without a doubt, official culture assimilates the other but, as it does so, it suppresses, *hierarchically,* the autochthonous or black values that confront it. In Brazil the predicament of the Indian and of the black is rooted in the hierarchization of values rather than in silence.

It was in this context that anthropology, a science forged from the wounds of European consciousness, came to play a particularly important role. Within the culture of the conquerors a special sacrosanct disciplinary place was established from which to evaluate the violence committed by colonization, a place from which one could attempt to preserve what could still be preserved—and, let us have no illusions here, to do so under the guise of scientific discourse. This addition to the specifically European disciplines is not as unimportant as anthropology's minor place initially seemed to indicate, for it ended up operating an important "decentering" of Western thought, in which European culture ceased to occupy its position as custodian of truth, culture of reference, and creator of hierarchies.

In the twentieth century the Brazilian intellectual undergoes the drama of having to resort to a *historical* discourse that explains him but has destroyed him, and to an *anthropological* discourse that does not explain him but speaks of his being as a site of destruction. This is precisely what Paulo Emílio Salles Gomes calls attention to in this perfect synthesis: "The painful construction of our selfhood unravels itself through the tenuous dialectic between non-being and being other." We are explained yet destroyed; constituted yet no longer explained.

How can we "explain" "our constitution"? How can we reflect on our intelligence? No disciplinary discourse will be able to do so alone. In universal History we are explained *and* destroyed because we have lived a fiction ever since European history became our story. In Anthropology we are constituted *and not* explained since what is considered by History to be superstition constitutes the concrete reality of our past.

Either we explain ourselves or we constitute ourselves—such is the *false* dilemma of the Brazilian intellectual since, in its simplification, it generates both populist and integrationist forms of authoritarian discourse among us. We must search for the "explanation" of "our constitution" (that is, of our intelligence) in our "betweenness," as we have said elsewhere, or in our "tenuous dialectic," as Paulo Emílio puts it.[1] Populist handbooks and *curupira*[2] folklore are the poles that must be avoided in order to achieve democratic socialism. Neither paternalism, nor immobilism.

The ethical drama for the Brazilian intellectual vis-à-vis all the minorities of Latin America resides in the ambivalent construction of his cultural existence. His understanding of these minorities through historical materialism is dependent on their total and definitive integration into Western globalizing processes; his anthropological understanding of others, however, has to question this historical integration, so that they do not have to continue living a "fiction" that has been imposed as a determining factor in their past, as well as in their future disappearance. The pact between the Latin American subject and Western History is problematic unless one indulges in certain determinations of a developmentalist character, in which the ideological praxis of progress takes the form of capital. It is worth noting, however, that although this category is present in Brazilian leftist thought, it is not explained by it.

We are already familiar with the praxis of progress as an ideological force. It supplies underemployment to the minority population (remember, for example, Juscelino Kubitschek's "golden period," or the recent years of the "Brazilian miracle"),[3] jeopardizes sociopolitical consciousness, and disallows culture by permitting television soap operas to dramatize effortless social mobility to the majority of a population profoundly marked by prejudice and authoritarianism. Progress incorporates minorities into its simulacrum of historical advancement and perpetuates a fiction that falls short of understanding the social mode of existence of those who strive to reveal its "meaning." It incorporates minority populations into the dominant class's self-promotion and, for this reason, social differences (in spite of the relentless messages of prime-time soap operas) become increasingly pronounced in the most acute moments of developmentalism. The greatest truth of Brazil's "miracle" is represented by the *bóias-frias;*[4] the greatest lie of the "miracle" is not the cake but the knife lying in the hands of whoever cuts it. As the proverb goes, "quem parte e reparte fica com a melhor parte" [he who slices and shares keeps the best part].

III

The digression that has brought us to the center of our discussion has been long but by no means irrelevant. It is particularly useful when questioning the foundational categories of comparative literature, for example. It is only within a historical-anthropological framework, an economic, social, and political perspective (cultural, in its broadest sense), that one can understand the need for Latin American intellectuals to confront certain disciplines whose origins lie in European thought. When the issue is the production of the Other, that is, of the indigenous and the black—such disciplines maintain a violent ethnocentric component which invalidates, a priori, all intellectual and analytical rigor and nullifies interpretive mastery.

Let us continue with a brief outline of comparative literature as an object of study. Basically, the object must be viewed as double since it is constituted by literary works that are created in different national contexts and contrasted with the goal of widening both the limited horizon of artistic knowledge together with the critical vision of national literatures.

It is obvious that a period such as the Renaissance lends itself considerably to this type of study, for the European nations of the time were constructing their cultural ground by consolidating regional differences that were nevertheless grounded in the common inheritance of Judaic-Greek-Roman foundations. Through this common ground of the past a vast array of similarities between Portugal, Spain, France, Italy, and so on, are forged, thereby dismantling the national frontiers that were established during that period. Regional differences born out of a common foundation create a double demand for *imitation;* on the one hand, of the Greek and Latin classics, and on the other, of the Renaissance author's contemporaries. This was considered a form of emulation and enhancement that motivated European authors always to search for inspiration in the other, in order to enrich their own production. Thus this ensemble of apparently divergent elements actually provides the origin for a single European culture, which lends this period in particular to comparative studies. This is especially so since European "states" emerged from symptomatic differences that were all a product of the same economic, social, and political context and its contradictions.

However, the relationship of Latin American—and particularly Brazilian—literature to European literature in the past constitutes a much more problematic ground. The same is true nowadays of its relationship to North American literature. There is no doubt that the finest vantage point for studying Latin American national literatures is to be found in comparative literature. But as Antonio Candido warns us in the opening pages of *Formação da literatura Brasileira* [The fashioning of Brazilian literature]:[5]

There are literary traditions which one does not have to step out of in order to acquire culture and enrich one's sensibilities; others, however, can only occupy a fragment of the reader's life or they will irreversibly restrict his horizons. . . . Those who feed exclusively on the latter are easily recognizable, even when erudite and intelligent, because of their provincial tastes and a lack of a sense of proportions. . . . Compared to the great literary traditions, ours is poor and feeble. But, after all, it is this and no other that expresses us.

IV

Candido's position cannot be faulted: To believe that we can have a self-sufficient autochthonous thought devoid of "alien" contacts is little more than nationalistic daydreaming. And the following evaluation is equally fair: placing Brazilian thought comparatively, within the socioeconomic, political, and cultural contingencies that have constituted it, erases all traces of excessive jingoism. It remains to be seen whether Brazilian intellectuals have been propagating methodological flaws in spite of the accuracy and fairness of much of their thought. One must remain attentive to the method and the means of approaching cultural objects. In short, one must be heedful of the strategies for reading kindred texts.

For example, if we restrict ourselves to the appreciation of our literature in relation to European traditions, taking as our point of departure comparative literature's ethnocentric principles of source and influence, then we will be emphasizing little more than the dependent character of our own repetitive and redundant elements. The singling out of duplication is doubtlessly useful but, nevertheless, ethnocentric, and aims at accentuating the all-powerful course of dominant cultural production in those peripheral societies that have been defined and configured by it. In the end two similar parallel products will have been constituted, but will nevertheless present two major disjunctures, for they will both be responsible for the process of hierarchization that diminishes the value of the dominated society's cultural production.

There are two major dislocations, then, one temporal (the backwardness of one culture in relation to the other), the other qualitative (the lack of originality of a dominated society's cultural production). The dominated culture's products are always belated, towed along by the colonialist machine of yesterday and the capitalist neocolonialism of today. No doubt they are belated products because they are also products of a "memorized" form of existence. It is interesting to note how encyclopedism is the underlying tendency of colonized thought. This is so because peripheral knowledge is introjected, learned, and assimilated from an array of generous sources that are revealed only later in a cultural production whose underlying drive is synthesis. Indeed, it is worth noting how, in dominated cultures, the difference between a historian and an original thinker is often tenuous, whereas it remains of paramount importance in dominant cultures. Historical synthesis is not an original product, it is above all generous, inclusive in scope, equidistant and as liberal as the very thought that gave origin to it. Therefore it is hardly strange that the ideal of a colonized instructive "intelligence" is the endless recording of cultural facts, without any concern for anything other than the logic of their exhaustive progression.

Thought desirous of dependency does not come to us exclusively as a reflection on the empirical data of a given nation. It is and always has been a fiction maintained beneath (other than *on*) the occupying culture. It is always already a eulogistic appropriation of a dominant culture whose products come to hierarchize, restrict, and finally call into existence the ethnocentric view of the creator or the historian. Having said this, however, Brazilian modernism[6] created a number of antidotes to the erroneous good intentions of Eurocentric encyclopedic knowledge, which is useful if one's task is to write an encyclopedic survey but is totally devoid of interest if one's purpose is to highlight singularity. Let us view three of these antidotes.

First. The evil-minded notion of cultural anthropophagy, brilliantly invented by Oswald de Andrade in a creative attempt to incorporate his production into a universal movement. Second. The notions of the "betrayal of memory," eruditely formulated by Mário de Andrade in his research on music, designed to foreground national-popular production. Gilda de Mello e Souza, in *O Tupi e o alaúde* [The Tupi and the lute], has once again placed this notion in circulation with a very successful interpretation of *Macunaíma*. Third. The felicitous, possibly ideological notion of a "radical break," generally implied (though sometimes not explicitly) in the movement of successive avant-garde groups. This notion was recently coined and defended by the Concretist group of São Paulo as an appropriation of Pound's paideuma, revised by the ISEB group.[7]

In all three cases there is no claim that dependency does not exist; on the contrary, they foreground its inevitability. There is no attempt to deny the debt held to cultural domination. Rather, the coercive force of debt is emphasized. There is no satisfaction in the glorifying portrayal of the indigenous or the black, but rather a search for their differential insertion into universal totalization. Moreover, the possible originality of a derivative product is not allowed to be lost in a maze of ethnocentric lucubrations. Forms of hierarchization maintained through the imposition of criteria such as "backwardness" and "originality" are subverted and collapse on themselves. This is a subversion, however, that is not a gratuitous play forged from a limited nationalism such as that of the Integrationist movement of the 1930s,[8] but rather is grounded in the understanding that despite producing a culturally dependent work, it *is* possible to surpass imitations and ethnocentric, encyclopedic syntheses, in order to contribute something original.

Such a leap could not be produced by rational thought or through the practice of a complementary logic that integrated a multitude of parts into a single whole. In both cases one would fall into the famous traps of coloniz-ing thought, in which analytical or dialectical rationality becomes the inevi-table means for incorporating the indigenous and black populations into the whole. Complementarity, in this case, becomes a process of homogeniza-tion and totalization of difference.

It is necessary, therefore, that any preliminary questioning of source and influence as logical, complementary categories implemented for the understanding of dominant and dominated products proceed by means of an explicitly *paradoxical* drive. The force of this movement, in turn, will initiate a tactical deconstructive process within comparative literature that will facilitate avoiding the comparison of works from atop a homogeneous historico-cultural terrain.

I have explained this paradoxical drive in an essay whose Borgesian title, "Eça, Author of *Madame Bovary*," symptomatically surpasses the fields of historical and academic common sense. The choice of this title is not a mere game as it might seem to a scholarly historian, neither is it a gratuitous break with chronological causality as it might appear to the date-police timekeepers of the academy. It is not a case of originality for originality's sake with the aim of enchanting minds that find fulfillment in conceptualist aesthetics. Rather, it is a challenge to erudition, a break with chronology, and a search for originality that intertwines in order to constitute a paradoxical critical *supplement* which is both tactical and deconstructive.

Emphasis in this essay is given not to repetition (the marks left by Flaubert on Eça's text). Repetition is taken strategically as the invisible side of the dependent work. Rather, emphasis is given to the difference inaugu-rated by the dependent text in spite of its subjection to the dominance of French culture in the Portuguese society of the time. The difference that *O primo Basílio* is capable of instituting in relation to *Madame Bovary* is its visible side. The invisible side is, in itself, a coherent and organized whole (the elements of the first text repeated in the second). The visible side is merely the supplement constituted by creative rereadings, and this characterizes all meaningful production in a peripheral culture.

All in all, when the subjugated culture's text is made to operate retroac-tively on that of the dominant culture, a process which is, of course, an intentional inversion of chronology, one sees, for the first time, a concrete evaluation of the metropolitan text's universality. In truth, universality exists within this process of expansion in which non-ethnocentric responses come up against the values of the metropolis. If this were not the case, we would always fall within the rubric of tautological colonizing frameworks. If one avoids the demands of a strict internal economy of the work, then the decolonized text is seen paradoxically as the richest of the two precisely because it *contains within itself a representation of the dominant text and a response to that representation within its very fabrication.* And this is a cultural response that creates a means of gauging universality which would be as efficient as those already known and catalogued.

Universality is either a colonizing game designed to achieve the gradual Western homogenization and totalization of the world by imposing European history as universal History, or it is a differential game in which economically inferior cultures can operate within wider horizons in order to bring attention to the agency of domination and the reaction of the dominated.

The truth of ethnocentric colonizing universality is doubtlessly to be found in the metropolis, whereas, as Anthropology shows us, the paradoxical truth of differential universality is located in peripheral cultures. In fact, on the periphery, colonized texts proudly achieve an encyclopedic synthesis of culture, a generous whole in which the dominated is merely an insignificant and complementary appendix to the general movement of civilization.

In peripheral cultures the signifying processes of decolonized texts question both their own status and that of the colonial advances of cultural hegemony.

Translated by Ana Lúcia Gazzola and Gareth Williams

5. The Rhetoric of Verisimilitude

■

I wonder how someone can lie by putting reason on his side.
—*Jean-Paul Sartre*

All rhetoric aims at overcoming the discourse of sincerity.
—*Roland Barthes*

It is about time that Machado de Assis's works began to be comprehended as a coherently organized whole by perceiving that certain primary and principal structures are disarticulated and rearticulated in the form of different, more complex, and more sophisticated structures, in accordance with the chronological order of his texts. One must also urgently revise the kind of criticism, like Augusto Meyer's, that is made as to the monotony of Machado's work, the repetition of certain themes and episodes in his novels and stories that causes emotional weariness in the reader (or the impressionist critic): "[Machado] gains much in being read in passages, or at long intervals between readings, so that relative forgetfulness helps one feel, not the inertia of repetition and the weak sides, but the original grace of the best moments."[1]

Statements like this one cannot continue to have free passage in Machadian criticism. The search—whether for constant originality or intellectual excitement on a purely emotional level—that results in readings of the "best moments" of the novelist, has made difficult the discovery of what is perhaps the essential quality of Machado de Assis: the slow and measured quest of the creative force for a depth that does not originate in innate talent, but in the conscious and dual exercise of the imagination and the means of expression to which any and every novelist has access.

Already in the "Warning to the Reader," put at the beginning of *Ressurreição* [Resurrection], after introducing himself to the critics as a "worker," he refuses the adolescent presumption of what is commonly regarded as personal value, classifying it as "blind and treacherous confidence," and concedes all creative power to "reflection" and "study." He finally rejects for himself the condition and law of genius, to be content with the "law of medium aptitudes, the general law of the minimal intelligences." He ends by saying: "Every passing day makes me realize better the acridness of these library tasks—noble and consoling, surely—but difficult when the consciousness completes them."[2]

Even the abrupt division of his work into two distinct phases—fortunately already contested by critics—must also be refuted. On December 15, 1898, Machado clearly exposed the problem in a letter to José Veríssimo: "What you call my second manner is naturally more acceptable and right to me than the former, but it is sweet to find someone who remembers the former, who penetrates and excuses it, and even manages to find in it some roots of my present bushes" (3: 1044).

It would not be a critical fantasy therefore to find in *Ressurreição,* for example, the roots of the bush *Dom Casmurro,* to take up Machado's metaphor. It was, if we are not mistaken, the American critic Helen Caldwell, in her *Brazilian Othello of Machado de Assis,* who first pointed out this correspondence. Analyzed and catalogued, this correspondence was unfortunately brushed aside, for Caldwell examines the two novels separately. What needs to be done is to take the next indispensable step of studying *Dom Casmurro* within the internal economy of Machado's oeuvre.

It is even more important not to fall into another mistake of Machadian criticism that insists on analyzing *Dom Casmurro* as an addition, or even an excrescence, of a certain current of the nineteenth-century bourgeois (but with antibourgeois intention) novel, that of the psychological study of female adultery, whose examples for us Brazilians are *Madame Bovary* and *O primo Basílio.*[3] According to this critical view—which does not perceive that Machado's novel, if it is a study, is rather a study of jealousy, and only of this—two parties have taken sides and begun to dispute in papers, journals, and even books whether to condemn or absolve Capitu. This dispute has reached a point where a tireless Machadian, Eugenio Gomes, decided to enter the field and calm the opposing parties by writing two hundred pages with the unfortunate title of *The Enigma of Capitu.*

For the general joy or sadness of the nation, let me take up the problem once more, but by way of another door, since changing the key seems indispensable. Intellectual rust is still the most powerful and corrosive acid against good criticism.

Either of the two attitudes adopted in a reading of *Dom Casmurro* (condemnation or absolution of Capitu) will betray the reader's critical naiveté to the extent that he identifies himself emotionally with one of the characters, Capitu or Bentinho, and comfortably feels able to forget the very serious proposal of the novel: the thoughtful conscience of the narrator Dom Casmurro, this man now in his sixties, a lawyer by profession, ex-seminarian by education, a thoughtful and vacillating conscience, who feels the need to rebuild in his old age the Matacavalos house where he spent his adolescence.[4] The reader, forgetting the thoughtful conscience of this man in his sixties would take the position of a judge and feel obliged to give a verdict on the narrator's phantasms, when in reality the only interest that Machado de Assis wants to awaken is in the moral person of Dom Casmurro. To sum up: the critics were interested in seeking the truth about Capitu, or the impossibility of having the truth about Capitu, when the only truth to be sought is Dom Casmurro's.

On the other hand, a similar reading of the novel would let escape the essence of the aesthetic form chosen by Machado for his novels. The Machadian novel is above all an ethical novel,[5] where the reflection of the reader about the whole is sought, even demanded. In the specific case of *Dom Casmurro,* to identify with either Bentinho or Capitu is to not understand that the moral reflection demanded by the author requires a certain distance from the characters and/or the narrator, which is, in fact, the same distance that Machado maintains from them as author.

The problematic of Dom Casmurro overtakes, so to speak, the rigid scheme of the relations that hold only in this novel, for it is not only this novel that reflects the problem of love/marriage/jealousy in the Brazilian society of the Second Empire. In the same way, it is not the only one that shows the search for a definition, ever more precise and ambiguous and richer in details, of the complex and suffocating position of the adolescent in his desire for a place in the sun within the rigidity of the bourgeois and aristocraticizing society at the turn of the century, his condition of adult and peer, his impersonality and personality.

In my long and minute analysis of *Ressurreição,* published in the literary supplement of *O estado de São Paulo,* I tried to show how the problem of jealousy arose in the Machadian universe. It comes—I proposed at the start—from the characters' conception of the nature of love and marriage, as well as, on the other hand, the delicate games of *marivaudage* that man and woman have to represent to be able to arrive at union. I determined from the beginning that the concept of marriage restricts the free expansion of feeling, for love is a feeling caged in by Christian ceremony (marriage), and it is this which makes possible the establishment of the family. And therefore the universe of Machadian love is ascetic, formal, sane, rigid. His conception of marriage is also masculine and bourgeois. To love is to marry, to buy a deed of property. Any outside incursion into this property—a lover—occasions an emotional short-circuit that invalidates the first two terms.

On the other hand, to go from love to marriage, the man and the woman give themselves up to various social games. The various game forms are based on opposite and complementary positions, which define their place in society: freedom and imprisonment, feeling and reason. To the multiplicity of experiences that the man can have in his condition of being free, will correspond the young lady's use—if she wants her freedom—of multiple masks. The acceptance of any experience on the part of the woman, for that matter, requires dissimulation by necessity: to conceal is the habitual attitude, even because the very *reserve* that sweetheart/fiancé/husband demands of her is already a veil that covers her most legitimate feelings.

In general terms, I said that the man resorts to his reason (marriage) to restrict his freedom, by accepting the chains of virtue. Yet, the woman frees herself from her condition as slave by clutching at feeling (love), which to her seems superior to reason (marriage), and risking a false step. If the man feels right choosing reason, which controls feeling, the woman, for her part, feels like a woman when she gives herself over to the feeling that symbolizes her search for freedom.

Thus, the female character who has the most dramatic power for Machado de Assis is the widow—Lívia, in the specific case of *Ressurreição*. The widow, having experienced both reason and feeling, is the only one, in the event of a new suitor, who can live the dilemma to its full extent. She has the possibility of choice: *either* fidelity to the dead man (the belief in marriage, reason, as superior to feeling, love), *or* acceptance of a new husband (the belief in love, feeling, as superior to marriage, reason). If she accepts a new husband it is because she is capable of feeling successive loves. She might be unfaithful, thinks the new suitor. The marriage will not be eternal; love is not. Only total fidelity to the first husband is what would justify the acceptance of a new husband. How can so many contradictions be reconciled?

This is the drama that the jealous Félix has to confront when he decides to lead Lívia to the altar. Yet, the night before the wedding he receives a laconic, anonymous letter accusing the widow. A type predisposed to doubt, Félix doesn't think twice: He gives total credence to the letter and abandons his plans for marriage.

I am emphasizing this episode from the novel because it is the one that brings us to the ethical problem of the conduct of the jealous man in the universe of the Machadian novel. The letter—Félix surmises correctly—must have been written by Luís Batista, another suitor for the favors of Lívia who was passed over, and it is therefore not deserving of credence or trust, written as it was with the pen of envy or wounded pride. But this was not important for Félix, since for him the verisimilitude of the situation created by the letter counted more than the truth provided by the careful examination of the facts: "What he [Félix] thought to himself was that, with Luís Batista's villainy suppressed, the verisimilitude of the fact was not excluded, and that was enough to make him right" (1: 192–93).

Machado de Assis, still insecure with his tools and even more insecure of the ability of the reader to understand the moral drama of Félix, allows the narrator to intervene in the narrative and clarify his moral error for the reader: "Let us understand one another, reader, that I, who am telling you this story, can affirm that the letter was really from Luís Batista" (1: 189).

He clarifies (in a rather gauche way, it is not too much to point out) the true origin of the letter and the error of the doctor's attitude with respect to the widow's conduct, and finally leaves to the reader the terrible responsibility of judging Félix, of judging the slander that he brings against Lívia, of judging, in other words, his decision, which is based not on the knowledge of the truth but on the mere verisimilitude of the facts.

II

Félix's drama becomes even more serious when Machado de Assis writes his novel *Dom Casmurro*. He wishes the drama to become more ambiguous, more subtle, and for this reason suppresses the omniscient narrator who explained the facts from a divine perspective, and gives the entire responsibility of the narration to the jealous character. We shall see later how Dom Casmurro gets on in this enterprise. On the other hand, the author not only changes the profession of the character—he becomes a lawyer, and therefore a man linked to the art of writing, persuading, and judging others—but also makes him an ex-seminarian, a man who at least in theory should be more attuned to feeling moral problems. Machado marries him, makes him jealous of his wife, the father of a son. He lets him accuse the wife of infidelity, renounce her, and send her to Europe with the boy. Bentinho lies to his friends. In Europe, the wife dies alone. He is visited by his son, now a young man, and wishes for him death as a leper—his wish is granted, as the boy dies of plague in North Africa. All the decisions are not justified, as in the case of Félix, by the full knowledge of the truth, but by believing that the events fit and can be explained by verisimilitude.

Juge-penitant is how the lawyer-hero and narrator of *The Fall,* by Albert Camus, proposes himself to the reader, so destroying the gap between conscience and consequence, between judgment and expiation. Defendant and defense attorney are Bentinho and Dom Casmurro, respectively. Dom Casmurro, as the good lawyer he should be, takes upon himself the defense of Bentinho, designing a rhetoric whose properly judicial aspect (it was written by a lawyer) and moral-religious aspect (written by an ex-seminarian) become of primary importance to us.

At first, we perceive that the most salient feature of the rhetoric of the lawyer-narrator is its a priori nature. He knows beforehand what he wants to prove and his rhetoric is nothing more than the believable development of a certain reasoning that will lead us implacably to the conclusion he eagerly desires. His structuring of the facts, his presentation of the human behavior of the characters (including Bentinho) is informed by the rigor of the demonstration. Thus, for Dom Casmurro the essential thing was to prove (and emerge victorious by doing so) that the knowledge he had of Capitu's acts as a little girl made possible for him a secure judgment of Capitu as a mysterious adult. Or, using his own words, directed, of course, to the reader: "But I believe not, you will agree with me, if you remember well Capitu as a girl, you will have to recognize that one was within the other, like a fruit within its rind" (1: 942).

The only *memory* the reader can have of the young Capitu is that which is given by the writing of the narrator. It is not at all strange, either, as Helen Caldwell has pointed out, that he spends two-thirds of the book describing his impressions of Capitu as a girl and one-third of Capitu as an adult. Now, what would prove to us that Dom Casmurro's thesis is valid if not a certain preconceived notion, a certain prejudice, that the adult is already in the child, as the fruit is in the rind? The comparison comes as a proof grounded in the truth of nature. As another lawyer—this one our contemporary, the judge Profitendieu in Gide's *The Counterfeiters*—says, "After all, this is only a prejudice, but prejudices are the pillars of civilization."

After having proved the first part of his theory, Dom Casmurro can afford to pass over the second, just as Félix accepts the truth of the letter without having the curiosity to appraise its veracity. On the other hand, seen from Bentinho's point of view, one perceives that in this structural reckoning the two-thirds describe him in a favorable light, while the remaining one-third would surprise him when he commits the acts that he really tries to justify by Capitu's actions as a girl and that he wishes to remove from the reader's sight. In short, applied to Bentinho, the same *thesis* of Dom Casmurro (that is, proof of a human truth coming from a comparison with the "natural" truth) is not valid, for the docile and angelical son of Dona Glória has nothing of the suburban and "grouchy"[6] (whatever meaning one wishes to give to this adjective) lawyer.

This structural imbalance is justified, to use a familiar expression, by a shabby excuse. The narrator says: "Here ought to be the middle of the book, but inexperience makes me go after my pen, and I come to the end of my paper, with the best part of the narrative still to write" (1: 903).

How could he know at that precise moment that he had reached the middle of the book? What is the *middle* of a book? And the middle of a book that is being written? A book can be as many pages as the author wishes. Its size always depends on the *intentions* of the one who writes it, and it is no doubt its elasticity that destroys the lovely thesis of Borges in the Library of Babel. Therefore, to hurry a narrative, the best part of it, as he himself tells us, just because he had gone beyond a point that in reality does not exist, is because there is a reason. It is to incur a priori reasoning and rhetorical nervous tic.

Another precise and important feature to define the rhetoric of verisimilitude is the predominance of *imagination* over *memory* in the investigation of the past. Machado de Assis in at least two chapters makes it clear that he wanted to give the narrator the opportunity to point out the contrast between the two faculties and establish the clear-cut victory of fantasy: chapter 40, "A Mare," and chapter 59, "Banqueters with Good Memory." In both, as if to stress even more the victory of imagination, he furnishes a small detail that reinforces by comparison and contrast the lack of memory. He doesn't know, or is not certain about the name of the author of the different quotations with which he opens each of these chapters. He confesses in the first one: "I think I have read it in Tacitus . . . , if it wasn't in him it was in another ancient author." And in the other chapter, he says: "The proof that I have a weak memory is exactly that the name of this ancient [author] does not occur to me." It is sufficient to juxtapose the two following passages to be able to apprehend in all its richness the problem we are speaking of: "Imagination was the companion of my whole existence, alive, quick, restless, sometimes timid and friendly to balking, most other times capable of encompassing vast plains in a hurry. No, no, my memory is not good. . . . How I envy those who have not forgotten the color of the first pants they wore! I can't remember the color of the ones I put on yesterday. I swear only that they weren't yellow because I detest that color; but that itself can be due to forgetfulness and confusion" (chaps. 40, 59).

From this doubtless follows the great difference—not very respected by Brazilian criticism—between the narrator of *Dom Casmurro* and that of *À la recherche du temps perdu*, to the extent that, in the case of Machado de Assis, the reconstruction obeys deliberate purposes, obvious or disguised, but always under the due control of he who remembers, who writes, and who knows where the middle of the book is, while with Proust the past comes to him as a present, free and unexpected, offered to him by the acute exercise of his senses. In the case of Machado, the reconstitution of the past obeys a predetermined plan (whose concrete example within the narrative fabric would be the reconstruction of the Matacavalos house, which shows in itself all the artifice of the Machadian process) and, above all, a convincing intellectual arrangement of the narrator's life. I have emphasized these two last adjectives—convincing, because there is an intention to persuade someone, the reader, of something; intellectual, because the arrangement depends on the constant reflection of the narrator and does not betray a desire to let itself be passively invaded by the past, by fleeting, momentary, and delicate impressions. The Machadian narrator, unlike the Proustian narrator, is resentful, fearful of the past: "There you come again, restless shades," he quotes Goethe right at the beginning (chaps. 40, 59).

In the preface of *Contre Sainte-Beuve,* Proust makes his position clear: "Every day I give less value to intelligence. Every day I perceive better that only outside of it can the writer regrasp something of our impressions, that is, obtain something of himself and the sole material of art." Machado, indefatigable rationalist, could only with difficulty be put side by side with Proust's Bergsonianism. To place one alongside the other is to underestimate the philosophical formation of both.

Yet another aspect, no less negligible, of the rhetoric of *Dom Casmurro* is the fact of systematically refusing the search for perfect identity between two elements, attempting rather to impinge on the reader propositions that translate *equality* into *similarity*. Even leaving aside the comparison girl/adult: fruit/rind, we see, for example, that Bentinho, according to what José Dias and his mother say, "looks just like his father" (1: 904), which Dom Casmurro gives as his strongest argument for his wife's adultery: his son does not look like him so much as he does Escobar. This whole vision of family life reveals, of course, a certain prejudice, or in this specific case, is based on proverbs such as "Like father, like son," or "A chip off the old block." Persuasion, in the present case, arises therefore from offering what the reader's mind is already prepared to receive; it does not demand of him any effort at adaptation, any improvement. Conviction is not achieved with the hope that the reader will evolve his way of thinking or his way of facing problems, but by the fact of proposing to him as a basis for his judgment that which he already possesses: good sense.[7] To discover, therefore, the fallacy of the narrator-lawyer is to refuse the (false) situation of equilibrium offered by conservatism; it is to unmask its own language and infuse a certain uneasiness in the status quo.

If, in a sense, these are the predominant mechanisms in his way of thinking and, consequently, his way of convincing, one should not forget that the rhetoric of verisimilitude unfolds, causing a certain particular understanding of the behavior of the *others*. Two attitudes are typical of Dom Casmurro, when he analyzes those around him: (a) he puts the blame of the slander on the others, apparently removing himself from any responsibility, even claiming for himself the status of victim; (b) he confers on the others contradictions between what I will call for the moment internal and external.

In the first case, it would suffice to recall that the first accusation against Capitu was made by José Dias, when he describes "a gypsy's oblique and dissembling eyes," and it is the same José Dias who inspires the first crisis of jealousy, saying that Capitu will not rest "until she gets some fop from the neighborhood to marry her." Later, José Dias needs to confess his mistaken judgment, and by one of those usual felicities of the novel, will utterly destroy the thesis proposed at the end by Dom Casmurro. The passage from girl to adult is seen by José Dias as the transformation of flower to fruit, and if the flower is capricious, the fruit is healthy and sweet: "I thought of the contrary, long ago; I confused the ways of a child with expressions of character, and I didn't see that this mischievous little girl with eyes that were already thoughtful was a capricious flower of a healthy, sweet fruit" (1: 905).[8]

The lack of control of José Dias's judgment (first he criticizes, then praises) shows well the character of the slander that informs the first judgment he made of the young Capitu ("ways of a child" are not "expressions of character"—a good lesson for Dom Casmurro). Bentinho accepted the slanders and elaborated on them in his imagination, as is evident in the passage in which he describes his first fit of jealousy, when he constructs the scene in which Capitu is courted by a young man in the neighborhood and has even reciprocated the advances of the passionate young man. So sure is Bentinho that they have exchanged kisses, that he only wants to know how many. But if he was able to mentally work out the slander, he was not able to accept the correction in judgment.

That Bentinho confers mainly on Capitu and José Dias the contradiction between external and internal, between gestures/words and the true aspirations and desires, and accuses them therefore of partial conduct, of lack of sincerity and dissimulation, protects him in a certain way and at the same time calls the reader's attention, by contrast, to his sincerity as a victim. Now, as we have seen in the case of *Ressurreição,* where the skeleton of the jealous man's mechanism of thought is more openly displayed, owing to the inexpertness of the fledgling novelist, feminine dissimulation is a given that exists and will exist in the society that Machado de Assis describes, and that can be observed in any young woman who has a sweetheart and wishes to marry. It is a consequence of her own position with respect to the man in society and in no way can be taken as an example of future betrayal, unless, of course, more importance is given to verisimilitude than to truth.

I believe that what I am calling the rhetoric of verisimilitude is elsewhere sketched out in general terms and in its predominant features. I can therefore now conclude that the novel being analyzed dramatizes the "moral situation" of Dom Casmurro, to use Machado's expression in his criticism of *O primo Basílio.* Dom Casmurro's ethical-moral problem is obvious, his reconstitution of the past is egoistic and self-interested, fearful and complacent even with himself, for it aims at freeing him from those "restless shades" and from grave decisions for which he is responsible. The *remorse* (another term constantly on the pen of Machado the critic) will stalk his final hours. As in Baudelaire's poem, he should cry:

> In what philtre, in what wine, in what potion
> Shall we drown this old enemy?

Dom Casmurro gives priority to this "old enemy" in his concerns of the quiet suburbanite, and he drowns it in his *writing.*

Through his ordered, logical discourse, he tries to resolve his existential anguish. After persuading himself, he wants to persuade the others of his truth. One sees, however, that the ex-seminarian lawyer falls into two fallacies in establishing his truth. From the strictly legal point of view, he errs in basing his persuasion on verisimilitude, and from the moral-religious point of view in sustaining his justifications on the basis of probability.

Thus, Dom Casmurro, who didn't have the energy to write a treatise on "Jurisprudence, Philosophy, and Politics," was nevertheless familiar with these subjects when he wrote the work he is steadfastly offering to the reader. It would be, therefore, a pity if the critic did not take into consideration the cultural background of the one who narrates his life, somewhat motivated by the gazes of the four busts painted on the wall.

It seems to me, finally, that the intention of Machado de Assis in writing *Dom Casmurro* was to "put in action" two flaws of Brazilian culture, which had always lived under the protection of the attorneys and the moral approbation of the Jesuits.

In this sense, the reading of Plato's *Phaedrus* is of great importance for understanding the complexity of the problematic established by the novel and the richness of the ethical-moral drama of Dom Casmurro, that is, if in the end one considers him a "moral person" or representative of a collectivity of *chefs/salauds* (Sartre). *Phaedrus* is a dialogue in which Socrates discusses the problem of a rhetoric that uses verisimilitude as a strategy of persuasion. Likewise, the reading of *Les provinciales* (from the fifth letter on), where Pascal mercilessly criticizes jesuitical casuistry through what is called "probabilism," or "la doctrine des opinions probables," would also be relevant. The word *probable*, as the theologians teach us, keeps its etymological sense, which is the perfect equivalent of the concept of verisimilitude in rhetoric. Definition: an opinion is probable which commends itself to the mind by weighty reasons as being very possibly true.[9]

In a letter addressed to Joaquim Nabuco in 1906 and widely read, Machado de Assis himself confesses his predilection for Pascal: "From a young age I often read Pascal . . . , and I assure you that it wasn't for entertainment." As for Plato, although critics have not emphasized the importance of his thought in Machado's works,[10] it is interesting to note, with the aid of Luis Vianna Filho, the latest biographer, that several of the author's contemporaries compared him, while he was writing *Dom Casmurro*, to the Greek philosopher: "For them [his friends] Machado is a kind of Plato, whose distinguished and agreeable company they tenderly dispute. 'I have seen only the Greek in him,' Nabuco will say. It is notable that on several occasions Veríssimo and Mário de Alencar remember the Greek philosopher when they refer to Machado." And further down on the same page, Vianna Filho cites Mário de Alencar: "I showed him once a dialogue of Plato, a passage on the word of Socrates."[11]

The familiarity with these two philosophers and the reading of the *Phaedrus* (an indispensable dialogue in the education of lawyers), along with the *Gorgias* and *Les provinciales* (where Pascal stubbornly criticizes those responsible for our moral and religious education) can doubtless explain the distance between critic and narrator/character that is indispensable to an appreciation of the ethical-moral drama of Dom Casmurro, or of the Brazilian who has power in his hands. Machado decided that his narrator/character would systematically fall into that very thing he idealized as object of his criticism.

The main interest of the *Phaedrus,* as its modern exegetes have pointed out, is the opposition of the viewpoint of Philosophy, represented by the word of Socrates, to that of the Sophists and Rhetoricians, represented by

Phaedrus to the extent that he is the disciple and admirer of Lysias, and reproducer of his words. As a basis for this discussion, the whole first half of the dialogue is dedicated to the three discourses on love, one from Lysias himself, as it is repeated by Phaedrus, and the other two the responsibility of Socrates. For our purposes, what is interesting to note is that Socrates underlines the indifference of rhetoric—such as it was practiced at that period in Greece—its indifference with regard to the truth, exactly because the Sophist text is based on verisimilitude.

For Socrates, as for us, the word *rhetoric* is taken in its wide sense. This is how he defines the term: "It is that, to sum up, would not rhetoric be a psychagogy, a way to lead souls by means of discourse, not only in the law-courts and any other public place of meeting, but also in private meetings?"[12]

Rhetoric is, then, basically a method of persuasion, of whose use we take advantage to convince a group of people of our opinion. And is this not one of the main interests of the prose of Dom Casmurro as I have been showing? In what other way could his constant need to bring the reader to the arena of argument be justified? How otherwise could one justify the golden key of the book, whose final sentence invites the reader to contradict the Scriptures and impose the true word as the metaphor of the narrator? For Socrates, the great error of the teaching and practice of rhetoric in Greece is that, as Phaedrus says: "It is not necessary, for him who would become an orator, to have learned what constitutes the reality of justice, but rather to have learned what the multitude, which must decide, may think; nor what is really good or beautiful, but what the multitude will think with respect to that. Here then, in fact, is the principle of persuasion, but not that of truth" (60–61).

This educational defect in the formation of the orator results in a doubly bad professional habit: the complete disconnection from reality and consequent belief in the supreme value of rhetoric, and, on the other hand, the centralization of the motive of discourse, not in the discernment of the orator but of the listener. Thus, the point of reference for his ideas is not reality (to catch in the act—as one says in police terminology), but the probable, the apparently true, which as we have seen is the basis of Dom Casmurro's rhetoric. Socrates continues: "Look: in the law-courts no one has the least interest in the truth, but only in that which is persuasive. Now, this constitutes the apparently true, which must be applied by whoever proposes to speak artfully. There are even cases when the very act must not be stated, if it has not been done in an apparently true manner, but one should rather focus on only the apparently true, whether by prosecution or defense. In any case, it is necessary to seek the apparently true, saying repeated farewells to the truth!" (89).

Dom Casmurro applies in his prose the rules and laws he has learned in the (evil) exercise of his profession: "It is therefore verisimilitude which, traversing discourse from one extreme to another, constitutes the totality of art" (84).

Within the proposed scheme, in which defense attorney and defendant are the same person, it is important to note that persuasion is situated on two levels—Dom Casmurro is himself persuaded of his innocence and at the same time persuades others. But the method that he uses is already familiar to us. And within Brazilian society, it is often by persuading the other that one is able to persuade oneself of something.

Instead of verisimilitude, Socrates is going to propose, as is known, the philosophical method par excellence: dialectic. And the ideal vehicle for the expression of the orator is not the written but the spoken word, as he emphasizes at the end of the dialogue. Now, if we pay close attention to the prose of Dom Casmurro we will notice that on several occasions he insists on the fact that he *writes,* writes a book, unlike other narrators in the first person who create the illusion that they are speaking. It is certain that Socrates, defending the written word, would at the same time prevent the philosopher from falling into dogmatism, for he who speaks could find himself open to the suggestions and corrections of those who listen. And finally we could ask if the written word is not the basis of one of the great dilemmas of our civilization: to believe that one has learned the substance of a book by reading it.

The complacency that exists on the legal level with relation to the listener's thought—the total, conscious surrender of the rhetorical imaginary in the reconstruction of the past—finds its correlative on the personal and moral plane, in the benevolence that the Jansenists combatted in the casuistry of the Jesuits, the *adoucissement de la confession.* The casuistry was based not on the teachings of the Gospels and the church fathers, but on those of *summae confessorum,* which since the Council of Latran (1215) aided priests in the difficult and delicate mysteries of the confession.

This opposition between the word of the Gospels and casuistry is magnificently expressed and concretized in the last pages of the novel, when the narrator—in a last effort at self-pardon and convincing the reader— opposes the word of Jesus, son of Sirach and author of *Ecclesiastes,* to a metaphorical argument, typical of the apparently true, the probable: "Jesus, son of Sirach, if he knew of my initial jealousy, would say to me, as in his chapter 9, verse 1: 'Be not jealous of thy wife so that she will not deceive thee with the malice that she will learn from thee.' But I don't believe so, you will agree with me; if you remember Capitu as a girl, you will have to recognize that one was within the other, like a fruit in its rind" (1: 92).

As Pascal notes, in the baroque world of those versed in casuistry, thanks to the institution of probabilism as a theory, extraordinary mistakes were made.[13] One of the worst was the organization of a religion that did not lead to faith or to charity but that wanted through benevolence to receive in its bosom the great and the noble, to flatter them in order to receive their thanks. The system became so intricate that, as Pascal tells us, Father Bauny could affirm: "When the penitent follows a probable opinion, the confessor must absolve him even if his opinion is opposed to that of the penitent" (81).

This type of reasoning, which approaches the absurd and seems to be taken from the logic of Ionesco, is what Jansenism criticized. Therefore, the ex-seminarian, orienting his reconstitution of the past within the probable, would doubtless achieve (even we did not share his opinion) not only the serenity provided by the confessor, but, it seems to me, that required by his own conscience.

"The main objective that our Society took as the good of religion is that of not turning away anyone, no matter whom, so as not to cause the world to despair" (88), says another priest in Pascal's letters.

Another question for which Dom Casmurro is liable is the so-called process of "directing intention" (97), also criticized by the Jansenists. This consists of proposing as the aim of one's actions a permitted object. Thus, the majority of cases of revenge can be excused by the fact that the criminal is not really exacting revenge but defending his honor. The example chosen by Pascal is clear and needs no commentary: "He who receives an affront can have no intention of avenging himself but he can have the intention of avoiding disgrace and, consequently, immediately redressing this injury, even by a stroke of the sword" (98–99).

In the case of Dom Casmurro, many of his acts are justified by having "directed intention." It was always his honor that was at stake: "I embarked a year later, but I didn't look for her, and I repeated the voyage with the same result. On my return, those who remembered her wanted news, and I gave it to them, as if I had just been living with her; naturally the voyages were made with the intention of simulating that very thing and deceiving opinion." He did not take revenge on Capitu, only defended his honor. He did not lie to his friends, only concealed from them the slip of his wife. Perhaps he even felt generous.

Machado de Assis, we can conclude, wanted Dom Casmurro to unmask certain habits of thinking, certain mechanisms of thought, a certain rhetorical benevolence—habits, mechanisms, and benevolence that are forever rooted in Brazilian culture, insofar as it has been determined by religious instruction and "bacharelismo,"[14] which is nothing more, according to Fernando de Azevedo, than "a mechanism of thought to which the rhetorical and bookish form of colonial instruction had accustomed us." As a conscientious and upright intellectual, among the keenest of critical spirits, merciless scrutinizer of the Brazilian cultural soul, Machado de Assis ironically points out our defects. But this is a commitment much more profound and responsible than that which has been arbitrarily demanded of him. And to think that there are critics who speak of the philosophy of Machado de Assis, believing that the basis of his ideas is to be found in the "resentment of the mulatto!"

Translated by Tom Burns and Ana Lúcia Gazzola

6. Worth Its Weight:

Brazilian Modernist Fiction

■

FOR DAVI ARRIGUCCI JR., WHO INSPIRED IT

At this point in the twentieth century, it would be unwise to begin writing on contemporary Brazilian fiction without considering the fact that it is transmitted through the object we call a book. Not to recognize this would produce two serious errors, no matter how justified they appear to be owing to the natural vanity that writers customarily display. It would confer an importance that the literary text cannot have to think that it reaches different social strata and raises their consciousness. The book of fiction (as is the case for books in general) has an extremely limited circulation, with an average of three thousand copies (each edition) in a country with 110 million inhabitants, according to the latest statistics.[1] In the best of cases, twelve to fifteen thousand copies (four or five successive editions) circulate in the country over a period of fifteen years, so that the total number of novel readers can be optimistically estimated at fifty to sixty thousand.

The proportion of sixty thousand readers for 110 million inhabitants, stated initially by Roberto Schwarz in 1970 and taken up again by Carlos Guilherme Motta in 1977, is ridiculous and depressing, but this inevitable asymmetry is also a point of departure for a rather unorthodox meditation on the knowledge that the book of fiction has brought to the inhabitants of this country called Brazil.

One must immediately exclude the possibility of disconnecting the reader of fiction from bourgeois cultural cosmopolitanism, since s/he has undoubtedly maintained direct and lasting contact with the classics of the genre both foreign and domestic. This leads firmly to the first pair of observations: since the reader of Brazilian fiction is hardly a xenophobe, universal quality is necessarily an important component of the new novel. This is proven by the observation that the discussions about such-and-such a novel are always preceded by comments contextualizing the work both in terms of the history of the genre and in relation to contemporary critical discussions in places like Europe, the United States, and, most recently, Hispanic America. Moreover, a novel is not criticized without prior detailed formal analysis and an initial examination of its technique.

As a result of the absence of xenophobia, together with the demand for bourgeois universalism, one encounters a sad situation: on the one hand, the foreign novel has a better market in Brazil than the domestic novel; on the other hand, we still have not achieved international recognition for our domestic production. Consequently, critical analyses of Brazilian works are incapable of understanding the quality of Brazilian fiction on its own terms. They attempt, in traditional works, to trace the foreign influences on the author and work, and, in recent academic studies, the shape of the intricate paths of cultural dependence.

Within this line of thought, one can say that, in spite of everything, the luxury is not in the technical or formal component of the text, inherent in the twentieth-century novel, but the luxury is the book itself—the book, in editions of three thousand copies in a country of 110 million inhabitants. It is an expensive object, for one thing, rather inconvenient for another, improper for circulation in a country of illiterates or semi-literates, for another, marginalized in a nation where everything is done to increase mass communications and nothing is done to improve the library system, for still another, and, finally, censored when it threatens to bare its teeth and devour other readers beyond its fifty or sixty thousand. It is in the restricted center of this five-point, low-magnitude star, that the book of fiction finds its space and its pride, a minimal area, one point perhaps, a limited pride, a dot of vanity perhaps, but not for this devoid of importance, as shall be seen.

The author of fiction cannot choose his readers. He writes so that he can be chosen (or elected) by the reader, and, for this reason, any displeasure that the novel may cause to the latter's austere habits causes him to be declassified critically at once. This is both good and bad. It is good because the book of low quality (lately characterized by the *tupiniquim*[2] publishing industry with the old label of best-seller) does not find the easy success that glorifies it in the United States or Europe. It is bad because the somewhat strange (i.e., experimental) book holds no surprises nor awakens any curiosity, since it is not expected to disturb but to please the refined, cosmopolitan, and self-sufficient "happy few." As an example, one may cite the fact that the boldest texts of the 1920s only began to be regularly consumed in the 1960s, or even in the year of the fiftieth anniversary of the Week of Modern Art. This is the case of the experimental novels of Oswald de Andrade (*Memórias sentimentais de João Miramar* [Sentimental memoirs of João Miramar] and *Serafim ponte grande*), or Mário de Andrade (*Macunaíma*). And one may raise the hypothesis that they would still be neglected by the common reader if it were not for the Concreto and Praxis groups from São Paulo[3] leading to Oswald's publicity, and the film version of Joaquim Pedro de Andrade promoting Mário's novel.

We therefore have an extremely reduced audience for fiction, which is both sophisticated and conservative, petulant and cosmopolitan, and ultimately superficial, a public which today puts on airs of living in the metropolis, where time is money, most sympathetic to short narratives (the story), or even to that developmental subliterature—the magazine or newspaper "chronicle," later collected in a book, serving as fodder for our indigent high school students and their enthusiastic teachers.

The reading public for fiction in Brazil lives in the big city and is made up of more or less predictable and similar levels of readers that reproduce themselves from state to state. These readers include the producer of literature himself (a novelist, poet, or critic reads novels), the dilettante ("I don't know why I read, I think it's a family habit"), the university professor and student (the professor assigns the book and makes the student read it), and finally opening out at random to the many and the few who need to impose some kind of order on their unrefined temperaments, individual nonconformity, and political and social malaise.

All these readers, we see, live in the well-being, leisure, and educational comforts inherent to the middle class, which is privileged by all the Brazilian booms, economic, social, and cultural, since the 1930s. The book, then, is a class object in Brazil, and when incorporated in a rich individual private library, is a sure sign of social status. As such, it addresses a certain class, expecting from it its applause and its most profound meaning, conferred by the act of reading, a reading that becomes a sympathetic echo of (self-) revelation and (self-) knowledge.

Writers cannot be professionals in a society in which their merchandise does not circulate and is not profitable, in which they do not believe in state or corporate mechanisms that protect them economically, and in which the competitive foreign product is more easily available. They end up availing themselves of the leisure time that their class and their professional activities (simultaneous and profitable) provide: the authors of the novels as permitted by time and readers, their slaves, in short.

Therefore, fictional discourse, reflecting on national or regional issues from different, complementary, or even opposing perspectives, rather than reflecting on the multifaceted and contradictory aspirations of the population in general, is the replica (in both senses: copy and reply) of the discourse of a hegemonic social class that wants to perceive itself better in its successes and failures, to know where it is headed and where the country that it governs or governed is headed, to be conscious of its orders and disorders or even of its gradually growing loss of prestige and power in the face of new groups or the modernizing transformations in society.

The Brazilian novel, despite a Jorge Amado (especially the novels of his early period) and a João Antônio leading with a great publicity campaign the *lambões de caçarola* group,[4] cannot avert its elitist tendencies, its commitment to *à la recherche du temps perdu,* or even more cynically, its obsession with the rearview mirror in a jalopy driving down an asphalt road, in which the signaling is evidently not very democratic. One concludes that it does not help to speak of the brightness of the headlights, or of the stretch of road ahead that it illuminates, as long as the eyes of the novelist and the middle class are glued to the rearview mirror.

The social function of the contemporary novel is to provide a critical, caustic, and rebellious space in the good cases; complacent and generous in the nobler texts; full of pity and compassion in the more traditional books; affected and merely narcissistic in the worst cases; a critical space in which the social groups who have been occupying the spheres of power, prestige, and decision on the farms and in the cities are reflected. It is a vicious circle, which can be broken only at the moment when a new and different reader emerges—a reader who requires of the novelist a different thematic agenda and attitude, and at the moment when a new and different novelist emerges—a novelist who can offer reflection for different social classes. But for that to occur, this individual must first be capable of rising to the condition of reader or novelist. How can we fulfill one of these conditions in a society like the Brazilian, where the problematics of literacy (that is, of having a primary command of the language) come up against state-run literacy campaigns?

It is easy, now, to map the quite unenviable dilemma and frustration experienced with every attempt at populist fictional writing. (The attempt in the 1930s, that of 1961–64 promoted by the Popular Center for Culture, the recent invasion that took by storm not only the novel but also poetry—such as Thiago de Melo—and the theater—such as Chico Buarque's *Gota d'água* [Last drop] or João das Neves's *O último carro* [The last car] or Gianfrancesco Guarnieri's *Ponto de partida* [The starting point]. Trying to raise problems of social classes or marginalized groups by the neocapitalist and repressive Brazilian political process, the populist makes use, as I am trying to prove, of an erroneous vehicle: the book (and, in the case of the theater, the commercial playhouse, where the price of admission is expensive). The denunciation of repression in populist fiction, whatever it is, falls either into the hands of whoever is conscious of arbitrariness and injustice and can do nothing, the text being used only to feed the already hungry bad faith, to use Sartre's expression, or into the hands of a more politically acute reader, who already knows the dramatized problems and dramatized facts and tries to act surreptitiously or secretly, the book coming to be a kind of crutch for the combative yet shaken yearnings for justice.

The populist social denunciation of repression functions within an ideological vacuum, which can only be activated if the members of the Brazilian ruling class (the possible purchasers of that novel) choose to annihilate those desires for power or to continuously destroy their own personal economic ambitions. But Brazil is not a country of political, business, or professional kamikazes.

The obliteration of the desire for power and destroyed personal ambition are not qualities of the emergent Latin American middle class, for even the rare passionate gestures of revolt (which are probably roused by the literature of denunciation, as in a Gorky play) become softened owing to the festive climate surrounding contestatory cultural activities, politically inclined toward social upheaval in the country. What is lacking in the populist text (which, in the last instance, is practically written for the middle class that consumes it) is the exhibition of the wounds of whoever has suffered persecution and mutilation, wounds that would be displayed in a harsh, stifling text, dismal, gray, self-critical and ruthless with itself, a text much closer to Graciliano Ramos's *Memórias do cárcere* [Prison memoirs], *Angústia* [Anguish], or *São Bernardo* [St. Bernard]. But what we witness is the continuous explosion of joy at the moments of political distension, as if the prior defeat were a motive for laughter and the exile-and-return of the leaders a motive for jubilation, and not an occasion for reflection on mistakes. What we see—on the other hand—is a student youth stifled by repression giving in to the populist text in a process of petty bourgeois liberation that cannot be confused with pungent, lasting political commitment. Or it can—and it is the intermittent spectacle that we see in the innocuous, festive university scene since the 1930s.

Shaped as a formally universal and modern work, with a precious and reduced set of readers, knowing even how limited and confined is its power of penetration and sociopolitical efficiency, the modernist Brazilian novel has consciously or unconsciously sought its most advanced ideological position in the discourse of memorialist fiction, as if to say that the individual adventure, because of its social rebellion and political audacity, its escape from and disrespect for the bourgeois norm, its ambition to be an authentic example and model of individualism during authoritarian regimes, would be worthy of the curiosity and interest of its peers. These people would see themselves reflected in memorialist fiction, and because of it could better know themselves, better know their social condition, better learn their importance and ineffectiveness within Brazilian society, thus closing the tautology of the sixty thousand readers in a country that had fifty million people and today has 110 million.

In our best modernist novelists, the text of memory feeds the text of fiction, the affective memory of childhood and adolescence sustains the literary pretending. This shows the importance that the narrative of the writer's life, his relatives and co-citizens, has in the process of comprehending the transformations undergone by the dominant class in Brazil, in the passage from the Second Empire to the Republic, and from the First to the Second Republic. Such importance comes from the fact that he—the writer or the intellectual, in the broad sense—is a constituent part of this power, insofar as his being is rooted in one of the "great families" of the nation.

In this sense, a reflection, even if in passing, on the *whole* of the poetic discourse of Carlos Drummond de Andrade would be revealing of the ideological ambiguity that maps the (mis)paths of the memorialist discourse of the dominant class.

In a surprising way, Drummond's text dramatizes the opposition and contradiction within the Brazilian thinking elite, between Marx and Proust, that is, between the longed for sociopolitical revolution, founder of a new universal and national order, exemplified by the poems of *A rosa do povo* [The rose of the people], and the appeal to traditional values of the family clan of the Andrades, its economic and cultural values, as can be seen in *Boitempo* [Ox-time] and *Menino antigo* [Old-time boy]. Drummond takes up, in a not-always-explicit way, two positions as bearers of these two ideological options: the position of the beginning and of the origin. These positions become concrete in autobiographical situations, for, as Décio Pignatari pointed out in the periodical *Invenção* [Invention], "The autobiographical Drummond is first of all autographical: he puts himself in writing in order to become."

By "the beginning" is understood an individual's desire to establish by his own means a society in which he can totally deny the values of the past and the clan. By not identifying with his forerunners, the poet can affirm with conviction and radicalism the values of rebellion and individualism that he thinks are just for a classless society. Such a myth is represented in Drummond's poetry by the story of Robinson Crusoe, a "long story that never ends." Removed from European culture by an unforeseen accident,

Robinson Crusoe is driven onto a deserted island where he has to retake all the cultural steps of humanity, beginning from zero. From solitude, he passes to the discovery of the other, becoming enthusiastic over the return to social life. It is a myth of rebellion and, in Drummond's case, of the denial of the Father as transmitter of culture, and of the Family as determining the sociopolitical situation of the individual. The past does not count, only the present, and even so everything is yet to be reinvented, as long as the hands are joined.[5]

By "the origin" is understood humanity's will to be inscribed in a sociocultural order that goes beyond the individual and in which individual values lose their reason for being, since they are traces of a mere passing insubordination or rebellion. Only the higher values of tradition and the past are eternal and valid. Thus, the individual takes off the temporary mask of a Robinson Crusoe and discovers that, in himself, he is worth nothing: he only *is* something when he is identified and is determined by his clan. Knowledge is not a Crusoevian adventure, but it is already completely codified by tradition and offered to him for free, and human potential—his own—is already predetermined by his class of origin. The brief adventure of the individual on earth is an infinite approach to this knowledge, that is, the return of the son to the Father's house, so that he may take his place after his insubordination, and the return to the bosom of the Family, so that he may become the patriarch. Such a form of social demand is authenticated by religious thought. The transmission of cultural goods takes place through *inheritance,* through the acceptance of the heavenly Father. Man, inserting himself in the patriarchal Christian family, transcends his own life and time, revealing his true "I" in eternity.

To crown this brief, and I hope, instructive parenthesis, I call attention to the fact that the intellectual-character, often narrator, always central and remembering, between Proust and Marx, is found in the novels I have mentioned by Oswald de Andrade, in *A bagaceira* [Cane-trash], by José Américo de Almeida, in the sugarcane cycle of José Lins do Rego, in the *Amanuense Belmiro* [Belmiro the amanuensis], by Cyro dos Anjos, in *Angústia* [Anguish], by Graciliano Ramos, in *O tempo e o vento* [Time and the wind], by Érico Veríssimo, in *O espelho partido* [The broken mirror], by Marques Rebelo, in *Encontro marcado* [The appointment], by Fernando Sabino, etc. And note that I do not mention the drama of Jorge de Andrade, synthesized in *Marta, a árvore e o relógio* [Martha, the tree and the clock]. Nor will I even touch on more complex problems, such as those that would involve a "literary" reading of *Casa-Grande & senzala* [The masters and the slaves] of Gilberto Freyre, our classic of sociological studies.

The memorialist posture of the fictional text can be proven concretely and without any tricks in an examination of the complete works of two representatives of different literary groups: Oswald de Andrade and José Lins do Rego. After publishing memorialist novels in the beginnings of their careers—respectively, *Memórias sentimentais de João Miramar* [Sentimental memoirs of João Miramar] and *Menino de engenho* [Mill-boy]—both feel the need, already in their old age, to rewrite the same book, the same book given as a gift by the text of remembrance, only now without the conniving frame of a "novel": *Um homem sem profissão* [A man with no profession] and *Meus verdes anos* [My green years]. This coincidence is all the more significant because it shows us how fragile the distinctions of literary schools are (Oswald, from the São Paulo group, versus Lins do Rego, from the Northeastern group) and how fluid and how barely pertinent the frontiers are between memorialist fictional discourse and autobiographical discourse in the Brazilian context.

With the barriers between one and the other discourse defined as fluid, note that the list hastily put together in the paragraph above (do not forget, dear reader, that it is not my intention to give the cast of a "history" of literature) grows very large, for large is the number of works with a clear autobiographical stamp written by the modernists. Let me cite a few: *Infância* [Childhood] and *Memórias do cárcere* [Prison memoirs], by Graciliano Ramos, *A longa viagem* [The long journey] (first and second stages), by Menotti del Picchia, *Idade do serrote* [Age of the hand-saw],[6] by Murilo Mendes, *Antes que me esqueçam* [Before you forget me], by José Américo de Almeida, *Baú de ossos* [Trunk of bones], *Balão cativo* [Captive balloon], and *Chão de ferro* [Iron ground], by Pedro Nava. And, again, I am being economical, since I have not even touched on the chapter of "testimonials" of politicians and important figures of the national scene.

It seems to have been Antonio Candido who noted with the greatest keenness and consistency the importance of this current in the process of the *coming of age* of Brazilian literature. Possibly only the complete abandonment of the dubious mask contained in the labels "novel" and "character" and the acceptance of the rules of memoirs could precipitate the critical-bourgeois reflection (its span, limits, and taboos), that is, activate the participation of any writing, of any book, in Brazilian intellectual and sociopolitical life. Oswald de Andrade, evidently grateful and encouraged, remembers, in the early pages of *Um homem sem profissão* [A man with no profession], the phrase and advice of his friend and reader: "Antonio Candido says that a literature only comes of age with memoirs, letters, and personal documents and he made me swear that I will now try and write this confessional diary."

And it is also Antonio Candido, the professor and critic from São Paulo who, in recent, unpublished lectures, has shown us the importance of memorialist writing in the return to political awareness carried out by the book in the 1970s, beginning with the analysis of the prose of Murilo Mendes, of the poetry of Carlos Drummond de Andrade, and of the memoirs of Pedro Nava. It is finally Antonio Candido to whom we owe the keenest perception—that this complex, intricate, and varied multicolored bundle of texts (all those cited above) can be reduced to a single and undifferentiated discourse of class. Let me cite unsparingly the opening paragraph of the preface he wrote, in 1967, for *Raízes do Brasil* [Roots of Brazil], by Sérgio Buarque de Holanda:

> At a certain point in life, it becomes possible to judge the past without becoming self-complacent, for our testimony becomes the register of the experience of many, of all who, belonging to that which denominates a generation, consider themselves by principle different from one another and little by little become so alike that they end up disappearing as individuals to be dissolved in the general characteristics of their era. Then to register the past is not to speak of oneself; it is to speak of those who participated in a certain order of interests and of a world view, at a particular moment of the time that one wishes to evoke.

Suddenly, an unheard voice makes itself present; "Sir . . . Give me some silence. I am going to tell a story." Shunning through significant displacement that encompassing and indifferent, masterful and cultivated memorialist discourse, the great novel of Guimarães Rosa, *Grande sertão: Veredas* [Devil to pay in the backlands] stands out.

It becomes pertinent to point out that the place occupied in the former discourse by the intellectual narrator is now filled by someone who obeys and disobeys the command of the boss, the gunman Riobaldo. Riobaldo who can only *speak,* and speaks "in ignorance" to this "boss" who at every moment emerges silent in the narrative. With this, the intellectual, city-bred and master of Western culture, becomes merely a listener and scribe, inhabiting the textual space—not with his enormous and inflated *I*—but with his silence. The intellectual is the clerk of "instructed ideas," who can only *punctuate* Riobaldo's text, as psychoanalysis says, and the narrator himself: "As it was, I tell; you put a full-stop to me."

Despite the differences, Riobaldo's narrative preserves the same autobiographical aspect as before, except that this element no longer belongs to a Luso-Brazilian "great family," builder of empires and republics. On the contrary: he is the antipode of the "rancher's son," as he did not even know his father: "For me, what I thought, was: that I didn't have a father; it means that, since I never officially knew his name." Because he was disinherited by the masculine and traveling fate of the backlands, disinherited also by successive violent processes of conquest, of colonization and of local bossism, Riobaldo's life is a search for his real name, but one that will never be the family name. Without a fixed name, without a definable socioeconomic position, going from boss to boss, he lives the logic of change, of journeying and of transformation. His successive names translate the dependence on others and the successive metamorphoses of the search for meaning: Cerzidor, Tatarana, Urutu-Branco . . .

The narrative displacement pointed out above contributes to the gunman's speech affirming itself without the certainty of command and the serenity of power, certainty and serenity found in the masterly and cultivated memorialist texts and which he, Riobaldo, seeks exhaustively in his silent interlocutor. The speech of Riobaldo is symptomatically characterized by a constant stammering of doubts and uncertainties, a good example of which would be this passage: "May you bear the bad digressions in my telling. It is ignorance. I don't talk right with anyone from the outside, hardly. I don't know how to tell it right." The "telling right" does not belong to the dominated.

This anguished faltering of the narrator corresponds to the ambiguous situation, socially speaking, which Riobaldo lives: He always wants to affirm himself as boss but lacks the boldness and manliness necessary. From this also result certain doubts as to his own individuality, as to his own name. "The gunman Riobaldo. It was I? It was and it wasn't I. It wasn't I!—because I am not, I don't want to be." Transported from the rural surroundings, circumscribed geographically as the backlands, *Grande sertão: Veredas* creates, in its own way, an eternal dimension that recovers the narrated acts and facts, a dimension that was also characteristic of the cultivated memorialist discourse, but with a difference. Instead of the family and cultural Catholicism of which we spoke in Drummond ("the tables of the family law of Minas"), what is proposed is a conferring of meaning on discourse defined by the special use of the preposition *above* placed with a concrete noun. Let us go back to the quotation from the previous paragraph: "I don't know how to tell it right. I learned a little from my compadre Quelemém; but he wants to know everything differently: he wants not the thing complete in itself, but the thing-above, the other-thing. Now, in this day of ours, you—listening to me with such devoted attention—is that gradually I'll be learning to tell corrected."

The "telling corrected" is the way that the narrated facts transcend the first, common meaning, "they rise out of the real," acquiring a value *above,* supernatural, if you like, serving to inscribe the fact and the hero in the pantheon of those disinherited and unsure of their own value. It is in this way that the narrative of Riobaldo oscillates, first, between the telling and the telling right and, later, between the telling and the telling corrected. It oscillates between the crossing that is the real, the lived-life and the blindness as well, and the places of departure and arrival (the *arché* and the *telos* of Greek tradition). This oscillation translates a curiosity and an inquiry beyond-the-fact, in the last instance giving a dimension to the writing as a teleological search: "Ah, there's a repetition that always happens at other times in my life. I go across things—and in the middle of the passage I can't see!—I was concentrating on the idea of the places of departure and arrival."

Let us see how the novel of Guimarães Rosa (like *Os sertões* [The backlands], of Euclides da Cunha, within premodernism) shows an indispensable and important current within the memorialist discourse of the dominant class, for here the intellectual only serves to reap the discourse of the non-city-bred individual, of that being not incorporated into the so-called cultural and Europeanized values of Brazilian society, of the country fellow, in short. Similar experiences, although without the silent radicalism of the interlocutor of *Grande sertão,* are found in Lins do Rego, in Ariano Suassuna (*A pedra do reino* [The rock of the reign]), in Autran Dourado (*Os sinos da agonia* [Bells of agony] and *Novelário de Donga Novaes* [The lifetime chronicles of Donga Novaes]), in Clarice Lispector (*A hora da estrela* [The hour of the star]). This national-popular current (as perhaps Alfredo Bosi would call it) of Brazilian literature, completely different from the discourse that I have called populist and denunciatory, will affirm itself in a very positive way in the general picture of Brazilian culture. Note that one cannot tear out of Guimarães Rosa, for example, a definition of popular and, by extension, of the people, according to a Marxist conception. His letting the Other speak also comprises an elitist vision of literature, the vision of the dominant class: the "telling right" and the "telling corrected." The very conception that he has of the profound meanings of the dramatized acts and facts is not at all materialist, but rather naturally idealist and spiritual, as I have shown. The people are given to know through their own manifestations: stories, tales, romances, proverbs, and so on: given to know by their own poetic production, in the widest meaning.

Nevertheless, it is this same popular current that will sustain the possibilities of a discourse that modernizes, without prejudices or demagoguery, the native element. It modernizes it without denying it, for it is not merely a tabula rasa, the metaphor used by the jesuitical letters to characterize it culturally. It modernizes it without falling into the romantic idealization of José de Alencar or Gonçalves Dias. It modernizes it without destroying it, contrary to Machado de Assis: "It is certain that Brazilian civilization is not connected to the Indian element, and has not received any influence from it; and this suffices not to go look for the titles of our literary personality among defeated tribes." Contrary as well to a Graça Aranha in full effervescence of "pau-brasil":[7] "Brazil has not received an aesthetic heritage from its first inhabitants, poor primitive savages."

Insofar as the novelist merely listens to the popular poetic production, merely wants to serve as a vehicle so that this nonprivileged manifestation makes itself heard far from the place of enunciation, serving as an alert to our cultural forgetfulness and as wealth for literature, to that extent does his work resemble that of an anthropologist. In the case of Euclides da Cunha, we know how he kept a Field Notebook, we know also how he changed his mind about the massacre upon witnessing the day-to-day life of Conselheiro's men, we know how he noted with the minuteness of a linguist the country people's expressions and speech. In the case of Guimarães Rosa, we know—from his constant journeys through the backlands of Minas Gerais—of his informants, of his flesh-and-blood ear and his mechanical ear, the tape-recorder he used to capture with greater precision the slippery voice full of doubts of the gunman.

Two other, more obvious examples would serve to better show the debt of the Brazilian novelist to anthropology: *Macunaíma,* by Mário de Andrade, and *Maíra,* by Darcy Ribeiro.

Cavalcanti Proença, in his indispensable *Macunaíma Guide,* calls attention, in the chapter with the suggestive title of "The Guide-Books," to the three main readings used by Mário de Andrade to nourish his novel: "The greatest number of motives was reaped in the legends collected in the second volume of Koch-Grunberg's work [*From Roraima to Orinoco*], and which in most cases furnished the central theme, to which are attached, as secondary themes, elements from other sources. A study which is spread throughout nearly the whole book and furnishes the central theme of Chapter IV and Chapter XIII is Capistrano de Abreu's book *Língua dos Caxinauás* [Language of the Caxinauás]. As for the 'Velha Ceiuci,' the theme is based on the legend of the same name that Couto de Magalhães registered in *O selvagem* [The savage]." In the case of Maíra, its author is too well-known as an anthropologist and social scientist to place in doubt the legitimate ethnological setting on which his fictional discourse is built.

As important as noting this joining of the erudite narrative with the popular or mythic narrative would be to say that, in both cases, it is a question of the search for a discourse that would be exemplary of Brazilian culture in all its extension and with all its ambiguities. Macunaíma, the hero without character, is not only a figure taken from a legend; he is first the melting-pot where Mário de Andrade fuses the complex Brazilian people as he sees them and conceives them with his irony, roguishness, and erudition. A people who, as he affirms in the unpublished preface, "are like a boy of twenty: you can more or less perceive general tendencies, but it is not yet the time to make any affirmations." Mário de Andrade abandons his preface and these words, but the paternalism of erudite reflection on popular production is revealed through them. The Brazilian people are shown to be like the young Alcibiades in trouble, confronted with the dialectic and wise word of the novelist Socrates.

Macunaíma, the novel that desired to be a "rhapsody," is like the *Bachianas* of Villa-Lobos, works that navigate as much in European waters as in those particularly national ones, showing themselves in the end to be a journey of Brazil's discovery in reverse. The European went from the sea to the center of the country. Macunaíma goes from the center of the country to the sea. This intersection of journeys gives the origin, in the novel, to the splendid chapter 9, "Letters to the Icamiabas," where, through pastiche and parody, the novelist allows the text of Pero Vaz de Caminha's *Carta* [letter] to intersect with his own satirical text.

It is in this intersection of discourses, since it is impossible to erase the European discourse and it is no longer possible to forget the popular discourse, it is in this intersection of discourses that the silence of the intellectual narrator is imposed and that the battle of parody and sarcasm is begun, it is there that the conflict between the discourse of the dominator and the dominated is made to be heard. It is in this not very pacific space in-between that the Brazilian intellectual finds today the volcanic soil where he may unrepress all of the values destroyed by the culture of the conquerors. It is there that the text-of-the-difference is constituted, of the difference that speaks of the (still) very limited possibilities of a popular culture for filling the place occupied by the erudite culture, presenting itself at last as the legitimate Brazilian expression. It is also in this space in-between that the novelist sees in the mirror, not his own reflected image, but that of an anthropologist, an anthropologist who does not need to leave his own country. And as such, the novelist lives the same ambiguity and the same contradiction of that social scientist, so well expressed by Lévi-Strauss in *Tristes tropiques:* "Frequently subversive among his own and in rebellion against traditional usage, the ethnographer seems to be respectful to the level of conservatism, provided the society looked upon is different from his own."

In the ambiguity of the subversive and the conservative a certain *tardiness* of literary discourse can be perceived in relation to the more active values of sociological discourse. The latter has more rapidly assimilated and utilized the current and universal categories for the comprehension of social stratification and economic imbalances, imposing, with its "revolutionary" reading of Brazilian society, a model of action for the nonprivileged classes quite different from the paternalistic, or Socratic, attitude we find in the schematically analyzed novels. There is no doubt that, if sociological discourse incites an immediate practice that would be responsible for a violent reversal in the social conduct of the proletariat, literary-anthropological discourse—on its conservative side—would be inclined to constitute temples of knowledge, which would serve to keep and preserve the whole verbal production that would be destroyed forever thanks to the good and bad modernizations.

But, at the moment in which the social realities to be discussed are inverted, it is also perceived, not without a certain malevolence, that sociological discourse is often blind in relation to the petit-bourgeois values it carries with it, thus becoming very "respectful" about what touches on the values of the sociologist's class origins. Not only respectful, but even reactionary, because these values, transmitted to the ideology of the class struggle, are found solidified and hardened by the dogmatic certainty of the scientific word.

It is there that the literary scalpel, more merciless and less compromised by bourgeois institutions (whether the university or the research centers), more anarchic and outlawed, more on the margins, in short, can cut with rigor and vigor the sclerotic flesh of the Brazilian dominant class. It is a shame that the knowledge practiced by this surgery be restricted to an edition of three thousand copies in a country of 110 million inhabitants. What efficacy can it have?

Translated by Tom Burns and Ana Lúcia Gazzola

7. The Permanence of the Discourse

of Tradition in Modernism

■

I would like to begin by affirming that this is not one of my favorite topics, as it is not for most of the people who were formed and continue being formed by what is today considered the modernist tradition. We are more used to confronting modernism within the tradition of rupture, to use Octavio Paz's expression, or within the aesthetic of "make-it-new," to use Pound's, or even within Rosenberg's tradition of the new, and so on ad infinitum. Our formation was always shaped by an aesthetic of rupture, of breakage, by a conscious destruction of the values of the past. "Destruction was my Beatrice," wrote Mallarmé, declaring the name of the modern Muse. Therefore, one of the most privileged discourses of modernism, above all in the last twenty years, has been that of parody. It is not accidental that, among the first famous modernists, Oswald de Andrade[1] is the one who has won the greatest approval of the younger generations. It is he who, in modernism, took the aesthetics of parody to its ultimate consequences. For example, there is his celebrated line, which takes up the line of Gonçalves Dias "My homeland has palm trees": "My homeland has palmares."[2] This type of aesthetic—of rupture, of diversion, of irony and laughter, of the transgression of the values of the past—is what has the right of citizenship, so to speak, in the Dadaist reevaluation through which modernism has passed since 1972.

Now, suddenly, I am called on to speak about the discourse of tradition *tout court* within modernism. I will not deny that I enjoy these commissions. I might not even completely endorse the words I shall use today with the design of convincing you of the interest and importance of the topic for the widest understanding of modernism. But I always like to think about what I haven't yet thought about. It is in this sense that I would say that today I am advancing along a path where I feel like a novice, as much perhaps as most Brazilian professors of literature, writers, and intellectuals who were conditioned by the modernist aesthetic of rupture and, in particular, by the strong, overwhelming presence of so-called concretism. It is concretism (in its multiple manifestations) that profoundly affects, within the modern movement in Brazil, the aesthetic of the new for the sake of the new.

Please do not be surprised if, suddenly, instead of quoting Pound, as is the rule, I quote T. S. Eliot, and if, instead of saying modern (that is, of the modern tradition which has its beginning in romanticism, or the end of the eighteenth century), I am, even if half-unconsciously, putting off the question to what must yet come, or is arriving, that is, the *postmodern*. The impression that I have is that the topic proposed to me by FUNARTE[3] was not done so innocently.

The question of tradition—in the 1980s—would be linked to a critical revision of the modern, and in particular of modernism, opening the way to the postmodern and postmodernism, respectively. Before going on, it should be clear that I will be using the expression *modern* to refer to the aesthetic movement that is generated within the Enlightenment, and *modernism* to refer to our own critique of the fixation on the past, made concrete in the Week of Modern Art of 1922. Therefore, *modern* becomes a universal term, much more comprehensive, while *modernism* is a much less inclusive and more localized term.

To organize my presentation in a better way, let me offer a kind of plan that I would like to follow. This plan begins with an initial question and subsequently is divided into four parts, which I shall treat separately.

Here is the initial question: What is the reason for the return of the question of tradition today, and more incisively, why would we be interested in the question of tradition now that modernism has arrived at its end? Or rather, why delegate to the second plane, in the evaluation of the modern and modernism, the aesthetics of rupture, of make-it-new, of the new for the sake of the new? In 1972, on commemorating fifty years of the Week of Modern Art, we have reexamined modernism through the Dadaist perspective. Now the perspective is different, less innocent in its questioning of the pillars of modernity.

In the response to the question, I shall try to prove to you that the question would be linked to two ideas. First, we have gone today through what Octavio Paz calls, not without malice, "the decline of the avant-gardes," and it is at this moment that the emergence of the postmodern condition seems to appear as inevitable. Second, I am already on the way to the basic proposal of the essay: to inquire, in this present revision of the modern and modernism, if the question of tradition (of the so-called *passadismo* [fixation on the past] as the tradition was seen by the eyes of the 1920s) was really absent from the theoretical production of some modern authors, or from the artistic production of the Brazilian modernists. The answer is no. There is a symptomatic permanence of the tradition within the modern and modernism. I advise you in passing that I would be falling into a series of clichés, commonplace for us today, if I had adopted the opposite position, that is, if I wanted to discover, within the modern and modernism, the distinctive features of the aesthetics of rupture and of parody. My proposal—may it be very clear—is the inverse of that which was the glorious course of the modernist movement: to know if, in a period in which the valuing of novelty, of originality as a concrete given of artistic manifestation was predominant, there were traces in this same manifestation which would indicate, according to the title of the lecture, the permanence of a discourse of tradition.

The "no" uttered above opens the way to discuss, at the level of the modern theoretical production that lends strength to the tradition, the very positive presence of a poet like T. S. Eliot. In his famous article of 1919, entitled "Tradition and the Individual Talent," Eliot opposes the emergence of a poet by way of distinctive, personal features to the maturity of the poet himself, a moment determined by the fact of his inscribing his poetic production in a discursive order that precedes him. Therefore, the modern poet for Eliot, in his mature age, does nothing more than activate the poetic discourse that is already made: he receives it and gives it new talent. He lends strength to the discourse of tradition. If one is interested in modernism, one sees that this article was not unnoticed by Brazilians. It had much success among the poets of the generation of 1945. There is no doubt that a first sign of the presence of tradition within modernism would begin with a reading of the poets of the generation of 1945.

I will have to speak, after Eliot, of Octavio Paz, to take up again some reflections from the book *Los hijos del limo: Del romanticismo a la vanguardia* [Children of mire: Modern poetry from Romanticism to the Avant-Garde]. I will slight a little what he calls the "tradition of rupture" (the modern) in order to enter into what he calls the "tradition of analogy." Paz defines two forms of tradition: the tradition of rupture, which I referred to before, as being that of the glorious "make-it-new," and the tradition of analogy. The critical approach of the two forms of tradition never quite emerges in the reasoning or in the text of Paz. Here is a book to be written which would investigate the role of the tradition of analogy alongside, or even within, the tradition of rupture, as articulators of modern thought.

I will conduct, therefore, the reading of modernism through the reflections of Eliot and Paz with the purpose of seeing if, among us, the discourse of tradition (or of analogy) was active.

Here there is a less interesting problem and another, more interesting one. The less interesting revolves around the discourse of tradition in 1945. In a general way, the poets of '45, with Ledo Ivo (1924–) in the lead and João Cabral de Melo Neto (1920–99) to a certain extent, would have a curious position in relation to tradition. And their relationship with tradition was so strong that it contaminated a poet already formed, like Carlos Drummond de Andrade (1902–87). He—the poet of the present time, of the present life, of present men[4]—will be producing, in 1949, a "remake" of the classical theme of the world machine. The ninth canto of *Os lusíadas* [The Lusiads, of Camões] deals with the world machine and Vasco da Gama, and Drummond makes of it what is perhaps the first great remake of modernism.

This topic is less interesting than the following one. Here, perhaps, I will provoke a small scandal. The discourse of tradition was activated by the first modernists, and right at the beginning of the movement: since 1924, with the journey to Minas Gerais made by the São Paulo modernists, guiding Blaise Cendrars. I think that the journey is a chapter still relatively unstudied, and, when it is explored, it is through ways that do not approach the reasoning I shall try to develop. The journey sets a date, an important moment to discuss the emergence not only of the native past (Mineiro, Baroque, etc.), but of the past as in an instrument for a primitive (or naive) aesthetic manifestation. It was Brito Broca (1903–61), in an article from 1952, who called attention to the contradiction between the future and the past in 1924.

Finally, I must concentrate on the presentation of two poets: Oswald de Andrade and Murilo Mendes,[5] concentrate on two themes that they worked on and that are fascinating: the notion of time and the question of utopia. The question of utopia, in both poets, is detached from a notion of deterministic and linear time and from a progress also seen as linear and evolutionary advancement. Both thematize—here is one originality of this work—the question of the eternal return. In a cultural area that was eminently dominated by Marxist thought, we have two poets who no longer activate the discourse of parody but prefer to activate the question of tradition. We shall see that the two have quite curious philosophical positions.

In the case of Oswald de Andrade, utopia would be connected to the matriarchy of Pindorama,[6] a contradiction that he expressed very well in a formula: one day we will be the technicized barbarian. In the case of Murilo Mendes, a Catholic poet, it would be connected to the Apocalypse, to

biblical discourse: Mendes—the poet of the Apocalypse, awaiting and an-
nouncing the second revelation of Christ.

Let us return to the question initially posed: What is the reason for this
return of tradition today? And mainly: Why are we interested in investigat-
ing the traces of tradition within modernism? The answer that I proposed is
that this question would be connected both to the decline of the avant-
gardes and to the rise of still undefined and uncharacterized problems that
revolve around what postmodernism will be. As to the question of the
decline of the avant-gardes, it would be well to perceive that in a chapter of
the same title in Octavio Paz's book *Children of Mire,* we will be led to the idea
that, in order to question the glorious tradition of rupture, it is also necessary to question four inseparable notions: that of time, of history, of ethics,
and of poetics. Paz's reasoning is brilliant and convincing; it homogenizes
these four elements in such a way that we finish the reading truly committed
to the end of modern action and thought and predisposed toward a new
aesthetics, which, for its part, would lead to new thoughts and actions as
well. All there is that is new today, Paz declares, is being articulated around
the notion of *now.*

As for the notion of time, Paz will tell us that, in spite of the modern
(when I refer to Paz, I mean much more the modern than modernism
properly speaking), in spite of the modern poet anchoring himself in the
present, there is at bottom a slighting of the present with the not always
disguised intention of valuing the future. Paz will tell us that the proposal of
victorious time in terms of modernity is that of the "colonization of the
future." The colonization would take place starting with a concrete proposal
for utopia that would be present in the great modern authors. If you take,
for example, a poet like Carlos Drummond de Andrade, you will see that,
along with the praise he makes of the present time and present life, he displaces the questioning of politics to the dawn of the day to come (see "Night
dissolves men"). Today is dark, to take up a little of the old-fashioned verse
of Thiago de Melo (1926–), today is dark, but I sing. Today is dark, we are
going through historical darkness, but I sing because I believe in the utopia
of the coming day. I believe in the colonization of the future. The political
efficacy of the utopian vision has been discussed since the 1970s, because we
have experienced a need to devalue the future. The future is seen as a kind of
horror film, something that scares us, and scares us exactly because it is
leading us to a nuclear catastrophe that is right around the corner. It is to
that catastrophe and others related to modern action to which the ecological
movements call our attention. You can see that Paz's argument, as I said, is
quite seductive. He builds these arguments to conclude that the poetics of

today is the "poetics of the now," which would not make a rupture with the past nor would it see the present as reason and argument for us to think only of the future and of utopia. This, basically, would be Paz's reasoning in relation to time. Let's see what comes of this.

Moving to the concept of history, he proposes to review the under-standing of evolution as linear progress; obviously, the revision is a logical result of what had been said before. Paz invites us to conceive of a history where the paths of progress are plural. In this way, too, he will make us revise another basic idea that pervades all of modernity: the idea of revolution as rupture, such as that conceived on the model of the French Revolution, a model taken up again by the Russian and, more recently, by the Cuban Revolution. This model of revolution, Paz points out to us, begins to be reexamined during recent decades by what he calls the spirit of rebellion. Rebellion, for Paz, no longer expresses the anxieties of a class struggle; it is not a movement of a universal type, but is characterized by the struggle of the minority groups in search of identity. We would have, from the 1960s, a kind of politics that is expressed by the fragmentation of the social move-ment, by the fragmentation of the political field. You see that the notions of time, history, and tradition of the revolution are at the same time put in check by Paz. The modern, too, will be put in check.

Let us go on to the third notion, which in my view is the most evident: ethics. We would have, again from the 1960s, a devaluing of the Protestant ethic as a repression of desire and the proposal of an ethics of the body, an ethics that would take into account a whole political process of de-repressing the human potential of each individual. By locating the body firmly in the present, by putting the body as the place of authentic sensa-tions, of vital experience, this new ethical position also disconnects man from the possibility of overvaluing the future to the detriment of the past.

Finally, one would arrive at the poetics of the now. Paz says:

> The vision of the now, as the converging point of the times, originally the vision of the poets, has been transformed into an underlying belief in the attitudes and ideas of most of our contemporaries. The present has become the central value of the temporal triad. The relation be-tween the three times has changed, but this change does not imply the disappearance of the past or the future: on the contrary, they acquire a greater reality, both past and future becoming dimensions of the pres-ent; both are presences and are present in the now.

You see that within Paz's poetics of the now there begins to be a place for a conception of the past that would not be characterized by the rupture in the present, and for a conception of the future without an overvaluing by utopia. Not going either to the past or escaping through the future, but taking a foothold in the present, here we see by what surreptitious manner the past and tradition began to take part in the construction of the present. At the same time, we will detach ourselves from the aesthetic of the make-it-new, of irony in relation to the values of the past. Therefore, there is a confluence of the three dimensions of time in Paz that would be the opening for us to be able to discuss, within poetry, the new role of tradition.

Even in this first part of the work, I see, parallel to the configuration of the decline of the avant-gardes, the appearance of the notion of the post-modern. I would merely call your attention to a quite evident fact, in particular in the recent discussions on architecture: the postmodern architects are looking for a nondestructive coexistence with the past. A revealing example of the opposite position, the modern position, is found in the construction of the building that represents to us the maximum expression of the modern, the building of the Ministry of Education and Health in the 1930s. This ministry was earlier housed in a beautiful fin de siècle building in Cinelândia,[7] unfortunately now razed. The architects are now acknowledging the destruction of the past, without obviously falling into the recovery of the past by kitsch, as we find in Botafogo.[8] Kitsch, for me, is painting the fine two-story houses of Botafogo pink, strawberry, and so on. It is not this I am referring to. Neither kitsch nor the destruction of the past, and not irony or parody either, but the coexistence of styles from different periods, without the condition evident in Ouro Preto either, where the past is, so to speak, safeguarded in its own past, and without any contact with the present. A discussion of the postmodern is found in the book of Paolo Portoghesi on postmodern architecture, or in a recent article by Fredric Jameson; it would also be found in the disregard the latest generations have for parody, since they now work more and more with the style of pastiche. Thus, leaving parody and irony in relation to the past, and going over to pastiche, the postmodern artist incorporates tradition and the past in a way in which trustworthiness would be the tonic, smoothed over by pluralism.

Let us go on to the second part, where I intend to discuss the concept of tradition in Eliot and that of the tradition of analogy in Paz, to see how both work with these *reactionary* notions within the modern.

Eliot, in "Tradition and the Individual Talent" cited above, tries to unmask a typical process we find in the critique of the modern, a type of prejudice we have: the modern critic praises a poet only for that, in his poetry, which resembles less the poetry of others. The modern critic will always give emphasis to the individual feature, will always value the original talent of the writer. Eliot says that here is a prejudice that is fairly simple to unmask: "Whereas if we approach a poet without this prejudice we shall often find that not only the best, but the most individual parts of his work may be those in which the dead poets, his ancestors, assert their immortality most vigorously." It is through the commitment of the modern poet to the dead poets, through the affirmation of the immortality of the discourse of poetry, that the discourse of tradition would be defined in Eliot.

Eliot, of course, discards tradition in the sense of blind attachment to or timidity before the conquests of those who immediately preceded the new generation. I think it is important to give this definition of "false tradition" because it is in this way that we discard, in this revision of modernism, a group like "Festa,"[9] which proposed a discourse of tradition in modernism, but one that was a false tradition because it constituted a neo-symbolism. That is not the true tradition for Eliot; that is simply the recovery of an immediately prior generation, a recovery of the conquests of a prior generation within an aesthetic that no longer admitted the old standards. That, indeed, was nothing more than what is still today *passadismo,* academicism.

Eliot will tell us that the meaning of the real tradition is connected to the notion of what he calls the "historical sense": "The historical sense involves a perception, not only of the pastness of the past, but of its presence." And he goes on: "The historical sense compels a man to write not merely with his own generation in his bones, but with a feeling that the whole of the literature of Europe from Homer and within it the whole of the literature of his own country has a simultaneous existence and composes a simultaneous order." Eliot incurs an evident Eurocentrism, and it is here that he must be repelled. One of the characteristics of modernism is going to be the constructive attachment to our indigenous civilization on the one hand and to our African civilizations on the other. There is no doubt that the notion of tradition would be linked in Eliot to a single, exclusive Western tradition. This can be the case for Murilo Mendes, certainly our greatest Eurocentric modernist poet, but it will not be the case for Oswald de Andrade. In virtue of the vision of the past as our contemporary, by reason also of his Eurocentrism, Eliot has always been suspect in Brazil. His aesthetics, for example, did not suit the principles of historical revision preached by our poets in early modernism. And yet from the traditional soil that I am trying to define here, the value of tradition would emerge, and the possibility would emerge of modernism being understood today in a way that is no longer conventional. By conventional, I mean the way in which the movement was interpreted even by the textbooks. On the contrary but without slighting the victorious and dominant perspective, my attempt must be to try to understand modernism through speculations that take tradition into account (without falling into the false tradition).

To talk a little about the tradition of the analogy in the discourse of modern poetry, it is important to explain the reasoning of Paz on this subject. Paz perceives in the modern poet an always contradictory relation to history, saying that the modern poet always begins with an enthusiastic adhesion to history, to revolution, to then abruptly break with the revolutionary movements that he participated in, whether they be the French, Russian, or Cuban revolutions. I know everything that is arguable in Paz's "discovery"; nevertheless, the interest today is much more to reproduce another's view to show to what extent the discourse of tradition within the modern would be connected to neoconservative thought. Perhaps I have gotten ahead a little, but one of the points that could be discussed later is that Eliot and Paz maintain, with respect to politics, a new neoconservative attitude. Perhaps it is for this reason that I am concentrating on the two poets so that later I may articulate with greater assurance the fact that, when tradition is spoken of, it necessarily leads to a sharp criticism of the Enlightenment as critical reason, to a crushing criticism of the idea of revolution according to the model established by the French Revolution. I shall also expound for the poets committed to the revolutionary struggle this possible folly: the impossibility of a poet at a mature age to endorse the political values considered positive by modern history.

To return to Paz: in the era of the dominion of critical reason and the secularization of knowledge, the modern poet does not find asylum in the historical soil itself—he is religious. Not finding the historical soil of the present able to support his poetry, the modern poet, according to Paz, looks for what he calls the tradition of analogy, that is, the knowledge that defined the episteme in the sixteenth century, when the vision of the universe was given as a system of correspondences (see Foucault's chapter "The Prose of the World," in *The Order of Things*). When we begin to perceive the similarity, for example, that a certain seed has to the eyes, we are discovering that it must be good for the eyes. To discover the correspondence is to arrive at knowledge. The tradition of analogy is: a vision of the universe as a system of correspondences and a language that is a kind of double of the universe. The modern poet, for Paz, disconnects himself politically from a compromise with history and grounds himself in the sixteenth century, where the poetic language, for its correspondence between word and thing, founds the universe and knowledge. By the language of analogy, the poet is the founder of the universe and of knowledge: he names things. This position should not be confused with Nietzsche's, where naming things means also an act of power *over* things. This is not exactly what Paz is talking about. He speaks of the modern poet as a founder, of the poet as a religious man who for the first time names things, and by naming them, is creating poetry.

Tradition, in Paz's thinking, has the meaning of a historical soil of knowledge that the poet borrows from the past in order to be able to articulate his *reaction* against the revolutionary principles that are the motor of modernity. Therefore, the tradition of analogy, as I said above, is cloaked in the book *Children of Mire* in its function of reaction to the principles of modernity. It is reactionary, in the etymological sense given it by E. M. Cioran.

I shall now go on to a more concrete discussion: How do we judge the tradition when we speak of Brazilian modernism? I shall divide the answer. I shall pass quickly over the less interesting and detain myself at what I think the more interesting. There is no doubt whatever that, around 1945, there is in Brazilian poetry a positive return of the so-called classical forms of poetizing, the virus of *sonetococcus brasiliensis*. There is, for example, a return of the sonnet both in a Ledo Ivo and a Vinícius de Moraes (1913–80), and we will find the involvement with tradition even in João Cabral de Melo Neto, when he writes the poems using the verse taken from popular romance, or when, at the level of composition, he uses the *auto* within the tradition of Gil Vicente (1465–1536). It is in this period, too, that our first modernist historians of Brazilian literature emerge, like Antonio Candido (1918–) and Afrânio Coutinho (1911–); it is they who establish the modernist standards of the tradition.

This involvement of our new modernists with the tradition will influence the so-called first modernist poets: it is the case to which I have earlier referred, that of Carlos Drummond, in the poem "A máquina do mundo" [Machine of the world]. Drummond had clearly, up to 1949, up to *Claro enigma* [Clear enigma], taken on a political position of a revolutionary type, becoming closer and closer to that of the Communist party, when he suddenly returns to the Portuguese tradition of Camões. Note how Paz is right: the appeal to tradition in modernism will always come close to the poet's break with a line of political participation of the Marxist type and, at the same time, will begin a greater concern for poetry, for the being of poetry, the fact of poetry perhaps being irreparably disconnected from a mature commitment to the present history of the poet. At the moment in which Drummond detaches himself from the Brazilian Communist party, and relegates to a secondary level the "rose of the people," in which he opens a book by saying that "it darkens, does not seduce me even to grope for a light-bulb," at the moment in which he rejects the sunny, participant poetry, he begins as well to be interested, without irony, in the great themes of the Luso-Brazilian tradition.

The most interesting case, in my view, to speak of a tradition in modernism, and here I disconnect it from the notion of neoconservatism, would be the journey made by the modernists to Minas Gerais in 1924, a journey in which Mário de Andrade (1893–1945), Oswald de Andrade, and a Swiss poet based in France, Blaise Cendrars, among others, took part. These poets were all imbued with the futurist principles, all had confidence in the civilization of the machine and of progress and, suddenly, they leave in search of colonial Brazil. They come upon the national historical past and—which is most important for us—upon the primitive as a manifestation of the eighteenth-century baroque of Minas Gerais. I cite one sharp observation by Brito Broca on the journey:

First of all, what deserves attention on this trip [to Minas] is the paradoxical attitude of the travelers. They are all modernists, men of the future. And to an avant-garde poet who visits us, scandalizing the conformist spirit, what are they going to show? The old cities of Minas, with their eighteenth-century churches, where everything evokes the past and, in the last analysis, everything suggests ruins. It would seem to be only an apparent incongruity. There was an internal logic in the case. The divorce from Brazilian reality in which most of our writers have always lived made the landscape of Baroque Minas appear in the eyes of the modernists as something new and original, within, therefore, the frame of novelty and originality that they were seeking. And did they not speak, from the very beginning, of a return to the origins of nationality, of the search for the vein of ore that would lead to a genuinely Brazilian art? For there in the Minas ruins they were to find, surely, the suggestions for that art. . . . But that excursion was fertile for the modernist group. Tarsila [do Amaral] would find in the painting of the churches and the old houses of Minas the inspiration for many of her paintings; Oswald de Andrade took the theme of several *pau-brasil* poems, and Mário de Andrade came to write then his admirable "Noturno de Belo Horizonte" [Belo Horizonte nocturne].

Brito Broca, in my view, happily shows the tearing apart of modernism, right at its beginning: on the one hand, a futurist aesthetic that preached the disconnection from the past—and in this sense it is good to recall the "Futurist Manifesto," where Marinetti preached the burning of libraries and museums; and, on the other, the shock in the unexpected and fruitful contact with the Minas tradition. And what emerges from this contact? There is a chronicle by Mário de Andrade, written soon after the trip, in which he relates the experience of the group as they behold the scenario of the baroque tradition. I shall select from the chronicle just three topics in order to see how poets and thinkers plunge into the tradition who were not in any way predisposed to perceive the past without Dadaist irony.

The first topic I will choose refers to Tarsila's attitude toward Paris.[10]

Tarsila, in Ouro Preto, says she wants to return to Paris, but not to learn of the latest fashion. She wants to return there to learn how to *restore* paintings. Tarsila already sees Paris no longer as the place for the *dernier cri,* but the place where she might acquire knowledge to facilitate the restoration of the Brazilian colonial past, unfortunately in shameful condition. Here is the passage:

> But, returning to the subject, what a wonder fallen from heaven is our Tarsila! A sacred flame has now taken her. . . . Her eyes shine. Her voice has become vital, true. What of Paris? What of Cubism?—No, Malazarte [Malazarte is the name Mário de Andrade uses to sign the chronicle]. I return to Paris, but to perfect myself even more in the processes of restoring paintings. Afterward I come to Minas. It is necessary to *conserve* such treasures [my italics]. I am ready. And with no pay. What greater payment for me than to restore to the small, marvelous Rosário of São João d'El Rei the past splendor of its roof? My whole life would be summed up in this . . . I would be happy! I like great undertakings.

This short passage is quite significant because the kernel is here for one of the great "conservationist" projects of the modernists: they approach the Ministry of Education and Health in the 1930s to create SPHAN,[11] with Mário de Andrade in the lead. In my view, Tarsila's discourse, the remains of the discourse of tradition alongside the clearly futurist aesthetics or dada of the modernists, serves to erect the quite rapid institutionalization of the modernist credo in the Estado Novo.[12] It seems that Tarsila speaks here as if she were Rodrigo Mello Franco,[13] except that she is speaking in 1924, which is rather significant.

On the other hand, there is an amusing pun used by Oswald de Andrade in the same chronicle: they encounter an individual named Senna, who serves as their guide in São João d'El Rei.[14] At a certain moment, Oswald makes one of his fine puns: "Oswald swears that he never had the intention of leaving Paris to come and find the Senna [Seine] in São João d'El Rei." It is clear that both Tarsila and Oswald, at this precise moment of modernism, are imbued with the need for an appeal to tradition, the eighteenth-century colonial tradition of Minas. From there to the matriarchy of Pindorama will be merely a step.

The third example is the responsibility of the chronicle's author, Mário de Andrade. He makes a severe critique of the modern architecture that he finds in the big cities of Brazil. He says: "Well then, do you not see that they are filling the avenues of São Paulo with complicated little houses, real monsters of spas, of international exhibitions? Why do they not take advantage of the old eighteenth-century mansions, so noble, so harmonious, and especially so modern by the simplicity of their line? Instead, they do not sully the Avenida Paulista with excrescences that look more like pigeon-hutches made by a celibate who enjoys retirement."

And he goes on making a violent critique of what would be modern architecture in São Paulo at that moment and, an even greater target of his critique, the Cathedral of São Paulo, which was being built during that period.

I wish to call your attention to the fact that we do not need to go to the generation of 1945 to see the clear presence of a discourse of a restoration of the past within modernism. The contradiction between futurism, in the European sense of the word, and modernism, in the Brazilian sense, already existed in 1924, at the same moment that the young were trying to impose an aesthetics of originality among us. The emergence of the historical discourse in modernism aims at a valuing of the national in politics, and of primitivism in art. And there is no doubt that the greatest example of this valuing of the national and primitive is found in Tarsila's work in terms of painting, and in Oswald's poetry in terms of literature.

But here I would like to make an examination of Oswald distinct from the analysis of his work, which puts the emphasis on parody. If parody is valued in a reading of Oswald's poetry and thought, it is clear that it will not be possible to see the line I am attempting to make visible. Parody, by being ironic about the values of the past, makes the present break the hold of the past, cutting the line of tradition. In this way, if we are interested in seeing how the traditional line is manifested in the poetry of Oswald de Andrade, we especially have to abandon the reading made by the concrete poets of the 1950s and, in a certain way, fixed by the youngest poets in the 1960s and 1970s. We have to seek another Oswald, the one of the philosophical texts. I would say that most people who know Oswald's work well have not read carefully the author's philosophical texts, which also proves the idea that the reading of modernism was focused on the aesthetics of rupture and therefore ignores what the philosophical texts reveal.

It is quite rare within modernism for a poet to have a philosophical vision of the world made explicit in conceptual texts. And this vision of the world is in Oswald notable for its original notion of the concept of utopia, which would neither be the clearly Marxist utopia nor the utopias defined by the model of the French Revolution—for Oswald, utopia is Cariban. The savage way of knowledge, says Oswald, has been questioning the European way of knowledge beginning with the first contact of Europe with the Americas. From Montaigne to Rousseau, that is, passing from the critique of religious wars to the Inquisition and arriving at Rousseau's noble savage, without forgetting the Declaration of the Rights of Man, the savage has been the motor of European utopia. Oswald, with his anthropophagous thought and action, thinks of bringing the European utopia of the Carib Indians *to its proper place*—Brazil. Oswald's utopia questions even the fact of a Western society being patriarchal—and here is another slip in meaning offered by Oswald's extremely rich thought. We will have to reenter the matriarchal soil of Brazil, duly industrialized, to achieve full utopia. It will be realized in the concrete of the matriarchy of Pindorama, reviewed by technology.

I am going to read a sentence by Oswald that is quite revealing of the relation between a false utopia and a patriarchy, generated as it is by messianic movements: "Without the idea of a future life, it would be difficult for man to support his condition as a slave; from this comes the importance of messianism in the history of patriarchy." Within the patriarchal order, man is the slave of the present. The utopian future proposed by messianism ratifies the unhappiness of the present. The true utopia already begins to be its own present. To quote Oswald again: "And today, when by technical know-how and social and political progress we have reached the era in which, as Aristotle says, the spindles work by themselves, man leaves his condition as slave and penetrates once more into the threshold of the age of leisure, another matriarchy is announced." Technical know-how will reach a certain stage in which it will no longer allow man to work. He can dedicate himself to leisure (and not to business, as in the patriarchal society). Dedicating himself to leisure, in the eternal return to the matriarchy of Pindorama, and taking advantage of technology, man achieves the condition of "technicized barbarian." I insist on saying that utopia in Oswald already begins to take place in the present, as he himself says, and I repeat: "It is *today* when by technical know-how and social and political progress we have reached the era . . ." (emphasis mine).

I will not detain myself with Oswald; I want, however, to make it clear that the notion of time that he thematizes is not characterized by the linear progress of human civilization, but by a contradictory movement. It seems that technical know-how goes in a straight line in order to close in a circle afterward, taking up again the matriarchy of Pindorama, that is, for Oswald Brazil is the country of utopia par excellence, as long as (as the modernists thought) it becomes up to date through industrialization. Returning to the matriarchy of Pindorama, to the origin of Brazil and modern utopia in Europe, we arrive at the future. In this way, Oswald tries to conciliate the progressive linear vision toward the future with the return to matriarchy. It would be what can be called the eternal return with a difference. It would not be the eternal return of the same, since Oswald does not wish, as Policarpo Quaresma,[15] for Brazil to go back to being an indigenous country. This theory of Oswald, as incredible as it seems, has been reactivated by some French anthropologists, especially Pierre Clastres. Clastres has shown how the Brazilian natives have constructed a society without the notion of coercive power. This would be our basic difference with respect to the Incas and the Aztecs. This absence of coercive power (of repression, Oswald would say) is thematized in the best pages to be found on matriarchy. It is a utopia where there would be no bosses, where there would be a community of equals—no business, complete leisure.

Let us pass on now to Murilo Mendes. One important detail in his poetry is his conversion to Catholicism, in 1934, under the inspiration of the painter and poet Ismael Nery. The Christian discourse would be the other important point of the discourse of tradition in modern Brazilian poetry. In this sense, it is curious to observe how Murilo will resume the same attitude as Eliot, wishing not to affirm his individual talent, but trying to give some continuity to a discourse that already existed before him, the discourse of Christianity. In this sense, for those who are closely interested in his poetry, I recall a curious fact: he did not want to reissue one of his books, *História do Brasil* [History of Brazil], surely because it demonstrated his narrow concern with the national, in a parodistic style. The limited concern for the national did not make any more sense in the discourse of a converted man, in the universalizing discourse of Christianity. At a moment when he abandons the nationalizing current of modernism, Murilo Mendes ceases to be merely a poet to become a prophet. And it is not by chance that he moves to Rome, where later he will die. This is a question of coherence: he had to die in Europe. Here is the story of Peter, of the rock, and of eternity. The discourse of tradition that brings back the values of Christianity made the poet's daily relation to Brazil practically impossible. A similar fact would occur with Henry James and T. S. Eliot. Eliot abandons his American citizenship, becomes English, converts to Anglicanism, and ends up receiving the title of "sir" from the hands of the queen. It seems like whenever we speak of the discourse of the Europeanizing tradition and try to see the efficacy of this discourse within the modern, we always fall into a neoconservative type of thinking. In Mendes's case, the very definition of time is quite interesting. One of his poems, "A flecha" [The arrow], is symptomatic in the contradiction it offers to the very movement of the metaphor of the flow of time. As the poem says:

> O motor do mundo avança:
> Tenso espírito do mundo,
> Vai destruir e construir
> Até retornar ao princípio.
> [The motor of the world goes forward:

Tense spirit of the world,
It is going to destroy and build
Until it returns to the beginning.]

We have concluded, as well, that when the question of tradition arises in poets who have a vision of a wider world, the poetic discourse feeds on the problematic of the eternal return—in Oswald's case, as we have seen, the eternal with a difference, the technicized barbarian; in Mendes's case, the basic principle of Christianity, which says that the end is in the beginning. The motor of the world goes forward, but does so in the strangest way, for it is building and destroying until it reaches the beginning of everything, which, in its turn, is the end:

Eis-me sentado à beira do tempo
Olhando o meu esqueleto
Que me olha recém-nascido.
[Here am I sitting on the edge of time
Looking at my skeleton
Which looks at me new-born.]

"Edge of time" is a classic image used by Murilo Mendes to designate eternity. What is interesting is to call attention to the fact that we are before the eternal return of the same. The end is already in the beginning and the beginning in the end.

To move on, I may add that Mendes's poetic posture during the Second World War is rather curious, a still very misunderstood chapter in our literature. We know Drummond's attitude well, through the various studies that have been made of him. The victorious posture is always more attractive in these Brazils that detest losers. For Drummond, the poet plants his foot in history, enters Berlin with the Russians, gives us a vision of the martyrdom of Stalingrad, and so forth. The poet makes poems with the strong presence of the discourse of social and political history, reduplicating it, so to speak, in verse. Mendes, on establishing a dichotomy between time and eternity, complicates the temporal scheme of modern history. Historical time marches in a straight line, but Christian time, which redeems historical time, converts the straight line into a circle, reducing the paradox of the end in the beginning and of the beginning in the end. A phrase of Murilo Mendes's concretizes for us the political implication of the dualism of time and eternity. He affirms that capitalism, in relation to communism, is reactionary, but communism, in relation to Christianity, is also reactionary. For him there is the inevitability of a historical evolution that passes through capitalism, communism, and so on, but all this will be reactionary in the eternal dimension of Christianity. Let us recapitulate. Mendes elaborates the historical and social discourse of the Second World War, and even the critical discourse of the Vargas dictatorship, not with a language that reduplicates these discourses (Drummond's case, for example), but with the language of fable. He seeks to show that there always was the game between innocence and cruelty, and he utilizes the form of apologies and parables to speak of the conflict of war and of resulting authoritarianism. I will cite three short poems from *Poesia liberdade* [Freedom poetry] that are very instructive for revealing how the discourse of Christian tradition prevents him from discerning historical specificity. The first poem says this:

A inocência perguntou à crueldade:
Por que me persegues?
A crueldade respondeu-lhe:
—E tu, por que te opões a mim?
[Innocence inquired of cruelty:
Why do you persecute me?
Cruelty replied:
—And you, why do you oppose me?]

One feels persecuted, and the other as well. Cruelty cannot exist without the opposition of innocence, and vice versa. You can see that the clear support of the poem is the fable of the wolf and the lamb, and this is the commentary that Mendes makes on the essence of the conflict of war in combative contradictions.

The following poem speaks of the evidence, of the inevitability, of hierarchy in the world of men:

A aveia do componês
Queixou-se do cavalo do ditador,
Então o cavalo forte
Queixou-se das esporas do ditador.
[The oats of the peasant
Complained of the dictator's horse,
Then the sturdy horse
Complained of the dictator's spurs.]

We see that there is a hierarchizing, from the oats to the spurs of the dictator. It is in this form—by the inevitable conflict of hierarchy and the resulting violence—that Mendes makes his criticism of the period's dictators. But the dictator is not merely Getúlio Vargas, Hitler, or Mussolini—that dictator that we find, in disguise or not, in the committed poems of Drummond and so many others. It is a dictator reconciled to the conflicting relation between things and beings. It is a universalized, abstracted, symbolic dictator, manifested in the form of a parable.

And the last of the three poems makes a play on the two temporal dimensions: time, properly speaking, and eternity:

> O pensamento encontrou-se com a eternidade
> E perguntou-lhe: de onde vens?
> —Se eu soubesse não seria eterna.
> —Para onde vais?
> —Volto para de onde venho.
> [Thought met with eternity
> And asked him: whence do you come?
> —If I knew I would not be eternal.
> —Whither do you go?
> —I go back where I came from.]

In proportion to Murilo's taking up the discourse of religion, his poetry disconnects itself more and more from the contact with historical time, with the immediate present of the poet, and makes a commentary in fable and parable—in the sense of parable as it is found in the New Testament on the more burning questions of the poet's social and political experience.

I would terminate our conversation of today on the permanence of the discourse of tradition in modernism almost without words, or with a few words, saying that perhaps the fact is irremediable that, within the aesthetic of rupture characteristic of modernity and modernism, in the cases in which we searched for the strong line of tradition, or even the line slightly broken, we have come closer and closer to a poetry, to a poetic production that disconnects itself from the social as a dimension of history experienced by the poet. This often can border on—and often does border on—neoconservatism.

Translated by Tom Burns and Ana Lúcia Gazzola

8. Repression and Censorship in the Field

of the Arts during the 1970s

■

So, I write my column every day and I have one thing I have learned from censorship. *I saw, for example, that many people were being diminished by censorship, were being prevented from doing what they wanted to do, and were doing other things to get by; these people were either going crazy or losing their taste for life, killing themselves, all these things. And so I imposed on myself that every time the censors would forbid me from writing something, I would write three more.—Plínio Marcos,* Folhetim, *July 17, 1977 (emphasis added)*

I

The problem proposed here—repression and censorship in the field of the arts during the seventies—does not have a single, easy reply. Of course, a first attempt at a reply, divided in two complementary parts, could be given with a quantitative and factual perspective on the problem: on the one hand, one could show the harm and the mistakes of the censor's prohibitions, and on the other, one could offer a historical view of the process of softening the repressive mechanisms, which was controlled from the top and was therefore slow and gradual.

One could list the titles and number of books that were prohibited from circulating, of plays that were not performed, of national and foreign films that were not shown (or were cut up), of songs of Brazilian popular music that were not sung or played, of pictures or statues that were not exhibited, and so on. One could list as well the names of all the writers, filmmakers, playwrights, actors, composers, singers, and so on, who had problems with censorship.

One could also begin to weave the history of the hazards of the censors themselves and of censorship itself in relation to the executive power, from October 1974, when for the first time a president of the Republic deigned to speak in public on the subject, even if *en petit comité*. Both at the inauguration of the Guaíra Theatre (October 1974) and the reopening of the Amazonas Theatre (January 1975), the president, questioned by different groups of intellectuals, spoke a few words that sounded like a good omen. The floodgates were open: the flow continued till the moment of the words of the minister of education, who, on May 23, 1979, classifies censorship as "paranoid ethics for the salvation of culture." And, he goes on to say, "This is an aid, a salvation for which culture was not consulted, nor did it give its consent."

The first task referred to above—the inventory—has practically been done by several newspapers. Although the list has not been exhaustive and systematic, there is already, for example, the reporting of every banned play. In an article with the title "The shows/plays that Brazilians did not see because censorship would not allow it," in the *Jornal do Brasil* (April 8, 1979), names of writers, actors, titles of plays, and dates of the banning of the play or the show are listed. The same newspaper, on June 18, 1978, had already published the long list of the "censorship documents," that is, the text of 270 orders issued by the censors between September 9, 1972, and October 8, 1975, in which certain episodes, information, foreign telegrams, and interviews were prohibited. In an analysis of this strange *corpus,* the newspaper report concluded: "Censorship always knew what it intended to erase: the activity of the security apparatus and the dispute over the succession of President Médici."

The second task—writing the history of the softening or slow suppression of arbitrary censorship—as far as I know, has not been done. Given the limits of time for this paper, I cannot recommence and dig deeper into the information given above, so that the long, difficult, and agonizing dialogue of the intellectuals with power might be interpreted with greater assurance, with an eye to the softening, rationalization, or suppression of the mechanisms of censorship. The urgent need for this research is here merely acknowledged.

This attempt at a response, in two complementary parts, would not in my view exhaust the problem proposed. There would still be grounds for *reflection* for someone concerned with criticism of the arts and their role in relation to the reader and, by extension, to society.

To begin with, one can affirm, in an apparently paradoxical way, that censorship and repression have not affected, in quantitative terms, Brazilian cultural production. That is because in the specific case of the work of art, the creative process—like an ostrich—feeds on practically anything: flowers, nails, snakes, and thorns. Books, plays, songs continued to be written. And, as far as it is known, no artist changed his political party because of censorship, or stopped thinking, imagining, inventing, noting, writing, because of censorship. No one stopped saying what he wanted to, even if in a low voice, to the paper, to himself, or to a few companions. As long as there is a brain, paper, pencil, and hope, there will always be a Plínio Marcos, a Chico Buarque, an Antônio Callado, a Rubem Fonseca, and so on. Repression and censorship can, at the most, feed a certain latent laziness in every human being, can only justify rationally the idleness that often impels the artist to think today and create only tomorrow.

Nevertheless, the artist-individual and the artist-family suffer quite a lot in the hands of censorship and repression, both economically and morally. Censorship ends up by getting to, in a drastic manner, the human person of the artist, the physical being—and not the work. And it is here that the greatest injustice of censorship lies within a society.

Economically, the artist suffers insofar as his main source of income can be cut off from one hour to the next, sometimes causing formidable difficulties, as in the case of the more expensive arts, the theater, and the cinema. The very economic survival and that of the artist's family can, in this sense, be harmful and difficult, and one need not even mention the case of there being, for example, an accident or illness in the family. This economic squeeze can lead the artist to debase himself politically and professionally, to accept jobs or positions that he would normally not accept, to endorse economic schemes that, in normal circumstances, he would reject. It can even lead him to abandon his own country (and many did so), in the search for greater peace of mind to work and a better material situation for himself and his family.

Morally, the artist suffers not only from the strange and uncomfortable situation that he begins to have within the concrete social group in which he and his family circulate, but also because, once his work is banned, the abuses of interrogations, imprisonment, and even the pain of physical torture follow. Repression and censorship, in some cases, manage to make a sane man ill, a psychologically healthy being with a paranoid mind. All of this, of course, reflects in an extraordinary way on the artistic works of the time.

The ex-head of the Division of Censorship argues, on the contrary, that a prohibition only makes the work "hotter" from the commercial point of view, and for this reason the artist profits from censorship. There is here an obvious sophistry, that doubtless is happily helpful, but only for the businessman who industrializes art: the recording-company, the film-distributor, the publisher, the producer, and so on. An artist of Chico Buarque's calibre can first say "And I don't deny that on the part of the businessmen and even that of the recording-company there is an interest in stimulating this mystique of the thing that is liberated but can be banned at any moment," to then add: "Of course, if I put out a record normally and nothing happens as far as censorship, this myth disappears. In fact, I am rooting that this happens because I don't want to sell records just because I am a censored composer" (*Isto É,* November 11, 1977).

Let me summarize, with a concrete example, what I have said above: Graciliano Ramos did not stop writing in the years following *Memórias do cárcere* [Prison memoirs], even though he had suffered horrors in the prisons of the Estado Novo.[1] Only in this way could Brazilian culture enrich itself with a merciless description and a cold analysis of the arbitrariness of the repression and with an overpowering personal testimony on the hell of the prison underground. Through the intense physical and moral suffering of a person and the intellectual and political persistence of an artist we can better know the paths of authoritarian power in Brazil.

It is the lucidity of this brilliant artist Graciliano Ramos that brings to a close this part of my commentary:

> It would be great if every novelist in Brazil had spent some months in the Correctional Colony of Dois Rios, had known the admirable figures Cubano and Gaúcho. *You might take this as perverse; it is not.* I would think it a good thing if my best friends stayed a while in that dreadful cell. It is true that they would suffer a lot, but perhaps it would lessen other complicated pains that they invent. There exists there a reasonable sample of hell—and, in contact with it, the fiction-writer would profit. (*Linhas tortas,* p. 98, italics mine)

Aesthetics, the theory of art, for the writer Graciliano Ramos, was not disconnected from the theory of life, and to speak from the point of view of the oppressed in our society, it was necessary that the writer incorporate their experience in his own.

II

If the crime censorship commits is not against the work, but against the physical person of the artist and with repercussions of moral, political, and economic order, against whom does censorship truly commit the artistic, cultural crime?

The one who is most punished, unjustly punished, by artistic censorship is society—the citizen, any one. And taking up, with some modification, the Minister of Education's words, let me say that censorship brings a "salvation" for which *society* was not consulted and did not give its consent. It is the citizen who stops reading books, seeing plays, listening to songs, watching films, looking at pictures, and so on. It is he who receives a certificate for being an intellectual minor. Because of censorship, in these periods, society has its sensitivity hardened and its artistic (and its critical and scientific thought) blunted. In these circumstances, the person who enjoys the work of art is plundered of certain elements that would help it compose the whole panorama of the society in which it lives, for it only receives a single voice that circumscribes all of reality, the voice of the authoritarian regime, the only one permitted.

The one who appreciates art becomes a citizen of amputated thoughts and feelings, someone ill-informed about aesthetic, social, political and economic questions, someone who is out of date in relation to his colleague in other countries, someone, in short, who is disengaged from this place and time of contemplation and reflection that is the place and time of the work of art in our contemporary world, a time and space in which he—a simple citizen, paying out of his own pocket for his book, record, or ticket—can give himself not only to intellectual satisfaction and aesthetic enjoyment, but also allow his head, nerves, and feelings to deal parasitically with his problems within the perspective of the Other.

And if, by chance, that person has the misfortune to *grow up* in this period, his situation is even more serious, for he will have gaps in his intellectual formation, in the formation of his sensitivity, in his sentimental education, to recall Flaubert, gaps in the artistic knowledge of the sociopolitical problems of his time and society, gaps that will never be filled. The days and years go by and with them those hours of leisure that are more accessible in adolescence than in the period in which he will begin to confront hard work. This is the generation that we have in the 1980s and after and which Luciano Martins, in a recent article, baptized the "AI-5 Generation."[2]

III

If, as Plínio Marcos tells us in the epigraph, the artist writes three more for every piece that is banned, if censorship, therefore, does not affect in quantitative terms artistic production, it can nevertheless cause the emergence of certain formal *detours* that become characteristic of the works of the period. Taking literature as an example, one can see that there were two types of books that were successful during the period: texts that were affiliated with so-called magic realism and that, through metaphorical discourse and oneiric logic, intended to critically and disguisedly dramatize situations that might attract the attention of the censors, and the reportage-novels, whose fundamental intention is to defictionalize the literary text and thus crushingly influence the process of the revelation of the real.

This said, it would be mistaken to see a simple causality between censorship and the emergence of these two types of books in the 1970s in Brazil. Rather than being a feat of censors in the seventies, magical realism—just to stay with one example—is purely and simply one of the trends of the text of modernity (see Kafka, Julien Green, Lúcio Cardoso, among others). A violent censorship may signal the return of this option of fictional writing, it can speak of the contemporaneity of this option, it can acutely develop its need for authors already predisposed to it. Take the case of Murilo Rubião. He would write as he writes, as in fact he has always written, independently of censorship. Censorship merely made more significant and up to date the need he had to write as he writes. Censorship could even lead his enigmatic text to be understood in a more *concrete* way by his contemporaries. It is not a coincidence that Murilo Rubião, a writer scorned by the literary histories, suddenly emerged with great critical and commercial success. Censorship prepared the ground, the minds, to receive the impact of a text as strange and parabolic as his. It is easier today for the reader to tune in, with more pleasure and profit, to *O Ex-mágico* [The ex-magician]. During the fifties, a period in which the stories that have a success today were actually written, the reader was little prepared to receive Murilo Rubião's text and was therefore not very enthusiastic about reading it.

Now, insofar as there is someone "tuned-in" who is young and who is only reading works that are adequately expressed by so-called magical realism, both Brazilian (the case of Murilo Rubião and J. J. Veiga, for example) and foreign works (the case of the Hispanic American novel, especially those of García Márquez and Cortázar), there will be a *single literary form* predominant among the novices in literature. At this level, we can indeed see how censorship—with no programmatic intention, of course—caused a formidable restriction on the options the young writers had for fictional writing. It is not by coincidence that the boom of the short story form in the 1970s took place through magical realism. Both form and style are notably young and end up being one of the literary realities of the decade, when speaking openly and impudently became a danger, and the way out could only be discerned metaphorically in the text of the "suppression."[3]

The other predominant form—the reportage-novel—perhaps maintains a tighter connection to censorship and a less effective one with literature, since its reason for being is in the naming of the forbidden subject and in divesting itself of the properly fictional resources of fiction. As censorship did not keep in view only the arts, but all forms of expression within society, it happened that the newspaper could no longer say what it wished to. This took place above all in the area generally known as crime. The great crimes of the decade as well as the great reaction of the police to the increase in criminality (the Death Squad) could not be covered with the journalistic objectivity they deserved. Literature therefore began to have a parajournalistic function, as is the case of the prose written by José Louzeiro and Plínio Marcos, whose chief aim was the sociopolitical denunciation of the exclusion that characterized Brazilian reality and the denunciation of censorship itself, which was making it impossible for certain subjects to be discussed outside the closed rooms of power.

Precisely because it accuses censorship and accuses it within a style that is a simple *transposition* of the real, as is the journalistic style, this type of work had the greatest success in the period and was the most persecuted. In an efficient way, it was able to reveal the wounds of the time during the time itself, like the newspaper in democratic regimes. Let us hope merely that its luck lasts longer. That is what the critic Davi Arrigucci Jr. believes. According to a suggestion of Walter Benjamin's, Arrigucci sees a universalizing character of "allegory." To prove his point, he not only uses the parajournalistic work of José Louzeiro, but also that of Antônio Callado ("which is constructed on the basis of imitating the newspaper techniques") and of Paulo Francis ("who makes a kind of disemboweling of the large newspaper").

IV

Let us assume that the titles of the banned works and the names of the persecuted artists are listed, and the difficulty of censorship itself with respect to the executive power is narrated; let us assume that the conformist thought that believes it is censorship that can muzzle the true work of art is eliminated and that censorship itself is put on the witness-stand for making a moral, political, and economic hell of the human person of the artist and for attacking those who have to pay the piper—civil society, particularly the young; let us assume that we have concluded that censorship can only lead to certain formal detours on the works of the time; then it is now possible for us to make a value judgment on the artistic production during the period of repression and censorship. Because it is a value judgment, it is intimately connected to the opinion of the one who formulates it.

I do not believe that the works of the period have less value. What constrains me in rethinking the period is the complete lack of cultural interest and curiosity that the work of art had to confront, for censorship above all castrated, cooled, neutralized, blunted the critical thought and sensibility of the public. The works created in this cultural vacuum—a cultural vacuum that is not in the field of production, but in the society as a whole—do not end up being qualitatively better or worse than those created in other periods. Yet, the impression one has is that, like a car stuck in the mud, the wheel turns, the motor runs, a lot of sand is thrown up, but forward movement is nil. Stuck in the morass of society, the work of art stays either in the limbo of restricted reading, waiting for better moments in which a large and more mobilized band of the population can have access to it with pleasure, or in the limbo of artistic creation, the artist waiting for better moments to render it concrete.

Censorship and cultural repression accomplished something really fatal in this country of 110 million people: to reduce even more the tiny public that is interested in the arts in Brazil. During the period, we had one of the most fascinating flowerings of committed works of modern Brazilian culture, but its fruition was always reduced to the 3 percent of the population to which Paulo Francis refers in *Cabeça de papel* [Paper head]. And this discrepancy speaks much more against the country and its leaders than against culture.

With this in mind, these are some proposals to which our artists in the 1980s should be sensitive: a less elitist art, more in tune with the anxieties and will of the people (without necessarily falling into populism); a text that is less difficult because it is less enigmatic, more accessible to the general population because it has learned not to abuse the artifice of art; less expensive access to the work (price of the book, the ticket, the record, the picture, etc.); a more generalized and significant fitting together of the work of art and the mass of the population both literate and illiterate, which would make its fruition a real fact in sociocultural terms.

Translated by Tom Burns and Ana Lúcia Gazzola

9. Literature and Mass Culture

■

The sign perhaps that the millenium is about to end is the frequency with which we ask ourselves about the fate of literature and the book in the technological, postindustrial era. I do not feel tempted to take a risk in this type of prediction.—Italo Calvino, Six Proposals for the Next Millenium

I

Like every child who grew up and was educated in any Latin American city during the Second World War, from an early age I was a consumer of mass culture, which began to come over to us in an overwhelming way from the United States at the time. Along with the automobile, which had taken over the streets, and airplanes and zeppelins, which enchanted the skies, dazzling new kinds of technology were offered in the form of the small electrical appliances of daily domestic use. In the eyes of children and adults, the North American mass culture imposed itself in a marvelous way on movie screens by means of films, cartoons, and serials. In these there was both a style of behavior and clothing different from our own and a cosmopolitan and symbolic vision of reality; both the popular music of unintelligible speech and syncopated rhythm and the dance-steps that were more daring; both the dramatization of foreign experiences of daily life and the "allied" version of the great world conflict. The style imposed itself also through comic books, where the super-heroes of the good reigned supreme, or through the magazines intended for the great urban public, such as *Reader's Digest* (1942), where Dale Carnegie taught us how to win friends and influence people in the best style of "the American way of life." Great future Brazilian intellectuals were on the editorial staff of this magazine, among them the professor and critic Afrânio Coutinho, who introduced New Criticism in Brazil.

All this industrialized material, imported mainly from the United States, mingled in an unbalanced way with the incipient Brazilian cultural production for children. The latter was presented without the American technological apparatus and was led by Monteiro Lobato (1882–1948). The imported material also mingled—pushing them to the margins—with the traditional, nonurban forms of spectacle and entertainment, such as the circus, the amusement park, and religious festivals, with their booths of food, drink, and games, folkloric dances, and pastimes.

In a provincial town, such as Formiga, where I was born in 1936, the cinema every day informed the imaginary life of its inhabitants of all ages, literate and illiterate, of current, foreign behavior and situations, to which, in the past, only intellectuals from big cities had access by reading imported books and magazines or by foreign travel.

It was, therefore, to be expected that the divided mind of the child and the youth would serve as a ready-made dish for obdurate nationalists like Monteiro Lobato, or city-bred intellectuals cross-dressed as ethnographers, like Mário de Andrade (1893–1945), or novelists cross-dressed as authors of children's books.[1] It was the consensus among writers that the field of the traditional and authentic repertory of popular Brazilian stories was being mined, taken by assault and dominated by the culture of the American industrialized image, and it did not matter to them if at the time the nation to the north was our political ally in the fight against the Axis powers. Strategically, the Americans had chosen a perfect target to achieve the change in the habits of entertainment and leisure: the children and youths (at the time known as "Coca-Cola boys"). With the imaginary taken over from the tenderest age by the industrially produced image, we would all be easy prey for all time.

More attentive to the market and to consumption, Lobato is exemplary in this fury of nationalist rebellion, from which the first cries of "The oil is ours"[2] are not excluded, and is an alert to the irrecoverable backwardness of Brazilian industry, particularly, the publishers. Less concerned with the literary market, the iconoclastic modernist intellectuals were not enthusiastic about Lobato's exclusivist (or xenophobic) ideals, ecstatic as they were, on the other hand, with the technical conquests and praise of the machine of the current European avant-garde, such as were illustrated since the beginning of the century in the futurist manifestoes of Marinetti.[3]

Since 1928, the modernist Oswald de Andrade (1890–1954), in "Manifesto antropófago" [Anthropophagous manifesto], envisioned the possibilities of revolutionary human behavior in Hollywood films. He writes: "What confounded the truth was the clothes, the water-proof between the internal and external worlds. The reaction against man in clothes. American cinema will bring us information." But sixteen years later, in 1944, at the time when the Brazilian Expeditionary Force took part in the Second World War on the battlefields of Italy, the same Oswald de Andrade acknowledges a relative *mea culpa,* in a letter addressed to Monteiro Lobato (see "Letter to Monteiro Lobato," now in the collection of essays *Ponta de lança* [Spearpoint], published in 1945). According to Andrade, in the past the nationalist Lobato was, and was not, right. He had not been right because he had not managed to see that the modernists brought in their poems, "under the cover of futurism, the distress and the anger of the Brazilian land." He was right because he had been the first one of his contemporaries to call attention, through his suffering rustic character Jeca Tatu (*Urupês,* 1918), to the falsity of savage Brazilian modernization. It was for this reason and not the former that Andrade held out his hand to Lobato's "opportune and sacred xenophobia," which should not be confused with the vainglorious vision of a Cassiano Ricardo (1895–1974), called by him "voodoo for tourists."[4]

What was the concrete fact responsible for the change in the way of thinking of the modernist from São Paulo? The Brazilian soldier, called to the campaign in Italy, was becoming skilled in modern weapons, and was adept at becoming cannon-fodder, as they say. Few Brazilian citizens had access to the technological avant-garde, but for those who had it was in order to find death more quickly. In the meantime, the country itself and the rest of its citizens were fated to the eternal colonial backwardness, without access to the modern industrial goods that North America had. In the ambivalent reading of Lobato's ideas, made in 1944, Oswald de Andrade hit a double target: he both retrospectively beckoned to the "miracle of resistance" of the poor Brazilian people, which Euclides da Cunha (1868–1909) had heralded at the turn of the century, and prophetically intuited that embracing Lobato, at a time predictably including the boys of the Casa do Estudante do Brasil (CEB) [House of the student of Brazil],[5] would be behind the nationalizations of foreign companies. The national state would promote the modernization of the country in the course of the following decades. It would even be behind the armed resistance of the young guerrillas, inspired by the Cuban revolutionary model at the end of the sixties.

Financial poverty of the political actors and modest technical, even primitive, resources for the armed struggle; manly courage and suicidal fearlessness of the combatents in their resistance in the face of the enemy with the aim of achieving victory; a priori disqualification of the technological advantage of the enemy by praise of the unity of the people's efforts—here were the authentic "nationalist" values from Cunha's *Os sertões* [The backlands] (1902) up to the "new cinema" (from 1961). The classic example of the latter is Glauber Rocha's *Terra em transe* (1967) [Land in anguish], in which, according to the commentary of ex-guerrilla Fernando Gabeira, "the main actor, Jardel Filho, fires off his submachine gun randomly, symbolizing in this way an almost desperate and personal rebellion." We were always confronted with discourses that encouraged armed conflict, discourses reactivated at the various historical moments of national crisis, when politico-economic pressures of the hegemonic countries offer in a colonial or neo-colonial way the means to modernization and the progress of the country through advances of the higher technology.

If this historical scheme of nationalism, necessarily unilateral and, for this reason, simplistic, is accepted, it is understood why, in Brazil, unlike countries such as Argentina where, since the twenties, technique allied itself with ideology in the making of revolutionary popular utopia,[6] the technical imagination hardly entered—or enters—the heads of the popular classes in the struggle for the emancipation of oppressed people. For this reason, it is hardly a theme in our mass culture, or even in our erudite one. The possible forms of mass culture in the peripheral modernity of Brazil are reduced to the fanaticism for the highly sentimental and melodramatic serials, as one sees in a definitive way in the radio *novelas* (soap-operas) beginning in the forties and in the television novelas beginning in the sixties. In these works, one finds the ideal pasture for a discourse in which the popular and collective "happiness" is removed from any nuance relative to the industrial world and its conquests. The exception to the classic Brazilian model has arisen only in the 1990s, when the process of the development of the country is taken up again. In the field of the television serial, the 1990s work of the scriptwriter Glória Perez is an example: the melodramatic plot feeds primarily on themes like artificial insemination (*Barriga de aluguel* [Rented womb]) and, more recently, the highways of the Internet (*Explode coração* [Heart explodes]).

The nationalist reaction of Lobato, more similar in its explicit pragmatism to that of a Delmiro Gouveia (1863–1917), wishing to alone impose the model of modernization of the Brazilian northeast by setting up a thread factory in the little town of Pedra, has always pointed to the problematical autonomous industrialization of Brazil, despite the extraordinary natural resources the company has at its disposal. The contradiction between backwardness and peripheral modernity, sharply delineated by Oswald de Andrade, finds its cultural high-mark in the anthropophagous theory, or in the theses of dependency defended since the 1960s by CEBRAP [Brazilian Research Center in São Paulo] (of which the current president of the Republic, the sociologist Fernando Henrique Cardoso, was a member). For the present topic, Brazilian literature today, both nationalist reaction and the contradiction between backwardness and modernity continue to serve as an alternative backdrop to the model emerging from our tupiniquim[7] modernity and the recent history of Brazil.[8]

Let me sum up: to take up the question of literature in 1995 only makes sense if one goes first by way of the *detour* of mass culture, a detour that Brazilian criticism has avoided but which all of us in our daily lives take in one way or another. To introduce this unexpected perspective, I avail myself of Vinícius de Moraes (1913–80), at a time when he was a poet and film critic. In an article of 1942, "Two Generations of Intellectuals," he asked: "Can it not be the interest in *cinema as an art* a sign of the profound difference that marks the two generations of intellectuals that exist in Brazil today?" Then, with shrewd critical acumen, he named one writer after another, the various writers of modernist Brazil, separating them into two distinct groups. The cinephile group, he observed, is nicely distinguished from the other group, which scorns the seventh art. About this latter group, he writes: "Their interest [in the cinema] is fortuitous, as an echo of other interests. There is no vocation in them. They are inner men, standing over an intimate cinema, without any patience for the kind of extroversion that the cinema requires. They will be, at the most, poets who go to the cinema."

In the literary situation of the 1940s, even the text using introspective language (an allusion to the French genre of the *roman d'analyse,* then in vogue in Brazil, as a reaction to the northeast social protest novel) takes place in cinematic language. It is a matter, however, of "intimate cinema," where the eyes of the author are the camera that turns inward. The writers who are lovers of cinema turn "extrovertedly" to the cinema, supporting themselves on its narrative technique to compose properly literary texts. Moraes concludes by pointing out the limitations of the "intimists": "I don't believe that any of these men of whom I spoke could write a good script, build a continuity correctly or give cinematographic rhythm to a succession of images."

II

Walter Benjamin was perhaps the first great theoretician of modernity who did not fear the cinema. In 1935, he thought it was important to write an essay on the new process that represented the technical reproduction of the work of art in the frame of the capitalist mode of production, believing that the concepts derived from this theoretical reflection would in no way be "able to be appropriated by the Fascists" and could be used for the "formulation of revolutionary demands on the political artist." This is the essay "The Work of Art in the Age of Mechanical Reproduction," which underwent at least two versions. In this analysis, let us leave aside many of the classic points of the essay, such as the destruction of the aura, and concentrate our interest on only two points, which in a certain form have been neglected by the majority of the Brazilian students of Benjamin. One may hope that this new detour, now focusing on the German 1930s, will lead us with greater security to the question of Brazilian literature today.

Let us first take, in Benjamin's text, the play between public and private, touching on the questions of artistic production and its diffusion. According to him, the traditional arts (literature, painting, etc.) had their public diffusion as a consequence of an external factor, independent of the stage of its production that took place on the plane of the private life of the artist. A literary or pictorial work is based on itself, independently of its diffusion as a book or in a gallery or museum exhibition. The same does not happen with a film. Benjamin notes: "The technical reproducibility of the film has its immediate foundation in its production technique. This does not only make possible, in the most immediate form, the mass diffusion of the cinematographic work, but makes it mandatory. The diffusion becomes mandatory because the production of a film is so expensive that a consumer who could afford a painting could not afford a film. The cost of the film is covered by the sum of the tickets sold."

This means that the cinema, besides being a collective work of art (classical theme to which the individualism of the traditional artist is opposed), makes works that are paid by the *collectivity* of consumers. (The great spiral into which the national cinema went, after the creation of EMBRAFILM [Brazil Film Institute] (1969) by the military junta that took over from President Costa Silva, is the result of the fact that the producers and filmmakers wanted to replace a collectivity of consumers with a sponsoring.[9]) The book and the painting can be, and often were, produced by obscure dilettantes, works that ended up being posthumously elected to artistic glory, or definitively assigned to oblivion. If the film does not externalize contemporary time and taste and does not maintain an immediate and effective dialogue with the spectators, it is fated to failure or nonexistence. In this sense, the more expensive the film, the more absolute is the a priori demand for a large and varied consumer market. It is for this reason that the financial investment backing a film is not confused with the payment made to the group of artists and technicians involved. The cinema requires large capital, which, in its turn, is considered repaid by the commitment shown by *collectivities of consumers,* domestic or foreign, in paying off the financing. The artistic tendency of the cinema is its precocious internationalization. The cinematographic industry designs and is designed by the world market. In the best cases, the film is an art that, collectively and comprehensively, points to the transgression of the values established in the various collectivities of consumers, whether they be metropolitan or peripheral, urban or provincial.

Within this general perspective, one of the unsolvable contradictions of the peripheral contemporary avant-garde (scientific, artistic, and technological) encounters in the cinema a radical metaphor for the hazardous stage at which it lives, since the cinema points toward the two poles that sustain it, industry and knowledge. Both the updating and progress of "backward" societies, in terms of social life, art, and science, and the sociopolitical and industrial modernization of a given peripheral country, occur in the sphere of the consumption of works that a priori could not and cannot be produced there. It is starting from the consumption of possible imported models—or rather, of the reading and critical or passive assimilation of the production where great capital reigns and from which it expands—that the best and most decisive creations and inventions of the periphery intensify, freed from the isolationist and repressive values of provincial societies that seek self-sufficiency in umbilical explorations and daydreams.

For something new to be able to be produced in the interior of the peripheral country, there has to be a gap between what is produced abroad and consumed (that is, partially financed) at home. This irregularity has led intellectuals, united with generations and generations of students, to resort to protectionist laws for national cultural production, as is the case of the law of the obligatory screening of the Brazilian film *8 x 1,*[10] and has led other intellectuals, possibly "the neo-Enlightenment," to demand of national governments generous financial investments that allow for the uncommitted exercise of research, taken here in its widest sense. They forget that, in addition to financing, scientific or artistic research for the majority of the citizens of a country must come with a good education for the youth.

Let us be moderately merciless: just as it makes no sense to consume, as is done nowadays, a film made ten years ago, it also makes no sense to acquire, as is done today, a computer made ten years ago. This perishability of the machine and its products in the modern Western world was acutely observed by Jean Baudrillard in *The Consumer Society,* in which he says that in these societies objects exist for death.[11] The abundance (or the quantity), from which the search for quality is not excluded, points as well to the constant renovation of the old, by establishing what is newest. Baudrillard ironically reminds us: generations were born and died using the same object; today, in one lifetime, we see similar objects being born and dying.

The second point of Walter Benjamin's text that is important for the present discussion centers around the transformation of the social function of art made possible by the means of technical reproducibility. Benjamin begins with a basic idea: "To an ever greater degree the work of art reproduced becomes the work of art designed for reproducibility." With the "authentic" no longer existing and, with it, the dimension of "secrecy" that was, in a contradictory way, evidence of the full existence of the single and unique object of art, Benjamin points out that in the human appreciation of these new forms of art, what occurs is the gradual loss of the *cult value* and the appeal to another, novel value, which is that of *exhibition*. The loss of the cult value of a work of art, at the same time that it de-sacralizes it, makes impossible its being placed in the tradition, that is, indicates the loss of a place where it was theo(teo)logically an object of ritual. The work of art at the moment in which it begins to be technically produced and reproduced loses something, but gains as a result the infinite places and contexts of its reproduction. And if it loses its value as cult, it also acquires a new function when it starts to have a lay social praxis, which is that of immediate intervention in the political sphere. If fascism sought in all forms the aestheticization of politics, the cinema—justly stimulated by reflections like Benjamin's—foregrounds and continues to foreground the politicization of art in the twentieth century.

(As later I shall speak of *alternatives,* and not of *competitive* solutions, for literature in the face of the avalanche of mass culture in the twentieth century, let me first allow Benjamin to refer to these alternatives in the nineteenth century. According to him, the impasse undergone by the traditional arts in the nineteenth century under the impact of photography was confronted by the two formal alternatives: the first, by way of the theory of art for art's sake, with the signature of Mallarmé, which represented a return to the theology of art, and the second, by way of its negation, which is art for art's sake, pure art, that is, art which rejects any social function for art. As we have seen, in his essay I shall not propose any searches or forms of competitive solutions in traditional art compatible with the total hegemony of the arts of technical reproduction. The Futurist and Dada movements did seek competitive forms in their time. In this case, there will be no effort to propose an aesthetic where "distraction" in the appreciation of the literary object is opposed to the laws of "contemplation," to use the terms of the German essayist. Let this parenthesis remain as an alert to readers, so that they do not think, when I speak again of literature of this decade, that I did not take the necessary epistemological precaution.)

The political praxis of art, announced by Benjamin, had its corollary in the way in which the cinema could intervene, through an incalculably plural and simultaneous diffusion, in the present time, making of the present its best representation, and performing as well the widest diffusion of the great questions engendered by it. The literature of the 1930s and 1940s felt the problem raised by Benjamin and tried to compete with the cinematographic art, by establishing as its subject-matter the material of the present that was at the basis of the cinema. Among us, Carlos Drummond de Andrade (1902–88) wrote during the era of committed literature: "Time is my material, the present time, the present men, the present life." The intention of the Brazilian poet was that his poetic production, independent of any discursive specificity, be given over to the contemporary consumer in its contemporaneity. The cinema will bring us information, as Oswald de Andrade said. Under the influence of the cinema, the reading of any and every literary work gained in strength through its capacity of being exhibited, which is an evident contradiction in our consumer society. To nourish the difference between exhibition and consumption and to activate the discussion, let me take as a basis the distinction Benjamin makes between the painter and the cameraman. The former, like a magician, distances himself from the body that he wants to cure, while the latter, like a surgeon, makes an intervention in the body to cure it. Benjamin concludes: "The painter maintains in his work a natural distance from the given reality and himself, while the cameraman penetrates deeply into its web." The spectator (the individual who disappears within the infinite audiences in different places) follows the pirouettes and exercises of the successive images on the screen, exercising what Benjamin calls with propriety an optical "unconconscious." Just as psychoanalysis had disclosed the experience of the "unconscious impulses," the cinema opens itself to the experience of the optical unconscious. The process of reading the cinema (or the committed literature of the 1940s) does not occur through the hermeneutics of depth, but is nourished from "shock effects," similar to those that we encounter in our daily lives.

The art of our day leads me to take up once again the distinction between painter and cameraman, so as to establish the difference between the reading of a traditional work of art in the society of the spectacle and the reading of film. This is not the case, as I have emphasized, of the committed poetic art of Drummond in the 1940s; that art resisted the distinction between painter and cameraman only and exclusively to observe the rules of conduct dictated by the cinema: "The cinema is the form of art corresponding to the most intense existential dangers with which contemporary man is confronted. It corresponds to profound metamorphoses of the perceptive apparatus, such as those that the passerby experiences, on an individual scale, when he faces traffic, and such as those that, on a historical scale, everyone who combats the reigning order experiences."

Let me further exemplify a functionally cinematographic poetic art with the poem of Carlos Drummond de Andrade, "The Death of the Milk-man," published in the 1945 collection *A rosa do povo* [The rose of the people]. In this poem, the useful and innocent walk of the milkman in the early morning of the city is checked by the indiscriminate violence of the homeowner, who kills him. The poem, in its turn, will submit the (innocent) reader to a "shock effect," quickening his sensibility to better understand the problems of "our time." He (the character in the poem or its reader, the identity has to be established) should not commit thoughtless acts ever again. The (political) lack of conscience causes the petit-bourgeois (character or reader) to murder the milkman, a predictable act by virtue of the alienation in which he lives. The poem foresees the end of this alienation in the socialist utopia, in the dawn of the day to come,[12] drawn by the mixture of the red of the human blood with the white of the milk, both spilled on the ground (see also the poem, "The night that dissolves men"):

> From the shattered bottle,
>
> . . .
>
> two colors seek one another,
> softly touch,
> lovingly intertwine,
> forming a third tone
> which we call dawn.

III

Having passed through the experience of cinema as art, having recognized its presentness and political function, having perceived the exaggerations and impediments of the film industry for the art of the cinema, having understood the transformations that cinema, together with other arts that are technically produced and reproduced, has generated at the core of the aesthetic discussion in the twentieth century, why does anyone decide to be a writer? Why does s/he decide to work alone as an artisan with words with the view of writing a book, a book that becomes more and more an obsolete object in the era of mass culture? Does one have to be merely and exclusively pessimistic as to the future of literature? Is it fated to be a production of "hillbillies" from the nonindustrialized periphery? In other, final words: Does there still exist a social function for literature at this end of the millenium?

At this moment, when the work of art is going through the glorious period of its technical reproduction, now in electronic clothing, our speech will be based on arguments that are woven around a skeptical attitude in relation to the dialogue that the literary text can maintain with its contemporaries. That is, the reading of books is not easy, nor is getting readers of books easy. By virtue of this situation, and paradoxically, our speech can be, in its extreme, quite *optimistic* with respect to the future of literature and its social role. Let me begin by speaking of literature in its own time of production and in the time/space of its contemporary consumption.

Let me begin from a presupposition that must be faced with the optimism derived from the skepticism of which I have spoken: literature, even before the era of the cinema and other arts of technical reproduction, was already considered by its finest artisans as anachronistic and not very conducive to exchange with contemporaries. Let us not take as an example the cultivators of art for art's sake or of pure art. On the contrary. Among us Brazilians, the one who first raised the question was Machado de Assis. Everyone knows the prologue "To the Reader," which opens the novel *Memórias póstumas de brás cubas* [Epitaph of a small winner] (1881). There Machado de Assis gives due credit for the idea to the French novelist Stendhal, at the same time in which he inscribes his novel in a specific stylistic line that recognizes in advance the unseasonable place of literature and the book in modern society: "That Stendhal confessed to have written one of his books for one hundred readers is a thing that causes wonder and dismay. What does not cause wonder, and will not likely cause dismay is whether this book will have Stendhal's one hundred readers, or fifty, or twenty, and when many readers, ten. Ten? Perhaps five." Stendhal realizes that his novel will go unnoticed by his contemporaries and only be fully read at the end of the century.

A few years after the publication of Machado de Assis's novel, we come across Nietzsche and his urgency in writing *Ecce homo,* an autobiographical account in which he reveals, as the subtitle says, "How someone becomes what he is." From 1879, when he abandons the stability of a university, Nietzsche leads a solitary, wandering existence. During the 1880s, he travels, thinks, and writes ceaselessly, managing in each new work to go beyond the limits of the latest one. Certain of the intrinsic and revolutionary quality of his philosophical work and of the importance of his knowledge for the future of mankind, Nietzsche cannot obtain in the bookshops and in the press the recognition of his contemporaries. The published books sell badly, and for this reason, are little read. His name is ignored. This lack of balance between the value of his production and recognition by his contemporaries, presented in a summary manner, is the first delicate problem the philosopher outlines and faces in the opening of his autobiography: "The disproportion between the grandeur of my task and the smallness of my contemporaries has manifested itself in the fact that they have not listened to me or even seen me. I live on my own credit. Would it be a mere preconcept, that I live? It is enough for me to speak with any 'cultivated man' who comes to the Oberengadin in the summer to convince me that *I do not live.*"

The passage is crystalline. The philosopher begins from the apparently nihilist and castrating effect of disqualification inflicted on him by his contemporaries, an effect already pointed out by Stendhal, but from it he extracts a lesson. The great philosophical task, the great work that appears in the form of a book, is not for the immediate comprehension of his contemporaries. These people, since they are small or immature in the face of it, cannot establish the contractual rules of reading with an author of the great undertaking, the great work. For this reason, cultivated men (the irony is in the italics) do not know Nietzsche, do not recognize the philosopher. The lack of a reading contract creates the fact of the philosopher not having been listened to or seen. In the event he speaks with some lettered man in the region of the Oberengadin where he wanders, the suspicion is confirmed. Nietzsche is convinced that he does not live, although his name remains in the published book.

Now, *Ecce homo* is written so that another contract may be clarified: that which makes the life and the work of its author possible, the urgency of continuing his task. He says: "I live on my own credit." Jacques Derrida comments on the passage in *Otobiographies* (1984): "This identity he [Nietzsche] doesn't obtain in a contract with his contemporaries. He receives it from the unpublished contract he signed with himself." I live on the credit that I opened for myself, for only thus can I write the books I want. On being a contemporary of himself, Nietzsche ceases to be his reader's contemporary. Nietzsche is *not* saying that he writes for himself: he says he writes starting from the credit that he himself opened for himself, in the belief that we future generations will pay off or settle the contracted debt. The more time passes, the more the credit increases (with interest), the more difficult and complex is the process of paying it off. The reader, not the contemporary but the future reader, is, from the beginning of the philosopher's autobiography or of the work of the modern writer, "implicated" in the game of self-conceded credit. The return of the investment is not carried out by a collectivity (of consumers) at the very moment at which it would be receiving the product. On the contrary. The contract is with people placed in successive chronological trenches of reading, people who will maintain with the Nietzschean text a contract that attests to the perennial nature of the product and the immortality of the author after death. Only at that moment will the life of Nietzsche stop being a "pre-concept."

What is important in the intellectually ambitious book is not the value of its being exhibited in various *simultaneous spaces,* but *the inevitable error* or *silence* of the reader[13] that is at the basis of its reception at the moment it is published. What is important is the ability the book has to generate *posterior spaces,* chronologically differentiated, more and more complete and complex readings-responses-payoffs, which lay the foundation of its value and recognize it as contemporary out of its time of production. The present out of its period cannot be confused with the present within its period, although they complement one another.

Since the literature I speak of is that which was produced during the hegemony of mass culture, it is doubly untimely: it distances itself from consumption by contemporaries on the one hand, and on the other from greater financial and technical commitments that the industrial arts of our time require even to be able to give their product a start. Unlike the cinema and other mass artistic manifestations, the greatest commitment of the literary object is not with the infinite collectivity, which through publicity directly or indirectly will pay off the high cost of production. There are forms of literature that can, of course, be valued in the market, and from it be validated by way of a new genre, the best-seller; there are even beneficial confluences between literature and mass culture, as happens, for example, with the lyrics of popular music. But great literature (or the literary literature) does not depend on the market in the way the cinema and television do. The market is an option that can move the pen of a Harold Robbins or a Paulo Coelho, just as it can that of the late Vinícius de Moraes or the present Caetano Veloso: the market is in the desire to maintain a financially profitable dialogue with contemporaries and, for this reason, is within immediate reach. The best-seller and the pop form of art reproduce on a very small scale the profits of a film or a television soap opera in the cultural industry: they will be what they wish to be if they manage to sell extraordinarily well. They will cease to be what they want to be if they fail to sell.

Let me consider now a second and final presupposition: literature is functionally untimely in the era of the cinema and arts of technical reproducibility. If the cinema, attuned to our times, offered an extraordinary field for the spectator's understanding of his present time, literature offers another, alternative understanding of the present time, by seeking forms of knowledge that escape the epistemological field common to its contemporaries. The literary work begins to fulfill itself when it points to future readers who will attempt—from the historical level where they are located—to become acquainted with the foundations of that location. In the credit the author opens for himself for the purpose of being able to produce his work, his successive readers will be inserted. Literature offers through the future reader of the work a present vision of the past and a past vision of the present. Every literary text, however oblivious it may be to the values of the past, directly or indirectly sets into motion forms of tradition that are the stage on which present events develop, which are really or virtually represented in the anachronistic time and atopic space of writing.

Translated by Tom Burns and Ana Lúcia Gazzola

10. The Postmodern Narrator

■

The stories of Edilberto Coutinho are useful, both to ask in an exemplary fashion and to discuss exhaustively one of the basic questions of the narrator in postmodernity. Is the narrator of the story the one who experiences it, or the one who sees it? Or rather: is he the one who narrates the actions based on the experience he has of them, or is he the one who narrates the actions based on knowledge he has acquired from them by having observed them in another?

In the first case, the narrator transmits an experience of life; in the second, he passes on information about another person. An action can be narrated from within or from without. It is not enough to say that it is a question of an option. In concrete terms, I narrate the experience of a soccer player because I am the soccer player; I narrate the experience of a soccer player because I am used to observing him. In the former situation, the narrative expresses the experience of an action; in the latter, it is the experience given by a look. In one case, the action is the experience that one has of it, and it is that which lends authenticity to the material that is narrated and to its narration; in the other case, it is arguable to speak of an authenticity of the experience and of the narration, because what is transmitted is information obtained from the observation of a third party. What is in question is the notion of authenticity. Is the authentic only that which I narrate based on what I experience, or can what I narrate and know through observation be authentic? Will human knowledge always be the result of a concrete experience of an action, or can it exist in a form *external* to this concrete experience of an action? Another tangible example: I say that the narrative of a fire related by one of the victims is authentic, and I ask if the narrative of the same fire related by someone who is there observing it is not also authentic.

Let me attempt a first working hypothesis: the postmodern narrator is the one who extracts himself from the narrated action in a manner similar to a reporter or a spectator. He narrates the action as spectacle that he watches (literally or not) from the audience, from the grandstands, or from a chair in his living room or in the library. He does not narrate as an "actant."

Working with the narrator who observes in order to inform himself (and not with what he narrates immersed in his own experience), the fiction of Edilberto Coutinho takes a further step in the process of *discarding* and *distancing* of the classic narrator, according to the model characterization Walter Benjamin made of it in his remarks on the works of Nikolai Leskov. It is the movement of discarding and distancing that makes the narrator postmodern.

For Benjamin, human beings are today being deprived of the "faculty of exchanging experience," because "the actions of experience are at a low, and everything indicates that they will continue falling until their value disappears completely." As society modernizes, the dialogue as an exchange of options on actions that were experienced becomes more and more difficult. People today no longer manage to narrate what they have experienced themselves.

In this way, Benjamin can characterize three stages through which the history of the narrator has evolved. The first stage: the classic narrator (the only one valued in the essay), whose function is to give to his listener the opportunity of an exchange of experience; second stage: the narrator of the novel, whose function becomes that of no longer being able to speak in an exemplary way to his reader; third stage: the narrator who is a journalist, that is, he who only transmits the information through narrating, since he writes not to narrate the action of his own experience, but what happened to x or y in such and such a place at such and such a time. Benjamin devalues (the postmodern values) the third type of narrator. For Benjamin, the narrative should not be "interested in transmitting the 'pure in itself' of the narrated thing as information or report." The narrative is narrative "because it immerses the thing in the life of the narrator so as later to take it out of him." In the middle is the narrator of the novel, who wishes to be impersonal and objective in the face of the narrated thing, but who, at bottom, confesses as Flaubert did in a paradigmatic way: "Madame Bovary, c'est moi."

Let me repeat: first, the narrated thing is immersed in the life of the narrator and extracted from it; second, the narrated thing is seen with objectivity by the narrator, although he confesses to have extracted it from his lived experience; third, the narrated thing exists as pure in itself, being information external to the life of the narrator.

In Benjamin's reasoning, the main axis around which the "beautifying" (and not the decadence) of the classic narrative turns today is the gradual and constant loss of its "utilitarian dimension." The classic narrator has "practical sense," as he intends to teach something. When the sedentary peasant or the merchant seaman narrate, respectively, community traditions or foreign voyages, they are being useful to the listener. Benjamin says: "This usefulness [of narrative] can consist in moral instruction, or in practical suggestion, or in a proverb or in a norm of life—in any case, the narrator is a man who knows how to give advice." Benjamin ends with the following: "The advice interwoven in the living substance of experience has a name: wisdom." Information does not transmit this wisdom because the action narrated by it was not interwoven in the living substance of the narrator.

Let me attempt a second working hypothesis: the postmodern narrator is he who transmits a "wisdom" that results from the observation of a lived experience outside of himself, since the action that he narrates was not interwoven in the living substance of his existence. In this sense, he is the pure fictionist, for he has to give "authenticity" to an action that, since it is not backed up by lived experience, would be deprived of authenticity. The latter emerges from the verisimilitude that is the product of the internal logic of the narration. The postmodern narrator knows that the "real" and the "authentic" are constructions of language.

The loss of the utilitarian character and the subtraction of good advice and wisdom, features of the present stage of narrative, are not seen by Benjamin as signs of a process of *decadence* through which the art of narration passes today, as I have suggested above, which removes him at once from the category of anachronistic or catastrophic historians. In the writing of Benjamin, the loss and the subtractions referred to above are pointed out so that by contrast the "beauty" of the classic narrative—its perennial nature—is emphasized. The basic game in the reasoning of Benjamin is the valuing of plenitude, based on acknowledging that which has faded away. And incompleteness—rather than being inferior—is merely less beautiful and more problematic. The transformations that the narrator undergoes are concomitant with an "entire secular evolution of productive forces." It is not a question, therefore, of looking backward in order to repeat yesterday today (we would perhaps be happier historians, because we would be restricting ourselves to the reign of the beautiful). It is a question rather of judging beautiful what was and still is—in this case, the classic narrator—and of realizing what appeared as problematic yesterday—the narrator of the novel—and what appears even more problematic today—the postmodern narrator. (Benjaminians take note: I am using the concept of narrator in a wider sense than that proposed by the German philosopher. He reserves the concept only for what I am calling the classic narrator.)

By supporting myself in the reading of *some* of Coutinho's stories, I shall try to prove the working hypotheses and learn the significance and the extension of the proposed problems. All this with the aim of offering subsidies for a discussion and future typology of the postmodern narrator.

As I have said, only some of the stories will be examined. Let me justify this choice by stating that otherwise, there would be the possibility of confusing my aim, for the author's fiction has a wider variety of narrators than that which is here analyzed. Let me cite for example the story "Mangas de jasmin" [Jasmine mangoes], justly appreciated by Jorge Amado. The story avoids the postmodern narrative and approaches the kind of narrative that rewrites the traditions of a community; as such, it may be classified as a narrative of "reminiscence," as Benjamin would have it and which was typical of modernism (Mário de Andrade, José Lins do Rego, Guimarães Rosa, and so on). The reminiscence is what "weaves the net that in the last instance all stories constitute among themselves." My intention here is not to give one more brush-stroke to the "beautifying" of the classic narrative, a job that has already been brilliantly done by Brazilian readers of Benjamin, such as Davi Arrigucci Jr. and Ecléa Bosi. My idea is to contemplate with Benjamin the "Angelum Novus," of Klee, trying to comprehend the reason why the wings of the angel of history do not close when overcome by the storm that is progress. That is, to try and comprehend what is problematic in the present—a history of human flight in the storm of progress.

In the story "Sangue na praça" [Blood in the plaza], a Brazilian journalist on a visit to Spain (the narrator of the story) and his young lady companion meet at a bullring with the American novelist Ernest Hemingway. The Brazilian journalist is also a reporter and he meets with the American novelist who had also been a reporter: a fine occasion to thematize the classic narrator and dramatize an "exchange of experience." But this is not the intention of the narrator (or of the narrative). What interests him is to dramatize other questions. He presents the oscillation between two professions (the reporter and the novelist) and between two different forms of narrative production (the journalistic and the literary). This dilemma is certainly our own contemporary one and therefore not gratuitous. Nor is there, in the story, the final and definitive rapprochement between reporter and novelist, between journalistic and literary production.

The one who tried, unsuccessfully, to jumble the two things for Hemingway, was the novelist Gertrude Stein (in the story introduced as "that woman from Paris"). Hemingway informs the Brazilian journalist who interviews him: "I was trying to be a writer and she practically told me to give up. She said that I was and would be merely a reporter." The blow, as it seems, was hard at the time for the aspiring novelist, but it didn't last long, for he soon discovered that there would be nothing wrong with being a reporter-novelist, or vice versa. He concludes: "And it was writing for newspapers that I really learned how to be a writer."

It is of little interest now to comb through writings and biographies of those involved in order to inquire about the veracity of the situation and the dialogue. These are sustained by proposing themes that transcend the personalities involved. Let me be content, therefore, in taking them up, situation and dialogue, in the area of the story and discover that, not without interest, the story is paradoxically written as a news story. Hemingway arrived in Spain and, as always, attacked the press, violently refusing to give interviews as he unethically denigrated his colleagues. The narrator is not intimidated. He takes up the struggle with his companion, by the name of Clara. Part of the plot of the story is the reporter's insistence on obtaining a personal interview from Hemingway. The insistence is broken only by another incident, as journalistic as the former: the matador is wounded by the bull and taken from the ring.

News report or story? Both, certainly. Read other texts of Coutinho, such as "Eleitorado ou" [Electorate or] and "Mulher na jogada" [Woman in play]. In the universe of Hemingway (according to the story) and in that of Coutinho (in accordance with the characteristics of his production), there is imposed a lack of prestige toward the so-called romance forms (those that, in the story, would be defended by Gertrude Stein) and a favoring of the journalistic techniques of narrating. Or rather, the journalistic attitude of the narrator with respect to the character, the subject, and the text, is imposed. The narrator is there to inform his reader of what happens in the bullring. This aesthetic reversal is not without consequence for the topic that I wish to discuss, since the figure of the narrator basically becomes he who becomes interested in the *other* (and not himself) and who affirms himself by the look that he casts around him, taking in beings, facts, and incidents (and not by an introspective look that searches for experiences lived in the past).

In a still-simplified way, one can say that the narrator looks at the other in order to lead him to speak (interview), since he is not there to speak of the actions of his own experience. But no writing is innocent. As a correlative to the earlier statement, let me add that, in giving speech to the other, he also ends up giving speech to himself, but in an indirect way. The very speech of the narrator who wishes to be a reporter is the speech by an interposed person. The oscillation between reporter and novelist suffered by the character (Hemingway), is the same as that experienced, but only in silence, by the narrator (Brazilian). Why does not the latter narrate the things as being *his,* that is, based on his own experience?

Before responding to this question, let me look at another of Coutinho's stories of Spain, "Azeitona e vinho" [Olive and wine]. Summarily, here is what happens: an old and experienced man of the village (the narrator of the story), sitting in a cantina, drinks wine and watches a young bullfighter, Pablo (known as El Mudo), surrounded by friends, admirers, and rich tourists. Watching and observing like a reporter before the object of his news story, the old man gets drunker and drunker while he weaves conjectures about the life of the other, that is, what happens, happened, and should happen with the young and inexperienced bullfighter, laying on him the hopes of the whole village.

The characters and themes are similar to those of the former story, and what is important for us is that the very attitude of the narrator is similar, although he, in this second story, no longer has journalism as a profession, as he is just someone from the village. The narrator has everything to become the classic narrator: as an old and experienced man, he could concentrate on the actions of his lived experience and, reminiscing, mingle his story with others with whom he has lived in the community tradition. However, he does nothing of the sort. He watches the younger man and gets drunk on wine and the other man's life. A precise form of narrating, therefore, remains valid and is the backbone of Coutinho's fiction, even though this time the journalistic form does not coincide with the narrator's profession (where is authenticity as a support for verisimilitude?). It is a question of style, as it is said, or of world view, as I prefer, a characteristic of Coutinho's story that transcends even the minimum rules of a narrator's characterization.

The continuity in the process of narrating that is established among different stories affirms that what is essential in Coutinho's fiction is not the discussion of the narrator as reporter (although it can be in this or that story), but something that is more difficult to understand, that is, the very art of narrating today. On the other hand, parallel to this acknowledgment, arises the question brought up earlier and strategically abandoned: Why does the narrator not narrate *his own* life experience? The story "Olive and Wine" narrates actions insofar as they are lived by the young bullfighter; the story is basically the experience of the look cast on another.

Tying the acknowledgment to the question, we see that what is at stake in Coutinho's stories is not so much the whole plot of each story (which is always easy to understand), nor the characterization and development of the characters (which always approach a prototype), but something more profound, which is the dense mystery that surrounds the figure of the postmodern narrator. The narrator removes himself from the narrated events (there are degrees of intensity in this removal, as we shall see in the story "A lugar algum" [Going nowhere]), and, in doing this, he creates a space for the fiction to dramatize the experience of someone who is observed and often deprived of the word. Removing himself from the action narrated by the story, the narrator identifies with a second observer—the reader. Both find themselves deprived of the exposition of their own experience in the fiction and are attentive observers of another's experience. In the *poverty of experience* of both is the importance of the character in postmodern fiction revealed: narrator and reader are defined as spectators of another's action which excites, moves, seduces them.

The majority of Coutinho's stories are covered up and enriched by the enigma that surrounds the comprehension of the human look in modern civilization. Why does one look? At what does one look? The reason and aim for the look cast on the other are not given at first glance, because it is a question of a dialogue-in-literature (that is, expressed in words) which, paradoxically, is beneath or beyond words. Fiction exists to speak of the incommunicability of experiences: the experience of the narrator and that of the character. The incommunicability, however, is covered up by the weaving of a relationship, which is defined by the look. A bridge, made of words, involves the mute experience of the look and makes the narrative possible.

In the story "Olive and Wine," the narrator insists: "Pablito doesn't know what I am observing in that group." And also: "He will not remember me, but perhaps he has not forgotten the things I told him." The imperturbable fixity of a look that observes someone, beneath or beyond words, remains, in the present of the cantina (from a table one observes the other), or in the past relived by the memory (I still see him, but in the past).

The return of the look is not important. It is a question of an investment made by the narrator in which he does not earn any profit but participation, for the profit is in the very pleasure that he has from looking. I give you a hand, says the narrator. I feel your support, replies the character. Both are mute. There is no longer the game of the "good counselor" between the experienced, but one of admiration of the older man. The narrative can express a kind of "wisdom," but one that does not originate in the narrator: it is inferred from the action of the one who is observed and can no longer narrate—the young man. Wisdom is presented, therefore, in an inverted way. There is a devaluing of the action in itself.

Here in a general outline is the charm and sorcery of the experience of the narrator who observes. The danger in Coutinho's story is not the muzzles but the blindfolds. It is as if the narrator were demanding: let me look so that you, reader, may also see.

The look thematized by the narrator of "Olive and Wine" is a generous, friendly, even loving look, which covers up the young Pablito without his being aware of the gift that is being offered him. But, pay attention: the more experienced man has no advice to give, and it is for this reason that he cannot count on any profit with the investment of the look. He must not ask for any, so to speak. Here is the reason for the quarrel between Hemingway (observer and also man of the word) and the bullfighter Dominguín (observed and man of action):

> At that time Dominguín called him Father, Papa. Now he was saying that the old man was a little crazy. Mad father. A few days later he could show Clara an interview in which Dominguín said: "I was his guest in Cuba. Some journalists came to his house to interview me. . . . When one of them wanted to know if it was true that I was looking for *advice* from the owner of the house in order to improve my art, I understood well how the nonsensical rumor could have arisen just by seeing his face. I thought of giving a diplomatic answer, but I changed my mind and spoke with complete frankness: I don't believe, at the point I have arrived, that I need advice from anyone on the question of bullfighting." (emphasis added)

The "son" cannot look submissively at the face of the "father," without risking destroying the mystery of the affectionate investment given by the paternal look. Diplomacy is no help if the pact is broken—Dominguín is short and sweet. The son cannot recognize the father as source of advice, or recognize the debt provided by the old man's profit, for he himself is the source of wisdom. Father, Papa. Crazy old man. Mad father. Here are the metamorphoses of the old man who would usurp the value of an action that is *not* experienced by himself, but only observed. He is removed by the look—here is the only advice that he can give the observed, if there is any place for dialogue.

The lived experience of the more experienced man is of little value. A first conclusion: the postmodern action is young, inexperienced, exclusive, and deprived of the word—it is for this reason that it cannot be given as being from the narrator. He observes an action that is, at the same time, uncomfortably self-sufficient. The young man can be right by being wrong, or be wrong by being right. The responsible paternalism in the guiding of conduct is of no value at all, unless paternalism deprives itself of words of advice and is a long, silent, and loving slide along the avenues of the look.

In case the look wishes to be recognized as advice, there arises the incommunicability between the more experienced and the less. The word no longer has meaning because the look it covers no longer exists. The need for narrative disappears. There exists a heavy silence. To avoid it, the more experienced must remove himself to make the less experienced valuable, brilliant. For the experience of the more experienced to be of less *worth* in postmodern times, he removes himself. For this reason, too, is why the juxtaposition of mature, adult experiences in the mutual form of advice has become practically impossible in narrative today. This juxtaposition would be like that found in the classic narrative and which would lead to a practical knowledge of life.

By virtue of the *incommunicability of experience between different generations,* one perceives how it has become impossible to give linear continuity to the process of the improvement of people and society. For this reason, to give advice—contrary to what Benjamin thought—can no longer be "make a suggestion about the continuation of a story being narrated." The story is no longer perceived as weaving a continuity between the lived experiences of the more experienced and the less, since paternalism is excluded as a connective process between generations. Narratives today are, by definition, broken, always to begin again. This is the lesson that one deduces from all the great rebellions of the less experienced that shook the 1960s, to begin with the Free Speech Movement in Berkeley, and including even the events of May, in Paris.

And yet, the link of sympathetic complicity between the more and the less experienced (sustained by the look that is covered up by the narrative) assures the climate of the interchangeable actions. Human actions are not different in themselves from one generation to another; what changes is the way of facing them, looking at them. What is at stake is not a new type of action arising, something completely original, but a different way of looking. One can face it with the wisdom of experience, or with the wisdom of naiveté. For there is no victorious, privileged wisdom, although there is an imperious one. There is a conflict of wisdoms in the arena of life, as there is a conflict between narrator and character in the arena of narrative. As Octavio Paz tells us: "The confidence in the powers of spontaneity is in inverse proportion to repugnance in the face of systematic constructions. The disbelief in the future and in its geometric paradises is general." From this he can conclude: "In postindustrial society, social struggles are not the result of the opposition between work and capital, but are conflicts of a cultural, religious, and psychic order."

The old man in the cantina had already experienced everything that the young El Mudo had, but what counts is the *same difference* that the observer experiences, that the observed experiences in his youth of today. The action in the youth of yesterday of the observer and the action in the youth of today of the observed are the same. But the way of facing them and affirming them is different. Of what value are the epic glories of the narrative of an old man in the face of the lyrical ardor of the experience of the younger individual?—that is the postmodern problem.

Here one imposes an important distinction between the postmodern narrator and his contemporary (in terms of Brazil), the memoirist narrator, since the texts of memoirs have become very important with the return of the political exiles. I refer, of course, to the literature inaugurated by Fernando Gabeira with the book *O que é isso, companheiro?* [What is this, comrade?], where the process of involvement of the more experienced is at least presented in the form opposite to that of the postmodern narrative. In the memorialist narrative, the more experienced adopts a victorious position.

In the memorialist narrative, the more experienced narrator speaks of himself as a less experienced character, extracting from the temporal and even sentimental gap (in the meaning Flaubert gives the word in "sentimental education") the possibility of good advice on the basis of the mistakes committed by himself as a young man. This narrative deals with a process of "maturity" that takes place in a linear form. The narrator of postmodern fiction no longer wishes to see himself yesterday, but wants to observe his yesterday in the today of a young person. He delegates to another, who is young today as he was young yesterday, the responsibility for the action that he observes. The naive and spontaneous experience of yesterday of the narrator continues to speak through the similar but different lived experience of the young person that he observes, and not through the wise maturity of today.

For this reason, the memorialist narrative is necessarily historical (and in this sense it is closer to the great conquests of modernist prose, that is, it is a vision of the past in the present, trying to camouflage the process of generational discontinuity with the wordy and rational continuity of a more experienced individual). Postmodern fiction, going through the experience of the narrator who sees himself—and not sees himself—yesterday in the young man of today, is the priority of the "now" (Octavio Paz).

Let me return to Benjamin, who says: "With the world war, a process became manifest that continues till today. At the end of the war, it was observed that the combatants returned mute from the battlefield, not richer but poorer in communicable experience." By one of these fine games of irony, the one who speaks in the story, the old man, does not narrate his own life to the reader. What is important is merely the courageous youth of the young man whom he admires and who is called symptomatically El Mudo, The Mute, and who remains mute throughout the story.

What matters is to give the word to the look cast on the other (to the less experienced, to El Mudo) so that what the word does not say can be narrated. There is an air of wounded superiority, of narcissism drawn and quartered in the postmodern narrator, dauntless because he is still the carrier of the word in a world where it counts for little, anachronistic because he knows that what the word can narrate as a trajectory of life is of little use. It is for this reason that the look and the word are cast on those who have been deprived of them.

Postmodern literature exists to speak of the poverty of experience, I have said, but also of the poverty of the written word as a process of communication. It deals, therefore, with a dialogue of the deaf and dumb, since what is really worthwhile in the relation of the two established by the look is a current of energy, *vital,* silent, pleasurable, and secret.

The most radical answer to the question "Why does one look?" has been given us by Nathalie Sarraute: one looks in the same way as the plants turn toward the sun in a movement of tropism. Light and heat—here are the forms of energy that the sun transmits to plants, lifting them up, giving them tone. Transposed to the human experience with which we are concerned, the tropism would be a species of sub-conversation (*sous-conversation,* in Sarraute's words) in which, contradictorily, the sun is the younger, and the plant, the more experienced. The old plant feels itself attracted by the young sun without showing the motives for the sub-conversation. It is not strange, then, that Coutinho has created his fiction on this lack of evidence of reason and of the finality of the look. The story says that the narrator looks. The story says that the character is looked at. But the reason and the finality of that look remain as an enigma. In apocalyptic terms, one looks in order to give reason and finality to life.

In a subtle way, Benjamin makes the beautifying of the classic narrative parallel with another beautifying: that of the human being on his deathbed. The same movement that describes the gradual disappearance of the classic narrative serves as well to describe the exclusion of death from the world of the living today. From the nineteenth century, Benjamin informs us, the spectacle of death has been avoided. The exemplary nature of the classic narrative's authority, translated by the wisdom of advice, finds its ideal image in the spectacle of human death: "Now, it is at the moment of death that the knowledge and wisdom of man and above all his lived existence— and it is of this substance that stories are made—assume for the first time a transmittable form." Death projects a halo of authority—"the authority that even some poor devil has when he dies"—that is at the origin of the classic narrative.

Death and the classic narrative cross paths, opening a space for a conception of human becoming in which the experience of lived life is enclosed in its *totality* and through this becomes exemplary. To the new generation, the still living, what is offered is the total and static example of the old generation; to the young man, the model and the possibility of the dead copy. A furious iconoclast would oppose to the spectacle of death a piercing scream of lived life at the moment of living, the exemplary nature of which is incomplete: the matador in the arena being wounded by the bull.

There is—let us not doubt—spectacle and spectacle, the young iconoclast continues. There is a camouflaged eye in the writing about Benjamin's narrator that deserves to be revealed and that is similar to the look that I am describing, except that the movements of the looks are inverted. The look in Benjamin's reasoning is in the direction of the deathbed, mourning, suffering, tears, and so on, with all the variations of Socratic asceticism. The postmodern look (not at all camouflaged, merely enigmatic) looks in the eyes of the sun. It turns toward the light, pleasure, gaiety, smiles, and so on, with all the variations of Dionysian hedonism. The spectacle of life today is contrasted with the spectacle of death yesterday. One looks at a body in life, whose energy and potential for experience are impossible of closure in its mortal totality, because it opens in the now with a thousand possibilities. All the paths are the path. The body that looks with pleasure, as I have said, looks with pleasure at another pleasurable body in action.

"To live is dangerous," Guimarães Rosa once said. There is spectacle and spectacle, the iconoclast said. On the deathbed, the danger of living is also exhumed; even the danger of dying, because it is already there. Only the calm immobility of man on his deathbed reigns, the reign of the *belles images,* to take up again Simone de Beauvoir's expression on the funereal engravings of the history books. On the contrary, on the field of life exposed at the moment of living, what counts for the look is movement, movement of bodies that move about with sensuality and imagination, inventing silent actions within the precarious, inventing the now.

In a postmodern story, death and love meet in the middle of the bridge of life. The only question that the narrator of "Ocorrência na ponte" [Occurrence on the bridge] asks before the image of death, "a sad, ugly, mud-colored lady," the only question that he asks her is: "Was it possible to reinvent life for the river or for her?" The answer is also unique: life is reinvented in death by desire. And in that woman's face, after copulation, after death, the narrator tells us, "something like an absurd hope" was expressed.

The postmodern human look is desire and word, which move through immobility, a will that admires and retreats uselessly, an attraction for a body that, however, feels alien to the attraction, its own energy that feeds vicariously from another's source. It is the critical result of the majority of our hours of daily life.

Postmodern times are hard and demanding. They want action as energy (from this the privilege of the young as character and of sport as theme). Once it is used up, the actant becomes the spectator of the other who, like him, occupies the place that was his. "Olive and Wine." It is this final condition of vicarious pleasure, at the same time personal and capable of generalization, that feeds the present daily life and that Coutinho dramatizes through the narrative that observes. On dramatizing it in the form he does, he reveals what can be authentic experience in it: the pleasurable passivity and the critical immobility. These are the fundamental postures of contemporary man, still and always a mere spectator either of lived actions or rehearsed and represented actions. By the look, present man and narrator oscillate between pleasure and criticism, always holding on to the posture of one who, even having removed himself from the action, thinks and feels and is moved by what remains in him of body and/or mind.

The spectacle becomes the represented action. In this form, it takes from the semantic field of "action" what exists of experience, of living, to lend it the exclusive meaning of *image,* conceding to this action freed from experience the exemplary condition of an empowering now, although deprived of the word. Light, heat, movement—transmission en masse. The experience of seeing, of observing. If the represented action lacks the support of experience, this in turn becomes linked to the look. The experience of looking. The narrator who looks is the contradiction and the redemption of the word in the era of the image. He looks so that his look is recovered by the word, constituting a narrative.

The spectacle makes the action into representation, representation in its ludic variations, such as soccer, theater, dance, popular music, and so on; and also in its technical variations, such as film, television, the printed word. The observed characters, until then called actants, become actors in the great drama of human representation, expressing themselves through rehearsed actions, product of an *art,* the art of representation. The postmodern narrator—he himself retaining the art of the written word—exists to speak of the various facets of this art. He narrates rehearsed actions that exist in the place (the stage) and in the time (youth) in which they are allowed to exist.

Edilberto Coutinho's typical narrator, for the reasons I have been giving, will find in the "society of the spectacle" (to use Guy Debord's concept) fertile ground for his critical attacks. Society invests in him and he attacks it. In the story "A lugar algum" [Going nowhere], a literal transcription of the script of a television program in which a young hoodlum is interviewed, the concrete reality of the narrator is zero degree. He has totally removed himself. The narrator is anyone and everyone in front of a television set. This, too, I repeat, is the condition of the reader, for any text is for anyone and everyone.

In this story, the narrator is only the one who reproduces. Things occur as if the narrator were pressing the button of the television channel for the reader. I am watching—look, you too—this program and not another. It is worthwhile. It's worthwhile because we watch the final residue of an image that is still not rehearsed, where the action (crime) is backed up by experience, the experience of a young hoodlum in the society of the spectacle.

To be a witness of the look and of its experience is why the written word still survives in postindustrial society.

Translated by Tom Burns and Ana Lúcia Gazzola

11. Worldly Appeal:

Local and Global Politics in the Shaping

of Brazilian Culture

■

I

1900. In the year in which the last century comes to a close and at the same time opens out to the twentieth century, Joaquim Nabuco, a politician belonging to the Brazilian intellectual elite, publishes *Minha formação* [Self-fashioning], a book of memoirs in which the author presents a series of fictionalized essays written for the daily press during the previous decade. In that complex and crucial moment of nation building, in which the emperor was expelled from the country and the Jacobin military inaugurated the Republican regime, *Minha formação* foregrounded the political contradictions of Brazil's recent history. At the same time, it opted for an indispensable and enriching opening of the new South American nation toward the world, which had been expressed by the tardy abolition of slavery, doubtlessly the greatest accomplishment of the dying monarchist regime.

The exploratory richness of Nabuco's memoirs does not stop there. In the first place, it can be useful for a discussion of the antagonistic ideological positions held in the first century of national autonomy; second, it can help us indicate the more complex dilemmas to be faced by Brazilian intellectuals in the twentieth century; finally, it can aid us in clarifying the political-cultural trajectory of our late modernity. I wish to foreground one of the most astonishing chapters of the book, "Atração do mundo" [Worldly appeal], in which the author courageously expresses, as Antonio Candido would do half a century later, the major defining synthesis of Brazilian culture, namely its "particularizing and universalist tendencies."

I highlight a sentence from the chapter "Worldly Appeal": "I am more a spectator of my century than of my country; the drama, for me, is civilization, and it is being performed on all the states of mankind, each one connected today by telegraph." This is such a surprising and suggestive sentence that each one of its elements could develop into several other statements. Let us initiate the process of interpretation, beginning with a general clarification.

Upon entering a mandatory yet temporary retirement, due to the transformation in the country's political regime, one of the most influential Brazilian monarchists expresses himself by means of metaphors borrowed from theatrical representations about the multiple experiences of a well-lived public life. In such circumstances he chooses to present himself to his readers as a spectator rather than an actor or activist.[1] He prefers to characterize himself as a spectator more interested in the theatrical drama of the century than in that of his native country. He sees the spectacle of the century as that of a civilization in full dramatic ebullience, so that the great play performed on European stages attracts him irresistibly. Since he lives in a provincial country, he is far from the stage on which the great drama unfolds, but he can be its spectator in the coziness of his own home, due to modern means of mass communication such as the telegraph.

The opposition of Brazil, *country of origin* (or, rather, *country of beginning*, as we will see below), and Western civilization, the preference for the crisis of representation through which modernity passes, rather than for the search for a national identity for which the young nation strives, bolsters another distinction and preference in the chapter. Nabuco states that in his lifetime he has experienced "a lot of Politics with a capital *P*, that is, of the politics which constitutes history." Immediately afterward he refers to his double incapacity to fully experience "politics itself, with a small *p*, which is to say the local, that of the country, of the parties." The double incapacity to experience national politics and to participate actively in it is the individual's decision: on one hand, it is the consequence of a value judgment regarding the local situation; on the other, it results from intellectual curiosity for worldly matters.

The double incapacity also constitutes an oblique and paradoxically more correct way for the informed and aware Brazilian citizen to participate in the national project that is at hand. By equating Politics with a capital *P* to History, to the history of civilization, in this case to the history of Europe in its geographical, social, and economic expansion (we cannot expect from the author an attitude in any way different from the Eurocentric one), Nabuco not only considers politics with a small *p*, the national, to be inferior, localized, and characterized by backwardness and pettiness, but also proposes ways for the nation to move on from its backwardness.

As Flora Süssekind has recently shown, Joaquim Manuel de Macedo's journalistic and fiction work illustrates well the mediocrity of national political life. One may mention, for example, the way in which Macedo's narrator describes an apprenticeship in politics in the second half of the last century:

If he [the apprentice] is the son, nephew or close relative of any *senhor velho* [plantation master] or any member of that privileged class . . . , if he is *nhonhô* [young master], he is soon nominated for the presidency of any province; from this provincial presidency he moves to the temporary house of representatives; from there he jumps to the ministry: it is a question of three jumps in a few months, and in two and a half strokes, *nhonhô,* who did not go through the lessons of any teacher, who had no apprenticeship nor time to read anything beyond the *prologues* of a few books, is then declared to be a famous statesman and a savior of the nation.[2]

Thanks to Nabuco's self-fashioning (which is what the memoirs are about), the double incapacity to experience the mediocrity of national politics finally obliges him to look beyond Brazil, that is, toward "the point where the action of the universal contemporary drama is more complex or intense." For a learned Brazilian, political complexity and moral intensity, to the extent that they are universals, cannot be a matter to be directly experienced, but only to be appreciated from an orchestra seat in the provincial audience. The text offers an example: "In 1870, my main interest is not in Brazilian politics, but in [the battle of] Sedan [fought in France]. At the beginning of 1871, it is not in the constitution of Baron Rio Branco's Cabinet, but in the burning of Paris," and so on. Political complexity and moral intensity, to the extent that they are universals, might only occur or be witnessed in Brazil through divine intervention: "In 1871, [my main interest] has been, for months, the struggle for the emancipation of the slave [*Lei do ventre livre,* or The freeborn law]—but wouldn't Brazil be in this year the place on Earth toward which God's finger is pointed?" Brazilian political backwardness is above all a question of geography and can be adequately compensated for, given the lack of God's finger, with a trip abroad for studies and observation or, in the absence of the latter, through the telegraph. In the same way in which there is a gap between writing and performing a dramatic play, there is also a distance between political action and its representation on the European stage. Similarly, there is also a distance between that representation and its transmission through technologies of mass communication, to its other and distant site of mimicry.

The *self-fashioning* of the Brazilian intellectual in the nineteenth century confuses itself with another fashioning: that of the sedimentation of geological layers of the "human spirit" (the expression is in the text). There is a late and therefore double inscription of the Brazilian or of the American, for that matter, in the historical process of the cooling of the crust of human culture. Americans belong to Europe due to the resulting stratified layers, and to America on the basis of the new fluctuating sediment of their spirit. One foot in Brazil, one in Europe, in equilibrium—only apparent, of course, since one cannot attribute the same weight and value to the sentimental search for beginnings and the rational investigation of the origin. The Eurocentric Nabuco concludes: "As soon as we have the slightest culture, the supremacy of these [the stratified layers] over those [the new sediment] begins." He adds: "The human spirit, which is unique and terribly centralistic, is on the other side of the Atlantic." The geological investigation of the national should go only as far back as the Christian landmark of the discovery of the region by a European country, that is to say, to the First Mass performed by the Portuguese Jesuits in Brazil; from that point on the geologist should not attempt to restore the traditions of the natives; he should move away from that native soil, turn away, and, cloaked as a historian of ideas, should strive to search for the depths to be found exclusively in civilizations of humanity, such as the European ones. There is a common European foundation (I enrich Nabuco's word semantically, taking it in all its possible meanings: geographic, historical, economic, social, etc.) that is both defining of the yonder and, through our legitimate processes of *fashioning,* of the hither.

The homeland that fascinates the heart does not deceive the mind and, thus, the "great spectacle" of the world is that which "captures and commands the intelligence." In politics the "law of the heart" is strong and dominating only at the moment in which reason is disqualified due to the advanced age or unhappiness of the homeland. Nabuco the memoirist states: "I am more and more a serf of the Brazilian glebe, and am so due to the fact that the singular law of the heart binds a man to his homeland with ties that strengthen in proportion to its misery, and to the risks and uncertainties that he himself undergoes." An old body in a Republican homeland dominated by the Jacobin military deserves pity, hence the sentimentality of the aging narrator.

In the years of his youth and of his maturity, sitting in the audience of the Brazilian stage on which the minor drama of the young nation is performed, Nabuco dreams of being in the audience of the great playhouse of humanity, where the seductive and definitive plays of the century are performed. He says: "All the landscapes of the New World, the Amazon forest or the Argentine *pampas,* in my opinion are not worth a stretch of the Via Appia, a hop from Salerno to Almafi, a portion of the Seine quay in the shade of the old Louvre. In the middle of the luxury of playhouses, fashion, and politics, we are always squatters [in English in the original], as if we were still cutting down the virgin forest." The historical identity of new nations such as the American ones is not to be found where the nativists, that is, politicians with a small *p*, think that they will find it. It is outside national historical time and outside native space: for that reason it is lacunal and Eurocentric. In short, its location is "absence," determined by a movement of tropism.

From this point of view, the foundational novel of José de Alencar, a writer with whom Nabuco maintains a significant polemic in the 1870s, cannot fill the void of the place of nationhood as it had been configured by the intellectual elite. This is why, no matter how much Alencar claims to have found the symbols (or the myths, as we would say nowadays) of nationhood, he will never be able to establish them among us, leaving this task to the authoritarian regimes that always appeal to them in periods of institutional crisis. It would only be in 1937, at the beginning of President Vargas's dictatorial regime, that the state would build a belated and suspicious pantheon to the Homeland.[3] With the transportation to Ouro Preto of the remains of the participants of the *Conjuração Mineira,* a patriotic movement at the end of the eighteenth century, justly led by the protomartyr of Independence, Tiradentes, this Minas Gerais colonial town became the cradle of nationhood.

As for Alencar's foundational novel, attention has been called to the increasing retroactive chronology of his Indianist texts. The first, *O Guarani* [Guarany] (1855), defines the new "landowners" upon describing the inglorious struggle of the Indians against the Portuguese invaders in the first centuries of colonization; the second, *Iracema* [Iracema, the Honey-Lips: A legend of Brazil] (1965), allegorically dramatizes the initial contact between races at the time of the discovery; and the third, *Ubirajara* (1974), penetrates the pre-Cabralian period in search of ethnic purity, as an aesthetic counterpoint to the standards of Coimbran Romantic medievalism.[4] Here is an example of what the cosmopolitan spectator Nabuco would qualify as unfortunate: José de Alencar is a domestic spectator whose "curiosity is increasingly reduced to a limited visual field." Alencar suffered, Nabuco would affirm in 1900, from a "type of tunnel vision."

In the chapter on which we are commenting, Joaquim Nabuco's general attitude only reaffirms what the young Machado de Assis had defended in "Instinto de nacionalidade" [Instinct of nationhood], an essay written in 1872 which is parallel to the elaboration of his first novel, *Ressurreição* [Resurrection]. In order to celebrate with more dignity the fiftieth anniversary of the country's political independence, Machado de Assis believed it convenient to distinguish between national and literary independence, stating that "this other independence [the literary] will not be carried out [like the former] in one single day, but slowly, so that it will be more lasting; it will not be the work of one or two generations; many generations will labor until it is totally accomplished." For this enormous task, still way beyond the shy standards of the young nation, Machado de Assis drew up an extremely rigorous and original itinerary that started with a redefinition of the Brazilian writer: "What one must require from the writer is, above all, a certain intimate feeling which makes him a man of his time and country."[5]

Highlighting the search for national identity on the basis of "intimate feeling," Machado refuses the triumphalist exteriorizations of the nativist movement (speeches, novels, poems, symbols, anthems, public bravados, etc.), and considers these a mere *instinctive* force and form of nationhood. For Machado de Assis, Brazilian culture does not reside in the externalization (fictional or poetic) of the political values of our nation. This externalization of our *interior* (nativism) is nothing more than the ridiculous farce of the tropical paradise. For Brazil to be capable of artistic externalization it is first of all necessary that it accept its *exterior* in all of its concreteness. The consciousness of nationhood will lie less in the knowledge of its interior than in the complex process of interiorization of that which is external to it, that is, of that which is foreign to it.

The task of the generation contemporary to Machado de Assis— according to himself in a text written in 1879—would be to transform the instinct of nationhood into *conscious* energy and form by means of "external influx." "The present generation . . . cannot escape the conditions of the environment; it will affirm itself through personal inspiration, through the characterization of the product, but *what determines the direction of the movement is the external influx* [emphasis mine]; at this point one cannot find in our environment the necessary energy for the invention of new doctrines." And he closes the paragraph with a note of indulgent irony: "I believe this could even sound like one of La Palisse's truths."

The three aspects of nativist literary externalization, which, in the young Machado's eyes, are necessarily limited and mediocre, are a lexicon deemed to be typical of the country, a local subject matter, and an indigenous influx. Even before putting his cards on the table of literary creation, he considers it necessary to discuss these three questions and to reject their primacy in the Brazilian aesthetic project. Regarding the first question he states: "A poet is not national simply because he introduces in his verses many names of autochthonous flowers or birds, which can only provide a nationhood in terms of vocabulary and nothing else." As to the second question, he views it as originating in a doctrine that recognizes the national spirit only in works that deal with local subject matters. It is for this reason that he raises the following question: "Even though *Hamlet, Othello, Julius Caesar*, and *Romeo and Juliet* have nothing to do with English history nor British territory, is not Shakespeare, besides being a universal genius, an essentially English poet?"[6]

One cannot expect Machado to reject the narrow-minded values of nationalism because of the social exclusion of Africans by black slavery in Brazil. But it is sad to find, in an otherwise very courageous essay, the panicked silence of the mulatto intellectual regarding the contribution of Africans to the fashioning of nationhood. His most radical critical position vis-à-vis nativism is grounded in a Eurocentric attitude similar to that found and already identified in Nabuco. In a conclusive tone, he states that "Brazilian civilization is not related to the Indian component, having not received any influx from it; and this suffices for us not to have to search for the entitlements of our literary personality among the vanquished tribes." His contempt for the cultural contribution of the Indians is also regrettable.

When, in the 1950s, Antonio Candido proposes a different fashioning, now related to that of Brazilian literature, he does not recommend for the evaluation of a somewhat ailing Brazilian literature a method different from that proposed by Nabuco (except that he replaces the emblem of telegraphic messages sent from the hegemonic countries with that of the classics of world literature). After characterizing our literary production as a secondary branch of Portuguese literature which, in its turn, is a second-rate branch in the garden of the Muses, he adds: "Those who feed only on them [Brazilian and Portuguese literatures] are recognizable at first sight, even when they are cultured and intelligent, due to their provincial taste and lack of a sense of proportions. Thus we are predestined to depend upon the experience of other literatures, which can lead to a lack of interest in, or even contempt for, our own." However, he warns the reader: "Compared to other literatures, ours is poor and weak. But it is that, and no other, which expresses us."

This double movement, this interest in a minor literature which will be framed and energized through an interest in major literatures—wholly similar to the double inscription of the learned Brazilian in Western history, as Nabuco wants—founds the necessity for a *comparativist* methodology in the analysis of our artistic production. According to Candido, this is archaeologically present in the fashioning moments of Brazilian literature. In the eighteenth century, when this occurs, Brazilian writers are both attracted to and motivated by the neoclassic aesthetic. They benefit from its universal conception, formal rigor, emotional contention, and from the ideas of the Enlightenment that contributed to inspire and accentuate their *applied* vocation, transforming them into true delegates of reality in its relation to literature.

Returning to Joaquim Nabuco's *self-fashioning*, one observes that the contrastive spectacle of two dramas, the native and the European, cannot be more fascinating than the drama of the spectator. Nabuco, like Machado, prefers the cosmopolitan sanctuary of intimate feeling over the public field of triumphant externalizations. Due to the absence of a legitimate native grounding, the sad suffering that the Brazilian experiences functions as foundation and justification both for the flights of his Eurocentric imagination and for the exile's attachment to the country of birth: "On one side of the ocean, one feels the absence of the world; on the other, the absence of [one's] country." The question of power (of the *power owners,* to recall Raymundo Faoro's expression) and of Brazilian culture as an heir to European culture, is announced in an extraordinary manner in Nabuco by the double breach of *absence.* And it is reinvigorated by the double and sad sensation of *saudade* [nostalgia] in the same way a motor is charged by a new injection of fuel.[7] In Nabuco's text, the crisis of the subject and the political discomfort he goes through, are, rather than ideological, clearly personal and cultural.

In order to shed light on the way in which the Brazilian subject joins the citizen of the world and vice versa, Nabuco appropriates the sensation of saudade from the Luso-Brazilian cultural tradition and reaffirms it both in the realm of the private and in that of the public, rendering them indissociable. In this sense, saudade comes to refer to the absence of Brazil when in the European audience, to the absence of Europe when in the Brazilian audience, and evokes the classics of Portuguese literature that he values so much, as well as the most recent texts of Brazilian Romanticism. In *Leal conselheiro* [Loyal counselor], a treatise in which he attempts to establish norms of conduct for noblemen, D. Duarte, the king of Portugal (1391–1438), defines *saudade* as a "feeling of the heart deriving from sensuality rather than reason, and sometimes makes one experience feelings of sadness and mourning." Originating with the work that officially inaugurates Romanticism in Brazil, *Suspiros poéticos e saudades* [Poetic sighs and nostalgias] (1836), the poet Gonçalves de Magalhães presents himself as a wanderer in distant European lands who dreams of the destiny of his young homeland. Upon his return from Europe and at the sight of Rio de Janeiro, he writes on May 14, 1837: "Lands of my country, I salute thee, / After long absence! / I salute thee, oh my childhood sun!" Homeland and childhood—the object of nostalgia coincides.

In a book written in French and published in France in 1906, *Pensées détachées et souvenirs* [Detached thoughts and memories], which was later translated by his daughter Carolina, the aging politician Nabuco redefines saudade through the poles of the private and the public, imbuing the authentically Portuguese word with an internal primacy in the field of feelings: "Among all words there is not one as moving as the Portuguese word saudade. It translates the pain of absence, the suffering of separation, the whole range of privation of loved beings or objects; it is the word that one chips into gravestones, it is the message one sends to relatives and friends. It is the feeling the exile has for the homeland, the sailor for his family, lovers for each other when they are apart."

Guimarães Rosa, in a diary written in Paris, records: "Saudade is being after having." If Rosa is right, then the homeland was an object of possession for politicians and nativist thinkers, and stopped being so for intellectuals such as Nabuco, who preferred being in the audience rather than being on the stage and representation over action, in other words, thinkers who have chosen politics with a capital *P.* Seen from Europe, the Brazilian homeland is above all an ontological interrogation. It is the place in which an individual dwells in order to qualify as Brazilian. The ontological condition of the *Brazilian being* is what facilitates positive and productive intimacy with the Portuguese monarchy. And, paradoxically, at the close of the nineteenth century, this is precisely that which moves the Brazilian leading class, shaped by liberal ideology, in the struggle against their fellow countrymen who considered themselves owners of the nation because they possessed land and black slaves. The arrogance of those who do not inhabit the homeland but own it is found emblematically in Oswald de Andrade's short and ironic poem ("Feudal Lord") reminiscent of his "family's feudal origin": "If Pedro II / Comes over here / with his smooth talk / I'll throw him into jail."

In a counterpoint to Nabuco's transoceanic travels, another man from the state of Pernambuco, José Lins do Rego, describes in *Menino de engenho* [Plantation boy] the domestic travels of a Brazilian plantation owner, Colonel José Paulino, the narrator's grandfather, through his lands: "My grandfather's trips were like this: he checked every nook and cranny, scrutinizing all the trees of his plantation. No one touched a coppice of wood, it would be the same as tearing a part of his body." The security policy of the plantation owner is the fence that, while tracing the limits of his own body, extends to incorporate the whole area of owned land. It is precisely this fence that expels from the demarcated territory any force other than the power of the landed elite.

The absence opened up by the double exile (the Brazilian can be both distant from country and motherland) is constantly neutralized, as we have already mentioned, by the transoceanic trips back and forth, which render the various countries of Western Europe more recognizable than the dis-

tinct regions of Brazil. The transoceanic trip may constitute another crite-
rion by which we can establish a cleavage within the nineteenth-century
Brazilian elite. The most conservative prefer sedentariness, enclosure, and
safety, whose emblematic figure would be the slave-owning colonel. The
least conservative would choose intellectual curiosity, wandering, and in-
stability. South Americans travel frequently to Europe, says Nabuco, not as
a consequence of the "pleasures of tacky provincialism"; they are there
because of the "appeal of forgotten but not erased affinities for our common European origin, which remain in all of us."

If, on the internal level, transoceanic trips begin to be counterbalanced
by the expansion of the railroad network (in 1885 Brazil had only 7,602
kilometers in use; 2,268 under construction; and 5,060 planned), on the
external level they began to be replaced by the telegraph. Flora Süssekind, in
a groundbreaking work, *O cinematógrafo das letras* [The cinematograph of
letters], calls our attention to the fact that, at the end of the century, imported books gradually lose their exclusive influence and give way to curiosity regarding the technical horizons of Western modernity. It is the latter's
technical innovations that become the privileged interlocutor of Brazilian
literary production after the end of the decade of the 1880s. Flora Süssekind,
more interested in examining the way in which "a technical horizon affects
literary form," chooses photography, the phonograph, the cinematograph,
the automobile, and the typewriter as interlocutors of modern Brazilian
writers. Since we are more interested in the configurational processes of part
of the Brazilian elite in the concert of civilized nations, we will privilege
another technical innovation (the telegraph), one other means of circulation
for ideas at the time (the newspaper), and Nabuco, a basically political
writer, who would be a predecessor of the contemporary "wired citizen."
None of these is discussed in Süssekind's study.

Two simultaneous events in the history of journalism in Rio de Janeiro
reveal the monarchists' need to keep in touch with the world, in spite of
their being defeated—or maybe due to that—by the military forces that
established the Republic in 1889. In 1891, two years after the proclamation,
Rodolfo Epifânio de Sousa Dantas founds *O Jornal do Brasil* in Rio de
Janeiro. Joaquim Nabuco is among his collaborators in the editorial enterprise. Around the same time, as Juarez Bahia (a historian of the Brazilian
press) informs us, Brazilian newspapers begin investing in the exclusive
service of correspondents, something that was already common in Europe
and in the United States. They did this not only to attain prestige, but also to
compensate for the "insufficient service" of agencies such as "Havas." The
correspondents of *O Jornal do Brasil* operated through the Western and
Brazilian Telegraph Company.

With the recent publication of Mário de Andrade's multiple and varied literary correspondence, one can better evaluate how the aesthetic ideas of the Week of Modern Art (1922), which were of a clear cosmopolitan configuration, were initially rooted in, and circumscribed by, São Paulo provincialism; one can also see more clearly the extent to which the new ideas spread to the four corners of Brazil until they finally became, in a few years, a truly national movement. A reading of the correspondence highlights the pedagogical role of Mário de Andrade (1893–1945), as he dedicated himself to the didactic task of confronting the elite's Eurocentric outlook with the loathed national past, rehabilitating it through the prism of a multiplicity of cultures which, silenced by the elites, were nevertheless conveying unsuspected contours. In the give and take of epistolary writing, in the *hermeneutic exercise of the conversation,* as Richard Rorty would say today, Mário de Andrade gradually reworks the main questions of the time, disseminating his audacious ideas to new and distant fellows in a slow, selective, and persuasive manner.[8] In this way he creates the condition for his own intellectual leadership among his modernist peers.

Besides concentrating on the modernists' correspondence, the discussion of the influence of Nabuco (in this case a negative influence) on the twentieth century could be advanced by focusing on the trip undertaken by a group of young intellectuals from São Paulo to the historic towns of Minas Gerais in 1924, with the Swiss poet Blaise Cendrars. Brito Broca (1903–61) was the first to call attention to the "paradoxical attitude" of the modernist travelers. He comments: "They are all modernists, men of the future. And what are they going to show to an avant-garde poet who is visiting us, in such a way as to shock all conformist spirits? The old towns of Minas Gerais, with their eighteenth-century churches, old colonial and imperial houses, a sad landscape in which everything is an evocation of the past and, in short, a suggestion of ruins." The reading of the implanting of the avant-garde spirit in the tropics should not disguise the paradoxical way of life of modernism, but rather should reveal the "internal logic" of the movement. Brito Broca adds: "The divorce from Brazilian reality which characterized most Brazilian writers resulted in the landscape of a baroque Minas Gerais appearing to the modernists as something new and original, and thus within the frame of novelty and originality that they were after."

The underpinnings of this internal logic can be mapped in the correspondence between Mário and young Carlos Drummond de Andrade (1902–87), whom he met in Belo Horizonte toward the end of his trip. The spirit of the Minas Gerais poet was then completely dominated by Joaquim

Nabuco's sadness and pessimism, and especially by Anatole France's fin de siècle skepticism. Mário does not condone these two complementary yet harmful influences, but finds in them material for the enrichment of his political thoughts and his well-aimed and ironic one-liners. He thus highlights recent phrases from his friend's letter that indicate two revealing moments of his intellectual insufficiency. He first underlines the following: "Personally, I consider regrettable this business of being born among unlearned landscapes and uncivilized skies. I consider Brazil infectious." Later on Mário detects the origin of Drummond's cosmopolitan regret and repugnance, as he perceives that his feelings are the result of "Nabuco's tragedy, from which we all suffer." He also highlights the following: "I owe a lot to Anatole France, who taught me how to doubt, to smile, and not to be demanding toward life."

The first didactic task to which Mário dedicates himself is that of elaborating on the concept of saudade that had been propagated by Nabuco, aiming at dissociating the private from the public in order to reject one of the meanings. In an interview with a Rio de Janeiro newspaper, *A Noite,* published in December 1925, he comments: "The Brazilian modernist has eliminated saudade for Europe, saudade for the classics, for ideals, for the past, for the future, and only feels saudade for his beloved, for his friend." For Mário, the melancholy of separation can only be cultivated on the level of personal relationships. Besides that, he highlights the *displacement* of the Brazilian in relation to the reality around him. From this derives, according to Mário, the young Brazilian's impulse to "feel and experience Brazil not only in its physical reality but also in its historical emotivity."[9] Mário was taking the first steps in the long journey toward the "brazilianizing of Brazil." Above all, he preached, it was necessary to search not for the origin of Nabuco's tragedy, but for the nidus of creole *infection.*

He begins good-humoredly by proposing to Carlos Drummond that he should consider "Nabuco's tragedy" as equivalent to the tropical disease transmitted by the insects known as *barbeiros* and that carries the name of the scientist who discovered it—Chagas' disease. Nabuco's so-called tragedy would be nothing more than one other tropical malady transmitted to young people by the bacillus of European nymphs. Mário writes to the young Minas Gerais poet: "Dr. Chagas discovered that there was throughout Brazil, a malady that would be called Chagas disease. I discovered another and more serious malady, with which we are all infected: Nabuco's disease." In another text of the same year he states: "Nabuco's disease consists in your [Brazilians'] missing the Seine Quay in the middle of the Quinta da Boa Vista, in this cowardly posture of talking informally but writing according to the standards of continental Portuguese. Stylize your speech, experience the Quinta da Boa Vista for what it is and you will be cured of Nabuco's disease."

In the 1920s, the modernists affirm that the superiority of Europe, when recognized and mimicked by the Brazilian intellectual, leads him to face the Brazilian condition from two opposing yet complementary poles: on the one hand, the nativist trend would idealize the autochthonous element as pure and indomitable (the Indian and the landscape, for instance); on the other hand, the cosmopolitan trend would *repress* whatever resulted from the sociohistorical process of European acclimatization in the tropics (the mulatto and Aleijadinho's baroque art, for example). The vaccine against Nabuco's disease could be found in a manifesto of the European avant-garde only if the Brazilian reader had already gone through the step of coming to terms with the national past: "We already have"—writes Mário— "a *guassu*[10] and handsome past burdening our gestures; what we must do is conquer the awareness of this burden, systematize it and render it traditional, that is, refer it to the present." To refer the national past to the present means, first of all, to enter a mine field: to confront Machadian Eurocentrism in its subtly racist form, which was defended tooth and nail by Graça Aranha in the decade of the 1920s.[11] It then means that one must turn toward the lesson of the European avant-garde, searching no longer for the technical modernity of the futurists but rather for a grounding to be found in the artistic movements, which, in Europe itself, proposed questioning Eurocentric standards of art. Based on these movements, the questioning of the national past would produce a "localist unrepression," a task officially realized by the tropical avant-garde.

This grounding or, rather, this bridge between European and non-European cultures, is *primitivism*. In the interview mentioned previously, Mário criticizes Graça Aranha's[12] *saudosismo* since it attacks all forms of primitivism, which, as a matter of fact, have never been opposed to cultures. He adds: "Giotto was extremely learned and primitive. So was Monteverdi. But if primitivism is not opposed to culture it may however become opposed to a specific culture, which in this case is the European." In his *conversation* with his peers, Mário astutely implies between the lines that the Brazilian who turns nostalgically to Europe is the real savage: "I propose that the Brazilian who does not become brazilianized is a savage." Even more astutely, in the same letter he inverts Nabuco's play with capital and small letters: "The Tupi Indians in their villages were more civilized than we were, in our houses in Belo Horizonte and São Paulo. For one simple reason: there is no Civilization. There are civilizations. . . . We will only become civilized in reference to civilizations when we create the ideal, Brazilian orientation. Then we will move from the mimetic phase to that of creation. And then we will become universal, because we will be national."

In spite of a certain timidity in the critique of Eurocentrism, Antonio Candido, in a text written in the 1970s, points out very perceptively the change in reference proposed by the modernists: "In Brazil primitive cultures are fused into daily life or are live reminiscences of a recent past. The terrible darings of Picasso, Brancusi, Max Jacob, or Tristan Tzara, were, deep down, more coherent with our cultural heritage than with theirs." The Brazilian modernists recover "European influence by delving into Brazilian detail." Or, as Mário himself would say in 1925: "A certain appearance of primitivism in Brazilian Modernism results from the fact that we decided at a certain point to have the courage of our naiveté." Candido adds: "The mulatto and the black are definitively incorporated as topics of study, inspiration, and example. Primitivism has now become a source of beauty rather than an obstacle to the elaboration of culture."

Geological dissatisfaction in the search for both the historical soil and rudimentary cultural production carried out within it, which produces the Eurocentrism and the feeling of American inferiority in Nabuco's thinking, is thus nuanced by the first generation of modernists through their attachment to the universal naiveté of the primitive; shortly after, in the generation of the 1930s, it would be revitalized by the equally universal notion of *underdevelopment*, with all its clearly communist leanings, proposed by the regionalist novel. The modernist rejects with open eyes the idealization and repression of the national past mentioned before; he favors the adoption, as *an aesthetic strategy* and as *political economy*, of an inversion of the hierarchical values established by the Eurocentric canon. This strategy and economy of thought, necessarily peripheral, ambivalent, and precarious, both points toward the recovery of the ethnic and cultural multiplicity of the national fashioning, and highlights the link that the latter maintains with non-Eurocentric universal thought. Nevertheless, upon inverting the values and hierarchy in question, this strategy and economy aims at conferring value to peripheral cultural objects that, in European sciences and history, are a priori disqualified due to processes of centralization, or marginalized for economic reasons.

The aesthetic strategy and political economy of the first modernism cannot be differentiated from the rise and apogee of a European science that "admits in its discourse the premises of ethnocentrism at the precise point at which it denounces it," namely ethnology. According to Jacques Derrida (author of the previous quotation), ethnology "only had the condition to be born at the moment at which a decentering occurred: when European culture . . . was *displaced,* expelled from its place, ceasing to be considered as the reference culture." This decentering had extraordinary consequences for the modernist intellectual's process of *self-fashioning,* as well as for the configuration of the various ethnicities that exploded the yearning for national culture into several splinters.

It is not only Nabuco's system of ideas that reactively stirs the rebellious intelligence of the modernists. The strong reaction to Anatole France, a writer of great prestige in the first years of this century in Brazil, also raises questions regarding the fashioning of Brazilian artists, at a time in which avant-garde art was striving for the urbanization, modernization, and industrialization of the country. The Brazilian artist, who doubles as an intellectual, must become an actor rather than a spectator, teaches Mário de Andrade. This is why life is more important than literature, why caring for the body is as important as caring for the mind. Strolling and listening to one of Bach's toccatas, the pleasure of the body and the pleasure of the book— these are complementary rather than exclusive activities.

Reacting to the previous quote by Carlos Drummond de Andrade, about what he had learned from his reading of Anatole France, Mário de Andrade writes him: "Anatole . . . taught something else that you have forgotten: he taught us to be ashamed of frank, practical, vital attitudes. . . . He made literature and nothing else. And he acted in the same way in which you feel affected: he destroyed poor youngsters, turning them into weary, feeble creatures, doubtful of faith and hope, fully devoid of hope, bitter, maladjusted, horrible. This is what that son-of-a-bitch has done." The vulgarity of the artist's turn of phrase is a clear sign of the general process of liberation to be unleashed against the established mentality: sensations and feelings, upon attaining public exposures, would configure new personalities in the national scene.

As an activist in the field of the construction of a new society, Mário de Andrade temporarily renounces elite culture and devotes himself to the exercise of *solidarity.* Through this exercise, he searches for the knowledge that exists in the cultural expression of the descendants of the ethnic groups that have been decimated or exploited, and forgotten by the country's slavist and Europeanized elite. The most absolute form of knowledge attainable through solidarity with the ethnic and cultural other is to be found in *conversing.* This practice now transcends the limited field of literary correspondence, and of the private, and attains an all-encompassing public and brotherly sameness which is confused with love for humanity. It is important to point out that the praise of extensive conversation (the intellectual's oral and public dialogue with any and every individual) is restrained, and advisable only in restricted conversation (epistolary dialogue with peers) and is justified by it.

In a letter to a friend, Mário de Andrade clarifies his notion regarding socializing, undifferentiated, and happy brotherhood. He construes it as (a) an inner necessity, (b) a sociopolitical exercise, and (c) a will for knowledge: "How pleasant to stop [in the street] and converse with people considered low and ignorant! Let me tell you something, if you still don't know it: it is with such people that one learns how to feel, not with intelligence and erudition. They are the ones who conserve the religious spirit of life and do everything sublimely in an enlightened religious ritual." And he immediately gives the example of a black woman whom he saw "thoroughly experiencing the dance" in the Rio carnival of 1923: "That black woman taught me what millions, millions is an exaggeration, but many books have not taught me. She taught me happiness."

The linguistic contract established by *conversation,* more than constituting exclusively a field of social communication, is a discourse committed to social existence; moreover, it is a commitment to a construction of an urban society in which learned artists could better understand popular practices and the originality of their artistic expressions. "Puxar conversa" [to initiate a conversation], one of Mário's typical expressions, underlines the way in which the modernist intellectual approximates the Other in an aggressive, shameless, sensual, and fraternal fashion, and does so in order that the Other, as he passes from occupying the status of individual to that of citizen, and from object to subject of knowledge, consequently transforms the person who has just started a conversation into a reservoir of previously unknown knowledge that, as the result of their engagement, becomes his own. It is in this sense that we can best understand one of the most thorny problems raised by Mário de Andrade in the 1920s: "It is difficult to know how to know."

In what refers to the question of knowledge, one of the fascinating topics in the modernists' ethics is the way in which they deal with what was considered an *error* by Europeanized teachings and learnings; it is the way in which they receive and judge that error. It consists of the cultural responses of the popular classes—in their diversified ethnic constitution—to the centering of European teaching. As such, it ceases to be an error and presents itself as a deviation and transgression of the imposed model, thereby becoming a revealing indicator of what is seen, in reverse, as a shameful, repressed, false, and falsifying official nationhood. Oswald de Andrade, the most anarchical of our modernists, states in his *Manifesto* that poetry must receive "the enriching contribution of all errors," and preaches "the joy of the ignorance that enlightens." Mário de Andrade opposes this total lack of rules and states that there are errors and errors, and distinguishes the joy of the knowledge that enlightens from that of the ignorance that enlightens, pointing toward the equilibrium between the popular and the erudite. For Mário, the most authentic representative of the acclimatization of popular error to Brazilian erudite art is the painter Tarsila do Amaral. He observes that Tarsila "neither repeats nor imitates all errors of popular art, but intelligently chooses the most fecund ones, *those that are not errors* [his emphasis] and takes advantage of them." To know how to know is to learn to distinguish after having absorbed everything in solidary fashion.

Oral and public conversation with strangers—as Mário preaches— puts an end to habits rooted in the conservative mentality of Brazilian intellectuals. It eludes the passage of time and the need for long-lasting contacts in the maturing process of not only human relations but also of individual thought. It renders the subject indifferent to the quality of dialogic expression and to the high or low intellectual register of the interlocutor. It facilitates the overflowing of heartfelt speech into a language of affect and anger, abandoning consciously intellectualized writing for a black hole of purely elitist literary production. Since he had adopted the posture of public and oral conversation precisely at the peak of modernism, Mário confesses—mistakenly, in our opinion: "All my work is transitory and decadent, I know. And I want it to remain transitory. . . . But what do celebrity and an eternity among the men of the Earth matter to me? They can both go to hell."

III

The writer of the 1930s, by scorning the arguments of modernist hermeneutics as oriented by cultural *ethos,* and by implementing a Marxist analysis to understand Brazilian historical processes, a necessarily small and belated part of that immense History of humankind—returns to the path of a universal radical politics now culturally grounded in historical materialism. He avails himself of this analysis both for the evaluation of the national past and to propose a utopian system of ideas that might bring social and economic injustice in the country and the world to an end. Artistic production ceases to be an inaugural fomentation of multiculturalism laboring in the service of political speculation and aesthetic subversion, and now becomes tied to the critique of the economic structure of society (inspired at that time by realism, which was being disseminated through international literary colloquia promoted by the Soviets). Upon imposing itself as teleological, Marxist aesthetics represses the writer's imagination and, at the same time, radically sharpens and redirects his gaze toward the miserable spectacle of Brazilian reality, and in particular toward that of the northeast of the country. Antonio Candido observes that, in the literature of the 1930s, "the preponderance of problem over character is defining." This, he adds, is the origin of the strength and the weakness of this writing.

Like Joaquim Nabuco before them, the major Brazilian writers of the 1930s position themselves once again as spectators, but no longer of diverse dramas performed on all the stages of the world, but rather of one single drama that, depending on the national or regional stage on which the action evolves, acquires differential hues of a merely adjectival nature. Contrary, however, to Nabuco, the affirmation of the impending proletarian revolution allows these writers to dissect and denounce oligarchical power (and the intellectual elites constituted by it) in order to reveal the ways in which oligarchical violence has controlled, controls, and will continue to control Brazil's class relations.

In the 1930s a true and solid politics of national identity is rendered possible only if it is paradoxically abandoned in favor of Marxist praxis (which, in its turn, would place within the same ideological bag Latin American nationalisms and emergent nationalist forces on non-Western countries, and would do so in order to redirect them). Only this authoritarian force, dutifully put into practice by the national communist parties, would be capable of radically questioning the capitalist mode that governs a world Europeanized yesterday, and North Americanized today. The exploitation of labor in Brazil and the major inequalities in the international order are but reciprocal aspects of the same situation. Raymundo Faoro, in a brilliant preface to *Prestes: Lutas e autocríticas* [Prestes: Struggles and self-criticism], distinguishes between Soviet-inspired and Brazilian conservative authoritarianism. He states that the latter is "an authoritarianism, in fact, that is not traditional, disconnected, or hostile to oligarchical groups and to *coronelismo* [the power of the landed elites], but rather is anchored in the presupposition of immaturity, incapacity, and imprisonment of the Brazilian people, who are in turn incapable of deliberating and deciding their own fate."

In 1942 Caio Prado Jr. proposed one other form of *self-fashioning* (the third in the present text): it is now the fashioning of contemporary Brazil. In *Formação do Brasil contemporâneo* [The colonial background of Brazil], he presents an economic interpretation of the country that echoes and supports, a posteriori, the interpretation proposed by the best artistic works of the 1930s regarding the underdeveloped character of the nation. In his attempts to give a "meaning" to the historical evolution of Brazil, he glimpses it "not in the details of its history, but in the sum of essential facts and events that have constituted its history over a long period of time." This meaning is that of the colonization of Brazil by Europe. Accepting the teleological premises of Marxist historical reason, and thus recognizing the totalizing and totalitarian view that functions as its frame, Caio Prado Jr. defines the significance of colonization as an "uninterrupted rigorous master code of successive events, always evolving in one specific direction."

In obvious opposition to the fervor and cultural ideals of emancipation defended by the thinkers and artists of the 1920s, who proposed and initiated substantial transformations in the colonized thought of the nation, Caio Prado Jr. slows down the engines of national emancipatory processes by calling attention to the fact that Portuguese colonization in the Americas is only a part of a whole, and is thus obviously incomplete without a vision of the totality. It is just one more chapter in the history of European commerce. The European was scarcely interested in populating nations discovered in habitats different from his own, thus he would only go to those regions of Portuguese America "of his own free will when he could go as a manager," that is, as the impresario of a profitable business in which others—the slaves—would work for him.

In this sense, Brazil is only one of the end-products in the signifying processes of Portuguese tropical colonization. He states: "If we go to the essence of our self-fashioning, we will see that we have been in fact constituted to provide sugar, tobacco, and some other supplies for European commerce, later on gold and diamonds; then, cotton, and following that, coffee. . . . It is with such a goal, such an external goal, such a turning outwards of the country with little concern for anything other than the interests of commerce, that Brazilian society and economy were organized."

How could elements constitutive of our economic, social, and cultural fashioning such as the Indian and African cultures, which, by definition, escape processes of Marxist historical reason, fall within the meshes of his letter?

As Caio Prado Jr. studies the social organization of Brazil, or, more precisely, the doubly unfavorable character of slavery in our country, he cannot escape the Eurocentric view common to the radical Enlightenment thinkers who remain blind to the demands of the Other, and consequently hierarchize civilizations in order to locate Western civilization necessarily as the center. The aim of such positioning is to disqualify, a priori, those civilizations that are different from it. Initially Caio Prado Jr. highlights "certain American indigenous groups such as those from Mexico and the Andean plateau," and immediately affirms that the elements from which

American slavery could feed were "the indigenous groups of America and the African black, people of an insignificant cultural level in comparison to that of their conquerors." Without wishing to "underestimate" (the choice of verb is his) the cultural resources of Indians and Africans, but in fact underestimating them (now the verb is mine), he adds quite rightly that slavery was responsible for a process of distortion of the values of those ethnic groups, and he concludes, in a manner I consider rather problematic, that the Indian and African cultural contribution "acts more like a *corrupting fermentation* [my emphasis] upon the dominant culture, namely that of the white master."

In a footnote in which he sheds light on our religious syncretism, Caio Prado Jr. discloses the dubious character of his "esteem" for the black race. He defines syncretism in the following terms: "Above all it is a neo-African religion, which, if it has lost the greatness and elevation of Christianity, on the other hand has not maintained the spontaneity nor the richness of color of the black faiths in their native state." Neither the greatness and elevation of Christianity, nor the spontaneity and richness of African religions. The catalysis between religious Europe and its Other is achieved by means of a "corrupting fermentation."

Caio Prado Jr.'s reductive view, similar to that expressed in the nine-teenth century by Machado de Assis and taken up in the 1920s by Graça Aranha, is correct in that it perceives the great risks of incorporating, in a naive and careless primitivism, the atrocities performed by the Brazilian slavist and colonial economy with regard to aesthetic modernity. In this sense, the resulting analyses are correct to the extent that they consider such incorporation, first as a means of recuperating a romantic notion of history, in which the modern spirit's rejection of the past coincides with the adop-tion, in its place, of another repressed past, this time that which remains prior to the discovery of America by Columbus. Second, this incorporation is nothing more than a conservative, and therefore harmful, form of na-tionalism.

The reductive view is incorrect since it is unaware that, on the cultural level, it only reaffirms the *centering* of cultural truth in European reason. Thus, it transforms the famous question formulated by Max Weber (Why is it that beyond Europe, neither scientific, artistic, state, nor economic evolu-tion have evolved along the path of reasoning peculiar to the West?) into a single definitive answer, in its turn rendered a dogma.

Following this same line of analysis but now applying it to literary ideas, Roberto Schwarz, in a well-known essay on Machado de Assis written in the 1970s, "Misplaced Ideas," has highlighted and deconstructed so-called Brazilian "originality," that is, the intricate link of slavery and favor that has been ultimately responsible for the covering up of class relations in Brazil.[13] He proposes that black slavery, in spite of being the basic productive relationship, did not constitute the effective link of Brazilian ideological life. In order to reach its nerve center it was necessary to consider Brazilian society of the time in its entirety. The colonization of the country, as a result of the monopolization of the land, had created three classes in the population: the proprietor of the latifundium, the slave, and the free man in the slave system. Schwarz concludes: "Between the first two, the relationship is clear; our argument will hinge on the situation of the third [the free man]. Neither proprietor nor proletarian, the free man's access to social life and its benefits depended, in one way or another, on the *favour* of a man of wealth and power."[14] In this sense, if black slavery contradicts the liberal ideas of nineteenth-century Brazil, in an even more perverse manner they are contradicted by favor since it absorbs and displaces them, thus creating a singular pattern.

Liberalism in a slavist country, affirms Schwarz, meant that ideas were doubly misplaced: "Free labour, equality before the law and, more generally, universalism were also an ideology in Europe; but there they corresponded to appearances and hid the essential—the exploitation of labour" (p. 20). Among us, the same ideas would be erroneous in a different way, which we could call "original." In the Brazilian context, ideologies produce a comedy that is best appreciated through the ironic and pessimistic gaze of the analyst, since they "do not describe reality, not even falsely, and they do not move according to a law of their own" (p. 23). For this reason, liberal ideologies in Brazil could be considered "ideologies of the second degree" (p. 23). As in the case of nineteenth-century Russian literature, which Schwarz uses as an example for a better understanding of Machado's critical talent, "progress is a disaster and backwardness a shame" (p. 29).

Around the same time and with the critical acumen that characterized him, Antonio Candido selected for his analysis and interpretation the most original of Brazilian Romantic novels: *Memórias de um sargento de milícias* [Memoirs of a militia sergeant]. His analytical approach, as outlined in the outstanding essay "Dialectic of Malandroism," reveals a precise critical goal: to establish that this novel apprehended with extraordinary clarity the moral and political behavior of free men in the slavist system. To get to where he wants to be, Candido first unravels and reworks the interpretative tradition of this novel. He demonstrates the way in which the novel *Memórias* escapes the two characterizations that have guaranteed its place in the history of literature: it was not the only example of picaresque writing in Brazil, nor did its realism *avant la lettre* make it a document about daily life in Rio de Janeiro at the time of the arrival of the royal family.

The picaresque reading of the novel impoverished the role to be played in Brazilian culture by Leonardo, the protagonist. He was not a picaro in the tropics, as critics maintained, but above all the Brazilian trickster, a human type who would be elevated to the condition of national symbol by Mário de Andrade in *Macunaíma*.[15] If the novel were taken as a social document of the period, it would be a rather poor one since neither the royal family nor black slaves appear in it. Candido points this out: "By suppressing the figure of the slave, Manuel Antônio almost completely erased labor; by suppressing the dominant classes, he suppressed the control mechanisms of power." On the one hand, the novel's action remains limited to free men, what we would call nowadays the petty bourgeoisie; on the other hand, this is the only nineteenth-century novel in Brazil that does not express the viewpoint of the dominant class.

By paying particular attention to Leonardo's daily adventures, which sometimes bring him into contact with the established order and sometimes lead him away from it, guiding him toward clearly criminal behavior, and by equally focusing on the amorous affairs of Major Vidigal, the police chief who easily enters the pleasurable underworld of disorder, Candido underlines the way in which the characters' behavior oscillates between order and disorder, and the extent to which this pendular movement sustains the creative process and gives the novel its form. The whole plot appears to the reader as a fictional universe free from the burden of error and sin. The originality of the novel, according to Candido, "consists in a certain absence of moral judgment, and a condescending acceptance of 'man as he is,' a mixture of cynicism and bonhomie."

One should also point out that the novel escapes the model of the foundational Romantic novel. José de Alencar's novel, for example, intended to instill in its readers disciplinary concepts and forms of behavior, so that the native forces that modeled the new society could better adapt themselves to European standards of quality. In this same line of thought, *Memórias* scorns "repressive symbols, that seem to tame the explosion of impulses" and presents a fictional space ruled by an "almost prodigious freedom," "free from guilt and remorse, from repression and inner sanction." Above all, Candido's reading presents *Memórias de um sargento de milícias* as a solid base for modernism's most aggressive caboclo novels (*Macunaíma* [Macunaima], by Mário de Andrade, and *Serafim ponte grande,* by Oswald de Andrade). Within the context of the 1970s, that is to say, at the worst moment of military repression in Brazil, Candido's essay constituted the academy's outcry against the abuses of violence and torture that were being perpetrated on the Brazilian people by the dominant class.

IV

The models of analysis, grounded in the decades of the twenties and thirties respectively, share a clear universalist position, but differ in the way in which they are founded disciplinarily (culture versus economy, and vice versa) and in the way in which they conceive of the historical process (pluralism versus a singular, exclusive direction, and vice versa). As a result of such distinctions they differ both in the emphasis given to the question of the national, and in the way in which they evaluate it in the search for *moral* advancement in Brazil; furthermore, they differ in the conception of the sociopolitical development of humanity.

These two models, as I have attempted to demonstrate, were the prevailing models in literary theory in the first half of this century. They thus reveal the permanence of the modernist system of ideas, already institutionalized and transformed into an aesthetic canon by the histories of literature written in the 1950s. We have already mentioned Antonio Candido's *Formação da literatura Brasileira* [The fashioning of Brazilian literature]. One should also mention *A literatura no Brasil* [Literature in Brazil], a collective work organized by Afrânio Coutinho, as well as Alfredo Bosi's *História concisa da literatura brasileira* [A concise history of Brazilian literature]. Similar models can be found in other so-called third world countries, as can be witnessed by the reading of thinkers as diverse as Frantz Fanon, Roberto Fernández Retamar, and Edouard Glissant. Contrary to what a mind with an authoritarian inclination would suppose, each model supplements and sustains the other, dramatizing for future generations the conquests and predicaments of cultures that, in spite of being dependent, do not cease to yearn for universal values.

Nevertheless, both models, and the respective canons that they represent, are under the scrutiny of the newest generations, maybe more so in the case of the model of *economic* foundation (and its corresponding canon), than in the case of the model of *cultural* foundation (with its corresponding canon). There are various reasons for the *cultural* choice made by the new generations. They may be related to the collapse of Soviet communism, symbolically represented by the fall of the Berlin Wall, to the repercussions and academic victories of Anglo-Saxon multiculturalism, to the improvement and expansion of the technology that fuels the great advances of computer sciences, or to the resulting and increasing swift globalization of peripheral capitalism. But even before the questioning of these two models by the new generations, they were questioned by those who had previously defended them.

Due to the dictatorship that resulted from the military coup of 1964, the model of the twenties had to be considerably repaired. As a consequence of police repression and political censorship, the Brazilian intellectual engaged in the deconstruction of ethnocentrism came to lose the nationalistic optimism of the first modernists, cloning it in a more critical hue, as he became more sensitive to questions referring to power and violence in the historical process of nation building in Brazil. It is not difficult not to be complicit with a national society that ignores the minimal standards of being able to govern justly. As his interest in the microcosm in which he survives strengthens, the Brazilian intellectual becomes more sensitive to the miserable condition of the popular classes, always discriminated against in Brazilian society and thus easily manipulated by populist political forces.

The model of the 1930s, on the other hand, loses the safety and support of the party and its universal political force, which had persuaded and attracted the masses on the basis of major social conquests. In its turn, the corresponding theoretical reflection, not accustomed to the exercise of self-criticism, insists on the "ironic" mode to describe the "divorce between cultural aspiration and local conditions" in Brazilian art. It is for this reason that artistic productions that better dramatize this divorce have been privileged. In the committed art of the 1960s, the image of a modern and industrialized Brazil is opposed to that of an archaic and traditionalist country. They find here a "picturesque emblem of national identity," which "configures an extravagant disagreement, filled with enigmatic dimensions, expressing and symbolizing to a certain extent the unorthodox character of the developmental trend [in Brazil]," in Roberto Schwarz's recent words.

The harsh critiques that are being carried out by the new generations of the two universalizing cultural models result from tendencies that, in general, might be inspired by social movements responding to the hegemonic presence of U.S. culture on a world level and particularly among us. Such movements are antagonistic and complementary in the way in which they react: on the one hand, a sympathy for the presence of North American culture in Brazil, on the other hand an antipathy for this form of neo-colonialism. To the extent that the present Brazilian government strives for democratic dialogue with the avant-garde political forces, it has been sensitive to the demands of both groups. The theoretical territory of these new political activists is circumscribed by the university campuses, but their action acquires force by means of the space conquered in the media by organizations of civil society to which the activists belong.

On the one hand, as just mentioned, we have social movements that express sympathy for political conquests articulated by multiculturalism. In a context that is different from that of U.S. society, the ideas formulated by Anglo-Saxon multiculturalism have been used in Brazil to articulate necessarily localized movements of social, political, and economic liberation. Their basic presupposition is founded on the model of freedom and equality for all. This model was inspired by the struggle for citizenship that took shape in the last decade, during the rallies in which people demanded direct elections for the presidency of the Republic in order to bring the military dictatorship to an end. The politics of multiculturalism, which is quite rightly named a search for cultural identity by minority groups, is in general administered by grants provided by foreign foundations to special programs in Brazilian universities, and by nongovernmental organizations, these latter with a strong religious hue. The politics of multiculturalism support: (1) the demands of the population of African and Indian origin in a country of European colonization; (2) female emancipation in a patriarchal society; (3) the struggles of sexual minorities or other ethnic minorities (such as the Jews) against discrimination and for civil rights; (4) the struggle for a dignified life for children (the so-called street children) and adolescents abandoned by their families, who survive in a condition of poverty, violence, and moral misery in the major Brazilian cities.

Although the politics of cultural identity in Brazil appears in little niches that pop up in the daily life of major cities, each of the movements inspired by it maintains, within its own restricted economy of agency, powerful alliances with similar cosmopolitan groups usually located in the United States and in Europe. We are faced with an unprecedented phenomenon in Brazilian culture: among us, localized political groups traditionally tended to search for cultural and financial support in parties with national power, or with powers limited to one or another region of the country. The goal of the politics of cultural identity is obedience to those aspects of the Brazilian constitution that demand profound transformations in the carrying out of state policies and the practices of Brazil's citizens (goals that are far too ambitious in a country characterized by authoritarian tradition and economic nationalisms). These cosmopolitan alliances are completely justified and result in a stimulating political picture that is at one and the same time urban *and* cosmopolitan, very different from the traditional frame imposed by the white male elites, who are also cosmopolitan, as we have seen, but in their own way.

On the other hand, we have the political antipathy toward the process of globalization of (or inspired by) American pop culture. The diffusion of these new cultural products is carried out by the exclusive presence of electronic media in Brazilian homes. According to statistic data available to me, while the United States had 154 million homes with a TV in 1988, Brazil ranked fourth in the world with 28 million homes, falling behind only Japan and Britain. Good old times, those of Joaquim Nabuco, when Brazilian newspapers dreamed of a telegraph to keep their literate readers informed of what was going on in the world. Today, this information arrives by the minute directly to the homes of literate or illiterate families. These ideological groups reject the hegemony of national products made in the studios of the Globo television network and successfully exported all over the world, as well as the indiscriminate aperture of the Brazilian market to foreign "canned" TV series. Lately, educational television, TVE, with its very low percentage of viewers, has practically been the only channel in electronic media that gives time and space to the diffusion of "legitimate" Brazilian popular culture.

According to these new ideologues, the globalized and alienating sameness that is instilled among the popular classes by the electronic media in an authoritarian manner distances Brazilians from Brazil. Aversion to this sameness articulates social movements more and more entrenched in the conservation and preservation of regional traditions. Today regional demands appear somewhat beatified, contrary to what happened in the 1930s, when the poorest states of the nation were spotlighted by artists and social scientists in order to better characterize not only Brazil's backwardness in the context of developed nations, but also the disregard of central government for the vast and very populated regions dominated by drought and controlled by rural servility—whence the key notion of underdevelopment, which in its turn is the basis of every modernizing politics. Regional demands are duly supported by ecological thinking—and herein resides a universalizing component that unbalances the characterization of the ecological movement as exclusively located in certain regions of the country. They function as a kind of last resource that strives to preserve both the moral bastions of a wounded nationhood, and the practices of the authentically Brazilian art of living well. On the social level, the victorious banner of this group has been the campaign in favor of the landless in the desperate and bloody struggle for agrarian reform. On the cultural level, one may mention the emergence and success of so-called country music among the urban and rural masses.

Both forms of response to U.S. hegemony, to the extent that they translate the yearnings of marginalized groups, are above and beyond the national as it has been proposed by the classical theories of Brazilian identity, and as it is now proposed by Fernando Henrique Cardoso's government. The first tendency is, at one and the same time, urban and cosmopolitan, and thus frequently forgets small-town Brazil. The second rejects the federational composition of the nation as it demands a place under the sun for the forgotten regions; it even fuels nodal points of dissidence which have been embodied in minuscule and failed separatist movements such as the one in Rio Grande do Sul. According to the government ideologues, the necessary remedy for rearticulating these new political and social demands is the strengthening of the Brazilian state, a position which becomes evident in recent statements made by the country's present minister of culture. He recommends the return to respect for national symbols (such as the flag, the national anthem, etc.), that is, the return to a new cosmopolitan realignment of the instinct of nationhood, now dealing with a globalization produced by the hegemonic force of U.S. pop culture.

At this point in time, when the Cold War comes to a close, and the migratory movements of workers awaken racial hatred in developed countries, when peripheral nations give absolute priority to the privatization of national institutions (which we call *estatais,* i.e., pertaining to the state) by opening up to predatory foreign capital, the two responsive tendencies come to share a common path. This is so to the extent that, due to the radical fragmentation of power in the Brazilian state, both reject traditional theories of national identity as being mystifications. In the same way, both repudiate the now dominant theories of globalization as being alienating and paradoxically retrogressive.

Translated by Ana Lúcia Gazzola and Gareth Williams

Notes

■

WHY AND FOR WHAT PURPOSE DOES
THE EUROPEAN TRAVEL?

"Why and For What Purpose Does the European Travel?" (Por que e para que viaja o europeu?, 1984) was a review of the translation into Portuguese of the book by Umberto Eco. This essay is included in the book *Nas malhas da letra* (São Paulo: Companhia das Letras, 1989).

1   Some of the members of the mission were Paul Arbousse, Roger Bastide, Claude Lévi-Strauss, Émile Coonaert, Robert Garric, Etienne Borne, Jean Maugué, Fidelino Figuei-redo, and Giuseppe Ungaretti [Trans. note].

LATIN AMERICAN DISCOURSE:
THE SPACE IN-BETWEEN

"Latin American Discourse: The Space In-Between" (O entre-lugar do discurso latino-americano, 1971) was originally written in French, with the title "L'entre-lieu du discours latino-américain." Eugenio Donato, who invited the author for a lecture at the Université de Montreal, considered the title enigmatic and suggested another: "Naissance du sau-vage: Anthropophagie Culturelle et la Littérature du Nouveau Monde." The lecture was given at that university on March 18, 1971, and later republished in English, with the original title, "Latin American Literature: The Space In-Between," by the State University of New York at Buffalo (1973). The Portuguese version, written by the author, dates from the publication of the book *Uma literatura nos trópicos* (São Paulo: Editora Perspectiva, 1978). The English translation in this book was based on this version.

1   Emphasizing ethnology's contribution to undermining the effect of Western metaphysics, Jacques Derrida points out in *Writing and Difference:* "Ethnology could only become a science at the precise moment in which a decentering occurred: at the moment in which

European culture . . . was *displaced*, expelled from its location, ceasing to be considered a culture of reference." He adds, "This moment is not merely a moment of philosophical discourse . . . ; it is also a political, economical, technical moment, and so on."

2   *Tristes tropiques* (Paris: Plon, 1955), p. 82.

3   See note 3 in my essay "The Word of God," *Barroco* (1970).

4   *De la grammatologie* (Paris: Minuit, 1967), p. 25.

5   In an essay carrying the suggestive title "Sol da Meia-Noite" [Midnight sun], Oswald de Andrade acknowledged the values of *unity* and *purity* that lay behind Nazi Germany, and he commented with typically outstanding precision: "Racist, purist, and record-breaking Germany must be educated by our mulatto, by the Chinese, by the most backward Indian from Peru or Mexico, by the Sudanese African. And it must undergo contamination once and for all. It must be undone in the *melting-pot* of the future. It must become *mulatto.*" *Ponta de lança* (Rio de Janeiro: Civilização, 1972), p. 62.

6   We closely follow Derrida's teachings in relation to the problem of translation within the grammatological presuppositions: "Within the limits where it is possible, or at least where it *seems* possible, translation practices the difference between signified and signified. But since this difference is never pure, translation is even less so, and one must substitute it for the notion of *transformation*, a ruled transformation of a language by another, of a text by another." *Positions* (Paris: Minuit, 1972), p. 31.

"Eça, Author of *Madame Bovary*" (Eça, autor de *Madame Bovary*) was a lecture originally written in English and given on April 30, 1970, during the commemorative event "Generation of the '70s" organized by Heitor Martins at Indiana University. The translation into Portuguese, done by the author, dates from the publication of the book *Uma literatura nos trópicos* (1978). The English version here is based on the latter.

UNIVERSALITY IN SPITE OF DEPENDENCY

"Universality in Spite of Dependency" (Apesar de dependente, universal, 1980) was written as a preface to Heloísa Toller Gomes's book *O poder rural na ficção* [Rural power in fiction] (São Paulo: Editora Ática, 1981), based on a master's thesis supervised by the author at the Pontifícia Universidade Católica do Rio de Janeiro. The essay was republished in *Vale quanto pesa: Ensaios sobre questões político-culturais* (Rio de Janeiro: Paz e Terra, 1982).

1   See "Latin American Discourse: The Space In-Between," above [Trans. note].

2   *Curupira* is a Brazilian trickster from rural folklore whose feet point backward [Trans. note].

3   The references are to the period of growth during Juscelino Kubitschek's government at the end of the fifties, and into the seventies, when the developmental project of the military dictatorship led to a period of bourgeois euphoria known as "milagre brasileiro" [Trans. note].

4   Slang for urban workers who carried their lunch to work and always had to eat cold meals consisting of dishes that were meant to be heated before eating [Trans. note].

5   Antonio Candido's work has been translated into English as *The Development of Brazilian Literature*. We prefer *The Fashioning of Brazilian Literature* and have used this translation in "Worldly Appeal," above [Trans. note].

6   Brazilian modernism is the period inaugurated by the *Semana de Arte Moderna* [Week of modern art] in 1922, which was characterized by a break with academic traditions in

literature and plastic arts, and by a search for inspiration in Brazilian sources and reality [Trans. note].

7 ISEB is the Instituto Superior de Estudos Brasileiros [Brazilian Studies High Institute] in São Paulo [Trans. note].

8 A Brazilian right-wing political movement, based on fascism, that lasted from 1932 to 1937 [Trans. note].

THE RHETORIC OF VERISIMILITUDE

"The Rhetoric of Verisimilitude" (Retórica da Verossimilhança, 1969), was a lecture written at the invitation of Heitor Martins and given at the special session of the Modern Language Association in 1969, which was dedicated to Machado de Assis. After being published in various journals, it became a part of *Uma literatura nos trópicos* (1978).

1 Preface to *Memórias póstumas de Brás Cubas* (São Paulo: Melhoramentos, n.d.), p. 17.

2 *Ressurreição,* in *Obra completa* (Rio de Janeiro: Aguilar, 1994), vol. 1, p. 114. Volume and page numbers for *Ressurreição, Dom Casmurro,* and other works by Machado from *Obra completa* are given in parentheses in the text [Trans. note].

3 A novel by the Portuguese novelist Eça de Queirós. See the essay in this volume [Trans. note].

4 One could doubtless study in *Dom Casmurro* the isomorphic relation between house and romance, to the extent that the reconstruction of the one follows that of the other. We might propose, as a point of departure, in the first case a return-to-origins (mother), and in the second the negation of the return-to-origins (marriage). On the other hand, one must not forget that there is a symmetry within the romance, since the Matacavalos and the Engenho de Dentro houses are similar but not the same, the only different one being the house of Gloria, where Capitu reigned supreme as housewife. But it is a happy coincidence that the second house, despite being Capitu's, is always referred to in the text as the house of Gloria, which is the name of Bentinho's mother.

5 Cf. "Compte-rendu: *Estruturas,* de Rui Mourão," *Suplemento literário do Minas Gerais,* 2 Aug. 1969.

6 That is, "Casmurro" from the nickname given the narrator [Trans. note].

7 In a recent article on Afonso Ávila's poem "Ahs! e silêncio," I attempted to show how his poem is constructed by successive transgressions/betrayals of a common phrase or cliché, its maladjustment being responsible for the semantic and participant, anti-code and revolutionary leap.

8 No doubt the flower/fruit metaphor makes an evident contrast with Dom Casmurro's: fruit/rind. A microscopic analysis of the two metaphors would surely show the co-herence in both José Dias and Dom Casmurro, in that in the former there is a process of transformation, while in the latter what occurs is merely an *internal* ripening. It is obvious that the problem of coherence is utterly foreign to the tenor of my study.

9 *Encyclopedia of Religion and Ethics,* ed. James Hastings (Edinburgh: T. and T. Clark, 1918), vol. 10, p. 349.

10 Cf. "O astrológo e a velha," a chapter of my study of *Ressurreição,* published in the suplemento literário of *O estado de São Paulo.*

11 Luis Vianna Filho, *A vida de Machado de Assis* (São Paulo: Martins, 1965), p. 189.

12 The quotes from Plato were taken from a French edition: *Phèdre* (Paris: Les Belles

Lettres, 1966); the page numbers that appear in parentheses are from this edition (English trans. by the translators).

13 The quotations from Pascal have been taken from *Lettres écrites à un provincial* (Paris: Garnier-Flammarion, 1967), page numbers given in parentheses in the text (English trans. by the translators).

14 Predominance of the "bacharel," i.e., a person who concluded the first level of studies in a law school, in Brazilian cultural and political life [Trans. note].

WORTH ITS WEIGHT:

BRAZILIAN MODERNIST FICTION

"Worth Its Weight: Brazilian Modernist Fiction" (Vale quanto pesa: A ficção brasileira modernista, 1978), was originally published in the periodical *Discurso* 10 (São Paulo: Universidade de São Paulo, pp. 161–74) and later included in the book of the same title (1982). It was translated into French by Michel Riaudel and published in the periodical *Braise* 1, January–March 1985.

1 The original version of this essay was published in 1978. Brazil now has 160 million inhabitants [Trans. note].

2 An Indian tribe of Brazil; the adjective is used ironically as a synonym for Brazilian in the sense of provincial [Trans. note].

3 Experimental poetry groups originating in São Paulo during the 1950s [Trans. note].

4 Literally, "pot-lickers," or people who eat voraciously due to hunger and bad manners. It refers to the title of the book written by João Antônio that became emblematic of the populist literature of the period [Trans. note].

5 An allusion to Drummond's poem "Mãos dadas" [Joined hands], in *Sentimento do mundo* [Feeling for the world] [Trans. note].

6 Adolescent slang for male masturbation [Trans. note].

7 Literally, "Brazilwood," the name of an avant-garde movement in Brazilian poetry (1924) concerned with the revision of the history of Brazil as written by the colonizers [Trans. note].

THE PERMANENCE OF THE DISCOURSE

OF TRADITION IN MODERNISM

"The Permanence of the Discourse of Tradition in Modernism" (A permanência do discurso da tradição no Modernismo, 1985) was a lecture written for the symposium "Tradition/Contradiction," organized by Adauto Novaes. The first publication dates from 1987, as part of the book *Tradição/Contradição* (Rio de Janeiro: Jorge Zahar/FUNARTE, 1987). The essay is included in the book *Nas malhas da letra* (1989).

1 Oswald de Andrade (1890–1954), one of the participants in the Week of Modern Art (1922), author of the *Manifesto Pau-Brasil* [Brazilwood manifesto] and the *Manifesto antropófago* [Anthropophagous manifesto] [Trans. note].

2 Play on *palmeiras,* palm-trees, and *Palmares,* the African republic founded in the northeastern part of the country by Brazilian slaves under Zumbi. Oswald de Andrade is parodying the verse of the Romantic poet Gonçalves Dias (1825–64) in "Canção do exílio" [Song of exile] [Trans. note].

3　The National Foundation of Arts in Brazil.

4　A reference to the poem "Mãos dadas" [Joined Hands], published in *Sentimento do mundo* [Feeling for the world], 1940 [Trans. note].

5　Murilo Mendes (1901–75), modernist poet, author of *Poems* (1930), *History of Brazil* (1932), and *Time and Eternity* (1935), among other works [Trans. note].

6　Land of the palm trees; name given to Brazil in the Indian language Tupi [Trans. note].

7　Neighborhood in downtown Rio de Janeiro [Trans. note].

8　Beach neighborhood in Rio de Janeiro [Trans. note].

9　A literary group in Rio de Janeiro associated with the magazine *Festa,* whose first issue came out in 1927. It represented a spiritualist tendency of one of the trends of Brazilian modernism [Trans. note].

10　Tarsila do Amaral (1897?–1973), the painter who participated in the Week of Modern Art in 1922 [Trans. note].

11　Abbreviation for the Institute of the Historical and Artistic Patrimony of Brazil [Trans. note].

12　Referring to Getúlio Vargas's regime from 1937 to 1945 [Trans. note].

13　Rodrigo Mello Franco was the creator of the Institute of the Historical and Artistic Patrimony of Brazil, with the cooperation of Mário de Andrade and Carlos Drummond de Andrade, among other intellectuals [Trans. note].

14　A colonial town in the state of Minas Gerais [Trans. note].

15　Main character in Lima Barreto's novel *O triste fim de Policarpo Quaresma* [The sad end of Policarpo Quaresma], published in 1911 [Trans. note].

REPRESSION AND CENSORSHIP IN THE FIELD
OF THE ARTS DURING THE 1970S

"Repression and Censorship in the Field of the Arts during the 1970s" (Repressão e censura no campo das artes na década de 70, 1979) was a lecture given at the annual meeting of the Brazilian Society for the Advancement of Science. It was published originally and simultaneously in the periodicals *Encontros com a civilização Brasileira* 17, and *Cadernos de opinião* 14. It is included in the book *Vale quanto pesa* (1982).

1　"The New State," the corporate state established in 1937 during Getúlio Vargas's dictatorship [Trans. note].

2　AI-5 is the Institutional Act No. 5, in December 1968, a notorious decree by the military government that closed the National Congress and put an end to individual civil rights established by the constitution [Trans. note].

3　*Sufoco,* literally, "smothering," can also mean a hard time and is used to refer to the worst period of censorship and repression during the military regime [Trans. note].

LITERATURE AND MASS CULTURE

"Literature and Mass Culture" (Literatura e cultura de massas, 1993) was a lecture given at the annual meeting of the Brazilian Society for the Advancement of Science. It was originally published in the periodical *Novos estudos.*

1　In 1936, José Lins do Rego published *Estórias da velha Totonha* [Stories of the old woman Totonha] (who is not only a character of his first novel but also appears in the autobiography *Meus verdes anos* [My green years]), and Graciliano Ramos assembled his production for children in 1944 in the volume *Histórias de Alexandre* [Stories of Alexander].

2 In August 1936, Lobato published *Depoimento apresentado à comissão de inquérito sobre o Petróleo* [Statement given to the committee of inquiry on petroleum], republished under the title *Escândalo de petróleo* [Scandal of petroleum]. In *O poço do visconde* [The well of the viscount] published in 1937, Lobato taught the geology of petroleum to children.

3 From 1909, one could read in the "Futurist Manifesto" that an automobile at high speed is more beautiful than the Winged Victory of Samothrace. The magazine created by the participants of the Modern Art Week in 1992 was called *Klaxon* [car horn] (curiously, this word disappeared from the Brazilian vocabulary, being substituted by *buzina*. Flora Süssekind has published an excellent study of the imaginary of the machine in the pre-modernists: *O cinematógrafo das letras* [The cinematograph of letters].

4 In the volume of essays cited, see the article "Bilhete aberto" [Open note], addressed to C. R. [Cassiano Ricardo], a poet who worked directly with the dictator Getúlio Vargas.

5 It was under the auspices of the CEB that Mário de Andrade gave, in 1942, his famous lecture on modernism.

6 See Beatriz Sarlo, *La imaginación técnica: Sueños modernos da la cultura argentina* [Technical imagination: Modern dreams of Argentine culture].

7 Name of a Brazilian Indian tribe, the adjective meaning local and peripheral [Trans. note].

8 For a defense of the theory of dependency, in the context of the critiques formulated by the historian Maria Sylvia de Carvalho Franco, see the essay of Roberto Schwarz, "Cuidado com as ideologias alienígenas" [Beware of alien ideologies], in *O pai de família e outros ensaios* [The father and other essays].

9 Created by the military dictatorship, EMBRAFILME, despite having played an important role in the years following its creation, slowly deteriorated. One of the most curious phenomena it produced was the "ideological patrols." See the interviews made by Heloísa Buarque de Holanda and Carlos Alberto M. Pereira, collected in the book *Patrulhas ideológicas* [Ideological patrols].

10 It is worth remembering that the first law of the obligatory screening of a certain number of national films was decreed by the British Parliament, the Cinematograph Act of 1927. At the end of the twenties, leadership in film production was disputed by the United States and Germany. Less than 5 percent of the films shown in Great Britain were of British origin. The referred to Cinematograph Act specified that the movie theater operators would have to show in the immediate future an increasing quota of British films: first 5 percent, then 10 percent, then 15 percent, and finally 20 percent. In order to be able to double the number of films to be produced in 1928, that is, to go from 101 to 205 films per year, England had to import filmmakers and actors from Germany. That was the beginning of the famous "German Connection," which culminated in the years 1933–34, when three hundred major figures flew to the island, many of them already motivated by political reasons. The majority of the Germans, of course, ended up being seduced by Hollywood. England became the passport of entry for Europeans into the North American film industry. The novelist Graham Greene, who was a film critic in the mid-thirties, reacted to the invasion, taking literally the initial protectionist idea: "But can one at least express the wish that the immigrants work at professions in which their lack of knowledge of our language and culture may not be such an obstacle." In 1934, the ACTT, the cinema technicians union, was organized. According to one of the union directors, an English producer, before contracting a "foreigner," had to prove that there was no English national who, under the same conditions, could do the same job as the

other. With the declaration of war and more restrictions imposed by the union, many of the Germans immigrated to the United States. This information may serve to clarify the vicious circle of protectionism in the cultural industry: opening, closing, and dispersion.

11   The precocious perishability of the machine in the Western world has its metaphorical correlative in the perfecting of aerodynamic lines, or streamlining. It is not only the quest for greater speed that is desired, but the optimizing of the degree of efficiency of the object with a view to the economy of natural forces and the consumer's pocket. Speed is allied with the saving of energy and money. The technological object tends toward saving in all its possible and foreseeable forms. For this reason, aerodynamic lines, in their subliminal aspect, vitalize the consumption of their form by an aggressively erotic appeal in the configuration of the objects. One saves in order to spend more in another way. The renewal of the object is also related to the liberation of the libido, the consumer being caught in the meshes of another logic: the one who has and can, spends.

12   The return of this poetic discourse, now in popular music after the coup d'état of 1964, received a very acute critical analysis by Walnice Nogueira Galvão in the book of essays *Saco de gatos* [Bag of cats].

13   The silence, or the error of the contemporary reader is expressed in an exemplary way by Jane Smiley, editor of the anthology *The Best American Short Stories of 1995*. In the introduction to this volume, which is necessarily composed of stories that could sell, immediately attracting the attention of the contemporary reader, the first paragraph in which she identifies herself as a reader is revealing of the idiosyncrasies of the contemporary: "I am not a good reader. I am slow and not very determined. I never make myself read a book to the end if I get bored in the middle. I am not especially forgiving—there are whole oeuvres of important and profound writers that I haven't read because I was put off by some quirk in the author's style. I like murder mysteries and magazine pieces about the five types of relationships that will never go anywhere. When magazines about horses and others about important social and political issues arrive the same day, I always read the horses magazines first. I read Tina Brown's *New Yorker* more eagerly than I used to read William Shawn's *New Yorker*." And to think that she was responsible for selecting the "best"!

"The Postmodern Narrator" (O narrador pós-moderno, 1986) was the preface for an anthology of stories by Edilberto Coutinho, which was to have been published by Editora Global. The essay was published in the special issue of the *Revista do Brasil,* dedicated to the literature of the 1980s (n. 5, 1986). It is included in the collection *Nas malhas da letra* (1989).

WORLDLY APPEAL

"Worldly Appeal" (Atração do mundo, 1995) was the Una's Lecture at the University of California at Berkeley (fall 1995). It was published in Portuguese in the periodical *Gragoatá* (n. 1, 1996).

1   See, in the same chapter: "The author and the actor disappear; the spectator, however, feels his anxiety grow to the point of anguish."

2   Flora Süssekind observes that the mediocre, selfish, and rhetorical discourse of Brazilian politicians, rather than sustaining comments or descriptions in the text, is constitutive of narrative voice itself. She concludes that the narrator "is not an outsider who is watching and criticizing political behavior."

3   During the Estado Novo, martyrdom and the cult of the Homeland are identified by Plínio Salgado alongside the growth and affirmation of *caboclo* fascism: "During the great collective patriotic demonstrations, the *integralistas* were the ones who accomplished the maximum apotheoses of the Homeland and exalted legal authorities. If we ever underwent federal persecution, our growth would be astonishing, since it is in the character and nature of our movement to grow due to the mysticism of martyrdom."

4   In the "Advertência" [Warning] included at the end of the novel, Alencar severely criticizes the European missionaries and adventurers who left us the information we have on the Indians, since "they all agreed . . . to represent the Indians as human beasts." It was "necessary to purify the event from the comments that accompany it, to get a clear notion of the customs and character of the savages." Within this line of reasoning, Alencar ends up creating an extremely daring metaphor to convey the sacred value of anthropophagy: "The remains of the enemies thus became like a sacred Host conferring strength to the warriors. . . . It was not revenge, but rather something like a *communion of the flesh* through which the transfusion of heroism resulted" [emphasis mine].

5   See, in the same essay: "There is an impatience to write much and fast; one attains glory from this, and I cannot deny that this is the road to applause. There is an attempt to equate the creations of the spirit to those of matter, as if they were not irreconcilable in this case. A man may go around the world in eighty days; for a masterpiece of the spirit a few more days are necessary."

6   In "El escritor argentino y la tradición" [The Argentine writer and tradition] (1951), Jorge Luis Borges legitimates the Machadian canon as he states: "Gibbon points out that in the Arabic book par excellence, the *Koran,* there are no camels. This absence of camels would suffice to prove that it is Arabic. . . . The first thing a forger, a tourist, or an Arab nationalist would have done would be to multiply camels, caravans of camels on each page; but Mohammed, because he is an Arab, was not concerned: He knew he could be an Arab without any camels. I believe we Argentines could act like Mohammed, we can believe in the possibility of being Argentine without exaggerating local color."

7   The "discovery of Brazil," anachronically given by Oswald de Andrade as having taken place in 1923, is not expressed in a different manner of his writing. In the preface to the book of poems *Pau Brasil* [Brazilwood], Paulo Prado states: "Oswald de Andrade, during a trip to Paris, from atop an atelier at Place Clichy—the world navel—discovered, overwhelmed, his native land. The return to the home country confirmed . . . the surprising revelation that Brazil existed." As Carlos Drummond states in a poem written at the time: "And as one travels in the home country, one misses the home country." The ambiguity of loss and nostalgia is in the following two verses in the same poem: "In the elevator I think about the countryside / in the countryside I think about the elevator."

8   Cf. "Hermeneutics sees the relations between various discourses as those of strands in a possible conversation, a conversation which presupposes no disciplinary matrix which unites the speakers, but where the hope of agreement is never lost so long as the conversation lasts. This hope is not a hope for the discovery of antecedently existing common ground, but *simply* hope for agreement, or, at least, exciting and fruitful disagreement." *Philosophy and the Mirror of Nature* (Princeton, N.J.: Princeton University Press, 1979), p. 318.

9   Manuel Bandeira, older and wiser, writes to Mário: "It seems to me that we are still watching Brazil, we are still not living it."

10 *Guassu* is the Tupi-Guarani word for "grandiose"; Tupi-Guarani is an indigenous linguistic family of the South American tropical region [Trans. note].

11 Cf. "Our privilege of not having the past of indigenous civilizations will favor creative freedom. We don't have to return, like Mexico or Peru, to Mayan, Aztec, or Inca ancestors in order to search for national spirituality in indigenous groups. Brazil has not received any aesthetic inheritance from its primitive inhabitants, poor and rudimental savages. Our whole culture developed from the European founders." *O espírito moderno* [The modern spirit] (1925).

12 Graça Aranha (1868–1931), author of *Canaã* (1902), *Malasarte* (1911), and *O espírito moderno* (1925) [The modern spirit], among other works [Trans. note].

13 Roberto Schwarz obviously does not belong to the same generation as Caio Prado Jr. but was considerably influenced by him. In a recent essay, "Um seminário de Marx" [A seminar of Marx], Schwarz narrates the intellectual adventures of a group of professors from the University of São Paulo (in which he participated, among others, with Fernando Henrique Cardoso) that, from 1958 on, met informally to read *Capital.* In this essay, he states that up to that time, the Stalinist gauge, revolutionary populism, and corresponding persecutions by the police had contributed to confine Marxism "to a precarious intellectual universe, distant from the normality of studies and deprived of profound relationships with the culture of the country." He adds: "The exception was Caio Prado Jr., within whom the Marxist prism articulated critically onto the intellectual accumulation of an important family of coffee and politics, producing *a superior work* [emphasis mine], remote from narrow-mindedness and founded on a sober knowledge of local realities."

14 Roberto Schwarz, *Misplaced Ideas: Essays on Brazilian Culture,* ed. John Gledson (London and New York: Verso, 1992), p. 22.

15 Roberto Schwarz does not overlook this final slip in Antonio Candido's argument. He comments: "The transformation of a mode of being of a class into a national mode of being is the founding operation of ideology. With the specificity that, in this case, it is not a generalization of the ideology of the dominant class, but of that of the oppressed class."

Index

■

Adventure, ethics of, 14–17

Alencar, José de, 75, 89, 151, 168, 182n. 4

Almeida, José Américo de: *Antes que me esqueçam,* 86

Almeida, Manuel Antônio de: *Memórias de um sargento de milícia,* 167–68

Alterity, 3–4, 56; as the Other: 3, 6–7, 10, 13, 16, 19, 21, 23, 44, 53, 56–57, 59, 85, 89, 115, 137, 161–62, 165–66

Amaral, Tarsila do, 103–5, 163

Anchieta, José de, 4, 54

Andrade, Carlos Drummond de, 6, 84–85, 87–88, 96–97, 102, 108–9, 127–28, 157–58, 161

Andrade, Mário de, 6, 8, 61, 81, 90–91, 103–4, 120, 136, 157–63, 168; *Macunaíma,* 6, 61, 81, 90, 92, 168

Andrade, Oswald de, 22, 61, 81, 85–86, 93, 96, 100, 103–8, 121, 123, 127, 155, 162, 168; "Feudal Lord," 155; "Manifesto antropófago," 121; *Memórias sentimentais de João Miramar,* 81, 86; *Ponta de lança,* 121, 176nn. 5, 6; *Serafim ponte grande,* 81, 168; *Um homem sem profissão,* 86

Anthropology/anthropologist, 5–6, 9, 16, 19–20, 57–58, 63, 90–92, 107

Art, 17, 21–23, 31, 46, 51, 71, 76, 103, 105, 140, 145, 159, 161, 163, 170; and censorship, 111–18; cinema as, 123–31; narration as, 135, 138

Authenticity, 83, 98, 121, 122, 126, 133, 136, 139, 146, 163

Avant-garde, 30, 40, 61, 94–95, 97, 99, 103, 121, 125, 157, 159, 161, 170

Backwardness, 3, 7, 60–61, 120–21, 123, 126, 148–49, 167, 172

Barthes, Roland, 32–33, 39, 42, 64

Baudrillard, Jean: *The Consumer Society,* 125–26

Benjamin, Walter, 7, 117, 123–24, 126–27, 134–36, 141–44; "The Work of Art in the Age of Mechanical Reproduction," 124

Borges, Jorge Luis, 4, 35–37, 39–41, 43–44, 46, 70; *Fictions,* 39, 41, 44

Brazil: censorship, 7, 111–18, 170; criticism, 1–2, 6, 71, 123; culture, 2, 5, 8, 46, 73, 77, 89–90, 112, 114, 118, 120, 147–63, 168; dictatorship, 7, 109, 170, 172; intellectual, 4, 57–58, 60, 91, 120, 123, 147, 149, 159, 163, 170–72; intelligence, 5, 55–56. *See* Modernism, in Brazil

Broca, Brito, 96, 103, 157

Callado, Antônio, 25, 113, 117

Caminha, Pero Vaz de, 15, 28, 91

Camões, Luiz Vaz de: *Os lusíadas,* 9–13, 17, 56, 96, 102

Candido, Antonio, 3, 59–60, 86–87, 102, 147, 153, 160, 164, 167–69; *Formação da literatura Brasileira,* 59, 169

Cervantes, Miguel S. de, 36, 40–41; *Don Quixote,* 36, 39, 41, 46

Cesário Verde: "O sentimento de um ocidental," 45; Ramalho Ortigão's criticism of, 45

Chateaubriand, René de, 14, 35

Cinema, 7, 40, 113, 120–32

Colonialism, 19, 26, 46; colonizer, 10, 15–16, 19, 26, 30. *See* Neocolonialism

Comparative literature, 2–3, 58–60, 62; source and influence in, 2–3, 60

Conversation, 50, 110, 143, 157, 159, 161–63

Copy, 3–4, 6, 13, 21, 23–24, 29–30, 36, 39–41, 51, 82, 144. *See* Simulacrum

Cortázar, Julio, 34–35, 116

Cosmopolitanism, 7, 45, 79–81, 119, 151, 154, 157–59, 171–73

Coutinho, Edilberto, 133–45

Cunha, Euclides da, 89–90, 122; *Os sertões,* 89, 122

Dependency, 1–4, 53, 61, 123

Derrida, Jacques, 2, 18, 29, 130, 160–61, 175–76n. 1

Desnos, Robert, 4, 37, 41

Diderot, Denis: *Supplement to Bougainville's Journey,* 15–16

Difference, 2, 4, 6, 13, 16, 19–20, 30–32, 36–37, 39, 41, 46–47, 56–59, 62, 88, 91, 142

Eco, Umberto: *Travels in Hyperreality,* 3, 9, 20–23

Eliot, T. S., 22, 94–95, 99–101, 107; "Tradition and the Individual Talent," 95, 99

Ethnocentrism, 2, 4, 9, 15, 19, 55–56, 59–63, 161, 170

Ethnology, 27, 31, 90, 160

Eurocentrism, 61, 100, 148, 150–51, 153–54, 157, 159–60, 165

Fashioning/self-fashioning, 149–50, 153, 160–61, 164–65

Faith: and the empire, 9, 13, 15

Flaubert, Gustave, 39, 43–44, 47, 49, 51–52, 62, 115, 134, 142

Foucault, Michel, 21–23, 25, 33, 46, 101

Foundation, 21–23, 25, 46, 53, 58–59, 124, 131–32, 150–51, 154, 168–69

France, Anatole, 158, 161

Gide, André, 1, 15, 49, 51, 69

Globalization, 7, 8, 170, 172, 174

Gomes, Paulo Emílio Salles, 53, 57

Hermeneutics, 22–23, 127, 163

Hybridism, 1, 30

Identity: cultural and national, 3–8, 20, 23–24, 37, 41, 49, 148, 151–52, 164, 170–73

Imitation, 28, 32–33, 59, 61

Indian, 4, 13, 27–29, 35, 46, 54–57, 89–90, 106, 159, 165–66, 171

Invisibility, 4, 36–37, 41–44, 46, 52, 62

Irony, 27, 90, 93, 98–99, 102–3, 130, 142, 152

Knowledge, 3, 5, 10, 17, 18–19, 21, 31, 33, 59, 61, 69, 79, 81, 85, 92, 101–2, 106, 115, 125, 127, 131, 133, 143, 161–62

Latin America, 1–3, 8, 28, 30–38, 58–59, 83, 119, 164; Latin American literature, 2, 37; the Latin American writer, 32–38

Machado de Assis, Joaquim Maria, 5, 47, 49, 64–78, 89, 129, 152–53, 167

Marcos, Plínio, 111, 113, 115, 117

Marx, Karl, 22, 37, 84–85; Marxist thought and praxis, 8, 89, 96, 102, 105, 163, 165

Mass culture, 7, 119, 122–23, 126, 128, 131

Memoirs, 81, 83–89, 114, 142, 147, 149–50, 167

Memory, 4, 32, 55, 69–70, 84, 139; betrayal of, 61

Mendes, Murilo, 6, 22, 86–87, 96–97, 100, 107–10

Model, 3–4, 6, 12, 18, 23, 29, 31, 33–37, 39, 41, 46, 51, 54, 83, 91, 98, 101, 105, 121–23, 126, 144, 162, 168–71

Modernism, in Brazil, 6, 53, 61, 84, 93–110,

136, 157, 160, 163, 168; Week of Modern
    Art, 81, 94, 157
Modernity, 6–7, 17–20, 123, 124, 131, 148,
    149, 157, 160
Montaigne, Michel Eyquem de, 10, 20–22,
    25, 29, 105
Monteiro Lobato, José Bento, 120–23
Moraes, Vinícius de, 102, 123, 131
Multiculturalism, 163, 169, 171

Nabuco, Joaquim, 8, 74, 147–72
Narcissism, 5, 13, 56, 82, 143
Narrative, 7, 48, 50–51, 68, 70, 84, 87–90, 123;
    the postmodern, 134–36, 140–43, 145
Narrator, 5, 7; in Machado de Assis, 65–91;
    the postmodern, 133–46
Nationhood, 3, 8, 151–53, 162, 172–73
Neocolonialism, 19–20, 29, 31–32, 34, 37–
    38, 60, 171. See Colonialism
Nietzsche, Friedrich, 21–23, 101, 130–31
Novel, 7, 14, 22, 41, 43–44, 46–52, 64–92,
    116, 123, 129, 134, 136, 151–52, 160,
    167–68

Parody, 4, 6, 34, 91, 93, 95–96, 99, 105
Pascal, Blaise, 74, 77
Pastiche, 4, 6, 34, 91, 99
Paz, Octavio, 6, 93–99, 100–102, 141–42
Plato: Phaedrus, 74–75
Politics, 8, 97–98, 101, 105, 111–18, 126,
    147–172
Postmodern, the, 94, 99
Postmodernism, 94, 96–97, 99
Postmodernity, 1, 7, 133, 141, 145
Prado, Caio, Jr., 8, 164–166, 183nn. 13, 15
Prison form (genre), 4, 37, 42
Proust, Marcel, 71, 84–85

Queirós, Eça de, 39–52; O primo basílio, 39–
    51, 62, 65, 73

Ramos, Graciliano, 83, 85–86, 114
Rego, José Lins do, 85–86, 136, 155
Renaissance, 29, 59
Rhetoric, 5, 64–78
Rosa, João Guimarães, 15, 87, 89–90, 136,
    144, 155

Sartre, Jean-Paul, 34, 64, 74, 83
Saudade, 154–55, 158
Saudosismo, 159
Schwarz, Roberto, 79, 166–67, 170
Simulacrum, 4, 5, 29, 58. See Copy
Space in-between, the, 1, 3, 5–6, 8, 25, 91
Süssekind, Flora, 149, 156, 181n. 2

Technology, 106, 119–22, 125, 149, 169
Text: visible and invisible, 4, 36–37, 39, 41–
    44, 46, 51–52, 56, 62
Tourist, 20–21
Transgression, 4, 36–38, 41, 46, 51, 93, 125,
    162
Tradition, 6–7, 31, 60, 85, 88, 93–110, 126,
    132, 135–36, 138, 150, 154
Travel, 1, 3, 9–24, 35, 87, 103, 120, 155–57
Traveler: the European, 3, 11, 15, 19, 21, 35

Universality/universalism, 1, 3–4, 10, 53,
    62–63, 80, 167

Valéry, Paul, 9, 32, 36, 41
Values, 3, 5–6, 13, 26, 29–30, 46, 56–57, 63,
    84–85, 89, 91–93, 99, 101, 105, 107, 122,
    125, 132, 134, 152–54, 160, 166, 169
Verisimilitude, 64, 68–70, 72, 73–76, 135, 138

Silviano Santiago is a novelist and theorist. Among other titles, he is the author of *De cócoras* (1999); *Keith Jarret no Blue Note* (1996); *Viagem ao México* (1995); *Uma história de família* (1992); *Nas malhas da letra* (1989); *Stella Manhattan: Romance* (1985; Duke, 1994); *Vale quanto pesa: Ensaios sobre questões culturais* (1982); *Em liberdade* (1981); *Carlos Drummond de Andrade* (1976); and *O banquete* (1970). He has also edited *Intépretes do Brasil* (2000); (with Dietrich Briesemeister and Helmut Feldman) *Brasilianische Literatur der Zeit der Militarherrschaft (1964–1988)* (1991); and *Glossário de Derrida* (1976).

Ana Lúcia Gazzola is President and Professor of English and Comparative Literature at the Universidade Federal de Minas Gerais.

Wander Melo Miranda is Professor of Literary Theory and Comparative Literature at the Universidade Federal de Minas Gerais and Director of the University Press.

Tom Burns is Associate Professor of English at the Universidade Federal de Minas Gerais.

Gareth Williams is Associate Professor of Spanish American Literature at Wesleyan University.

Library of Congress Cataloging-in-Publication Data

Santiago, Silviano.

The space in-between : essays on Latin American culture / Silviano Santiago ; edited by Ana Lúcia Gazzola ; with an introduction by Ana Lúcia Gazzola and Wander Melo Miranda ; translated by Tom Burns, Ana Lúcia Gazzola, and Gareth Williams.

p. cm. — (Post-contemporary interventions) (Latin America in translation/en traducción/em tradução)

Includes index.

ISBN 0–8223–2752–x (cloth : alk. paper) — ISBN 0–8223–2749–x (pbk. : alk. paper)

1. Latin America—Civilization—20th century. 2. Latin American literature—20th century—History and criticism. 3. Literature, Comparative. 4. Literature and society—Latin America. I. Gazzola, Ana Lúcia. II. Title. III. Series. IV. Series: Latin America in translation/en traducción/em tradução

F1414 .S27 2001   980.03′3—dc21   2001051115